Mastering Yii

Advance your modern web application development
skills with Yii Framework 2

Charles R. Portwood II

BIRMINGHAM - MUMBAI

Mastering Yii

First published: January 2016

Production reference: 1210116

Published by Packt Publishing Ltd.
Livery Place
35 Livery Street
Birmingham B3 2PB, UK.

ISBN 978-1-78588-242-5

www.packtpub.com

Credits

Author
Charles R. Portwood II

Reviewer
Tomasz Trejderowski

Acquisition Editor
Divya Poojari

Content Development Editor
Anish Dhurat

Technical Editor
Edwin Moses

Copy Editor
Stuti Srivastava

Project Coordinator
Bijal Patel

Proofreader
Safis Editing

Indexer
Priya Sane

Production Coordinator
Shantanu N. Zagade

Cover Work
Shantanu N. Zagade

About the Author

Charles R. Portwood II has over 10 years of experience developing modern web applications and is well versed in integrating PHP with native mobile applications. An avid proponent of Yii Framework and open source software, Charles has contributed multiple guides, extensions, and applications to the Yii community. In addition to being a programmer, he is also a Linux system administrator.

About the Reviewer

Tomasz Trejderowski is a middle-aged developer from Poland who
has hands-on experience working with many programming languages and in
diverse IT-related areas. He has been programming computers since the very
first Commodore 64 and thus, he poses over 20 years of software development
experience. You can access repositories and contributions on his GitHub profile,
at `http://github.com/trejder`.

He is a full-time business analyst and free-time PhoneGap/Yii2 developer and
blogger. He is also a mobile market entrepreneur, constantly working on some
innovative projects. For more information, visit his company website at
`http://www.gaman.pl` or his blog network at `http://www.acrid.pl/`.

He is a happy husband of his wonderful wife and father of two beautiful daughters.

www.PacktPub.com

Support files, eBooks, discount offers, and more

For support files and downloads related to your book, please visit www.PacktPub.com.

Did you know that Packt offers eBook versions of every book published, with PDF and ePub files available? You can upgrade to the eBook version at www.PacktPub.com and as a print book customer, you are entitled to a discount on the eBook copy. Get in touch with us at service@packtpub.com for more details.

At www.PacktPub.com, you can also read a collection of free technical articles, sign up for a range of free newsletters and receive exclusive discounts and offers on Packt books and eBooks.

https://www2.packtpub.com/books/subscription/packtlib

Do you need instant solutions to your IT questions? PacktLib is Packt's online digital book library. Here, you can search, access, and read Packt's entire library of books.

Why subscribe?

- Fully searchable across every book published by Packt
- Copy and paste, print, and bookmark content
- On demand and accessible via a web browser

Free access for Packt account holders

If you have an account with Packt at www.PacktPub.com, you can use this to access PacktLib today and view 9 entirely free books. Simply use your login credentials for immediate access.

Table of Contents

Preface

Yii Framework 2 (Yii2) is the successor to the popular Yii framework. Like its successor, Yii2 is an open source, high-performance rapid development framework designed to create modern, scalable, and performant web applications and APIs.

Designed for both developers with no exposure to Yii and Yii2 and for Yii framework developers looking to become experts with Yii2, this book will serve as your guide to becoming a master of Yii. From initialization and configuration to debugging and deployment, this book will be your guide to becoming a master of all aspects of this powerful framework.

What this book covers

Chapter 1, *Composer, Configuration, Classes, and Path Aliases*, covers the basics of a Yii2 application. In this chapter, you'll learn the core conventions of Yii2 and how to configure it as a multi-environment application. You'll also discover how to use Composer, a dependency management tool for managing your applications' software dependencies.

Chapter 2, *Console Commands and Applications*, focuses on how to use the built-in Yii2 console commands as it guides you through creating your own commands.

Chapter 3, *Migrations, DAO, and Query Building*, teaches you how to create migrations in Yii2 and how to interact with your database using database access objects (DAO) and how to use Yii2's query builder.

Chapter 4, *Active Record, Models, and Forms*, teaches you how to create and use Active Record to effortlessly interact with a database. Furthermore, you'll also discover how to create models to represent information not stored in databases and how to create web forms based upon Active Record models and normal models.

Chapter 5, Modules, Widgets, and Helpers, covers how to incorporate modules inside of our application. This chapter will also cover how to create and use dynamic widgets and will additionally cover Yii2's powerful helper classes.

Chapter 6, Asset Management, focuses on how to create and manage our assets using asset bundles and how to manage our assets using the asset command. This chapter also covers several strategies to build and generate our asset library using powerful tools such as Node Package Manage and Bower.

Chapter 7, Authenticating and Authorizing Users, teaches you how to verify the authenticity of users in Yii2 using several common authentication schemes (such as OAuth authentication, basic HTTP authentication, and header authentication) as well as shows you how to grant them access to specific sections of your applications.

Chapter 8, Routing, Responses, and Events, focuses on how Yii2's routing and response classes work in Yii2. In this chapter, we'll cover how to handle data both in and out of our application and discover how to tap into Yii2's powerful event system.

Chapter 9, RESTful APIs, talks about how to quickly and effortlessly extend your application with a RESTful JSON and XML API using Yii2's ActiveController class.

Chapter 10, Testing with Codeception, helps you learn how to create unit, functional, and acceptance tests for your applications using a powerful testing tool called Codeception. In this chapter, you'll also learn how to create fixtures to represent your data for testing purposes.

Chapter 11, Internationalization and Localization, covers how to localize our applications and build them to support multiple languages. Additionally, you will master how to create and manage translation files using Yii2 console commands.

Chapter 12, Performance and Security, covers many ways to improve the performance of your Yii2 application and how to keep it secure against modern day attacks on web applications.

Chapter 13, Debugging and Deploying, helps you become well-versed in how to debug your Yii2 applications using both application logging and the Yii2 debug tool. Furthermore, you will discover the fundamentals of deploying your Yii2 applications in a seamless and non-disruptive fashion.

What you need for this book

To ensure a consistent development environment and prevent unnecessary alterations to your host operation system, it is highly recommended that you run all commands within a Linux virtual machine. This will ensure that your output both in your web browser and from your command line matches the output that is presented in this book. As setting up this environment on your own can be a daunting task, prebuilt virtual machines that use VirtualBox and Vagrant are provided to make this setup process easy.

To get started with this book, you should be running the latest version of either Microsoft Windows 7, 8, 8.1 or 10, Apple OS X 10.9 or higher, or a Linux operating system that can run virtual machines, such as Ubuntu 14.04 LTS. Additionally, you will need to install the latest version of VirtualBox (available at `https://www.virtualbox.org/wiki/Downloads`) and Vagrant (available at `https://www.vagrantup.com/downloads.html`).

 After installing these software dependencies, you may need to restart your computer for the changes to take effect.

After installing VirtualBox and Vagrant, you can then create a new dedicated development environment by opening a new command line or terminal window, creating a new directory for the chapter, and then running the following command to create your virtual machine development environment. These commands will download a prebuilt virtual machine containing all the software required to get you started and start your new development environment:

```
vagrant init charlesportwoodii/php56_trusty64
vagrant up --provider virtualbox
vagrant ssh
```

 More information on this specific Vagrant box can be found at `https://atlas.hashicorp.com/charlesportwoodii/boxes/php56_trusty64`.

Note that if you are on Windows, you may need a tool such as PuTTy to connect to your virtual machine over SSH. More information on how to connect to your new virtual machine over SSH on Windows can be found at `http://docs-v1.vagrantup.com/v1/docs/getting-started/ssh.html`.

Once your new Vagrant box has started, you can access the files of this virtual machine over SSH and access your webroot directory by opening a new browser window and navigating to http://localhost:8080. By default, when you open this web page, you will see the output of phpino().

Depending upon your operating system security settings, your computer may prompt or block you from accessing port 8080 on your computer. Ensure that you configure your firewall settings if you are facing issues and ensure that port 8080 is open on your computer and that VirtualBox can forward connections from your host operating system to your guest operating system.

As Yii2 is fully compatible with PHP7, it is strongly suggested that you develop and test your web applications against PHP7 as well. The following commands will allow you to provision a PHP7 Vagrant box:

```
vagrant init charlesportwoodii/php7_trusty64
vagrant up --provider virtualbox
vagrant ssh
```

As these virtual machines automatically configure port forwarding, it is recommended that you only run a single virtual machine at a time. Refer to the Vagrant documentation for a complete list of commands and configuration options at https://docs.vagrantup.com/v2.

Who this book is for

Mastering Yii is for intermediate to experienced software developers who want to quickly master Yii2. This book assumes some familiarity with PHP 5, HTML5, and rudimentary software development practices and methodologies.

Conventions

In this book, you will find a number of text styles that distinguish between different kinds of information. Here are some examples of these styles and an explanation of their meaning.

Code words in text, database table names, folder names, filenames, file extensions, pathnames, dummy URLs, user input, and Twitter handles are shown as follows: " This script tells Composer that when the `create-project` command is run, it should run the `postCreateProject` static function."

A block of code is set as follows:

```
"scripts": {
    "post-create-project-cmd": [
        "yii\\composer\\Installer::postCreateProject"
    ]
}
```

When we wish to draw your attention to a particular part of a code block, the relevant lines or items are set in bold:

```
// Define our application_env variable as provided by nginx/apache
if (!defined('APPLICATION_ENV'))
{
    if (getenv('APPLICATION_ENV') != false)
        define('APPLICATION_ENV', getenv('APPLICATION_ENV'));
    else
        define('APPLICATION_ENV', 'prod');
}

$env = require(__DIR__ . '/config/env.php');
```

Any command-line input or output is written as follows:

```
$ ./yii fixture/load <FixtureName>
$ ./yii fixture/unload <FixtureName>
```

New terms and **important words** are shown in bold. Words that you see on the screen, for example, in menus or dialog boxes, appear in the text like this: " Once we have specified all the necessary attributes, we can click on the **Preview** button to preview our form, and then we can click on the **Generate** button to generate the source code."

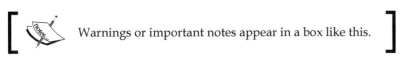

Warnings or important notes appear in a box like this.

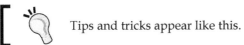

Tips and tricks appear like this.

Reader feedback

Feedback from our readers is always welcome. Let us know what you think about this book—what you liked or disliked. Reader feedback is important for us as it helps us develop titles that you will really get the most out of.

To send us general feedback, simply e-mail `feedback@packtpub.com`, and mention the book's title in the subject of your message.

If there is a topic that you have expertise in and you are interested in either writing or contributing to a book, see our author guide at `www.packtpub.com/authors`.

Customer support

Now that you are the proud owner of a Packt book, we have a number of things to help you to get the most from your purchase.

Downloading the example code

The latest and most up to date copies of source code for this book is maintained on the Packt website: `http://www.packtpub.com` and on GitHub at `https://github.com/masteringyii`, for each chapter where applicable.

Errata

Although we have taken every care to ensure the accuracy of our content, mistakes do happen. If you find a mistake in one of our books—maybe a mistake in the text or the code—we would be grateful if you could report this to us. By doing so, you can save other readers from frustration and help us improve subsequent versions of this book. If you find any errata, please report them by visiting `http://www.packtpub.com/submit-errata`, selecting your book, clicking on the **Errata Submission Form** link, and entering the details of your errata. Once your errata are verified, your submission will be accepted and the errata will be uploaded to our website or added to any list of existing errata under the Errata section of that title.

To view the previously submitted errata, go to `https://www.packtpub.com/books/content/support` and enter the name of the book in the search field. The required information will appear under the **Errata** section.

Piracy

Piracy of copyrighted material on the Internet is an ongoing problem across all media. At Packt, we take the protection of our copyright and licenses very seriously. If you come across any illegal copies of our works in any form on the Internet, please provide us with the location address or website name immediately so that we can pursue a remedy.

Please contact us at copyright@packtpub.com with a link to the suspected pirated material.

We appreciate your help in protecting our authors and our ability to bring you valuable content.

Questions

If you have a problem with any aspect of this book, you can contact us at questions@packtpub.com, and we will do our best to address the problem.

1
Composer, Configuration, Classes, and Path Aliases

Before diving into Yii Framework 2, we need to take a look at how it is installed, how it is configured, and what the core building blocks of the framework are. In this chapter, we'll go over how to install the framework itself and prebuilt applications via a package management tool called **Composer**. We'll also cover some common configurations of both Yii Framework 2 and our web server, including making our applications aware of the environment they are running on and responding appropriately to that environment.

 The most common ways to reference Yii Framework 2 are *Yii Framework 2*, *YF2*, and *Yii2*. We'll be using these terms interchangeably throughout the book.

Composer

There are several different ways to install Yii2, ranging from downloading the framework from source control (typically, from GitHub at `https://github.com/yiisoft/yii2`) to using a package manager such as Composer. With modern web applications, Composer is the preferred method to install Yii2 as it enables us to install, update, and manage all dependencies and extensions for our application in an automated fashion. Additionally, using Composer, we can ensure that Yii Framework 2 is kept up to date with the latest security and bug fixes. Composer can be installed by following the instructions on `https://getcomposer.org`. Typically, this process looks as follows:

```
curl -sS https://getcomposer.org/installer | php
```

Alternatively, if you don't have cURL available on your system, it can be installed through PHP itself:

```
php -r "readfile('https://getcomposer.org/installer');" | php
```

Once installed, we should move Composer to a more centralized directory so that we can call it from any directory on our system. Installing Composer from a centralized directory rather than on a per-project basis has several advantages:

- It can be called anywhere from any project. When working with multiple projects, we can ensure that we use the same dependency manager each time and for every project.

- In a centralized directory, Composer only needs to be updated once rather than in every project we are working on.

- Dependency managers are rarely considered code that should be pushed to your DCVS repository. Keeping the composer.phar file out of your repository reduces the amount of code you need to commit and push and ensures that your source code remains isolated from your package manager code.

- By installing Composer from a centralized directory, we can ensure that Composer is always available, which saves us a step each time we clone a project that depends on Composer.

A good directory to move Composer to is /usr/local/bin, as shown in the following example:

```
mv composer.phar /usr/local/bin/composer
chmod a+x /usr/local/bin/composer
```

 Throughout this book, we'll be using Unix-style commands when referencing command-line arguments. Consequently, some commands may not work on Windows. If you decide to set up a Windows environment, you might need to use Composer-Setup.exe (available at https://getcomposer.org/Composer-Setup.exe) to get Composer configured for your system. If you have any issues getting Composer to run on your system, ensure that you check out the Composer documentation available at https://getcomposer.org/doc/.

Alternatively, if you have Composer installed on your system already, ensure that you update it to the latest version by running this:

```
composer self-update
```

The commands that we use through this book are based on the assumption that you have sufficient privileges to run them. On Unix-like systems, you may need to preface some commands with `sudo` in order to execute the command with a high permissions set. Alternatively if you are running these commands on Windows, you should ensure that you are running the listed commands in a command prompt that has elevated privileges. Ensure that you follow best practices when using `sudo` and when using elevated command prompts in order to ensure your system stays secure.

Once Composer is installed, we'll need to install a global plugin called **The Composer Asset Plugin** (available at `https://github.com/francoispluchino/composer-asset-plugin`). This plugin enables Composer to manage asset files for us without the need to install additional software (these programs are Bower, an asset dependency manager created by Twitter, and Node Package Manager, or NPM, which is a JavaScript dependency manager).

```
composer global require "fxp/composer-asset-plugin:1.0.0"
```

 Due to the GitHub API's rate limiting, during installation, Composer may ask you to enter your GitHub credentials. After entering your credentials, Composer will request a dedicated API key from GitHub that can be used for future installations. Ensure that you check out the Composer documentation at `https://getcomposer.org/doc/` for more information.

With Composer installed, we can now instantiate our application. If we want to install an existing Yii2 package, we can simply run the following:

```
composer create-project --prefer-dist <package/name> <foldername>
```

Using the Yii2 basic app as an example, this command will look like this:

```
composer create-project --prefer-dist yiisoft/yii2-app-basic basic
```

After running the command, you should see output similar to the following:

```
Installing yiisoft/yii2-app-basic (2.0.6)
  - Installing yiisoft/yii2-app-basic (2.0.6)
    Downloading: 100%
Created project in basic
Loading composer repositories with package information
Installing dependencies (including require-dev)
```

```
- Installing yiisoft/yii2-composer (2.0.3)

- Installing ezyang/htmlpurifier (v4.6.0)

- Installing bower-asset/jquery (2.1.4)

- Installing bower-asset/yii2-pjax (v2.0.4)

- Installing bower-asset/punycode (v1.3.2)

- Installing bower-asset/jquery.inputmask (3.1.63)

- Installing cebe/markdown (1.1.0)

- Installing yiisoft/yii2 (2.0.6)

- Installing swiftmailer/swiftmailer (v5.4.1)

- Installing yiisoft/yii2-swiftmailer (2.0.4)

- Installing yiisoft/yii2-codeception (2.0.4)

- Installing bower-asset/bootstrap (v3.3.5)

- Installing yiisoft/yii2-bootstrap (2.0.5)

- Installing yiisoft/yii2-debug (2.0.5)

- Installing bower-asset/typeahead.js (v0.10.5)

- Installing phpspec/php-diff (v1.0.2)

- Installing yiisoft/yii2-gii (2.0.4)

- Installing fzaninotto/faker (v1.5.0)

- Installing yiisoft/yii2-faker (2.0.3)
Writing lock file
Generating autoload files
> yii\composer\Installer::postCreateProject
chmod('runtime', 0777)...done.
chmod('web/assets', 0777)...done.
chmod('yii', 0755)...done.
```

 Your output may differ slightly due to the data cached on your system and versions of subpackages.

This command will install the Yii2 basic app to a folder called basic. When creating a new Yii2 project, you'll typically want to use the create-project command to clone "yii2-app-basic" and then develop your application from there as the basic app comes prepopulated with just about everything you need to start a new project. However, you can also create a Yii2 project from scratch that, while more complicated, gives you more control over your application's structure.

Let's take a look at the `composer.json` file that was created when we ran the `create-project` command:

```json
{
    "name": "yiisoft/yii2-app-basic",
    "description": "Yii 2 Basic Application Template",
    "keywords": ["yii2", "framework", "basic",
    "application template"],
    "homepage": "http://www.yiiframework.com/",
    "type": "project",
    "license": "BSD-3-Clause",
    "support": {
        "issues": "https://github.com/
        yiisoft/yii2/issues?state=open",
        "forum": "http://www.yiiframework.com/forum/",
        "wiki": "http://www.yiiframework.com/wiki/",
        "irc": "irc://irc.freenode.net/yii",
        "source": "https://github.com/yiisoft/yii2"
    },
    "minimum-stability": "stable",
    "require": {
        "php": ">=5.4.0",
        "yiisoft/yii2": "*",
        "yiisoft/yii2-bootstrap": "*",
        "yiisoft/yii2-swiftmailer": "*"
    },
    "require-dev": {
        "yiisoft/yii2-codeception": "*",
        "yiisoft/yii2-debug": "*",
        "yiisoft/yii2-gii": "*",
        "yiisoft/yii2-faker": "*"
    },
    "config": {
        "process-timeout": 1800
    },
    "scripts": {
        "post-create-project-cmd": [
            "yii\\composer\\Installer::postCreateProject"
        ]
    },
    "extra": {
        "yii\\composer\\Installer::postCreateProject": {
            "setPermission": [
                {
                    "runtime": "0777",
```

```
                "web/assets": "0777",
                "yii": "0755"
            }
        ],
        "generateCookieValidationKey": [
            "config/web.php"
        ]
    },
    "asset-installer-paths": {
        "npm-asset-library": "vendor/npm",
        "bower-asset-library": "vendor/bower"
    }
}
}
```

While most of these items (such as the name, description, license, and require blocks) are rather self-explanatory, there are a few Yii2-specific items in here that we should take note of. The first section we want to look at is the `"scripts"` section:

```
"scripts": {
    "post-create-project-cmd": [
        "yii\\composer\\Installer::postCreateProject"
    ]
}
```

This script tells Composer that when the `create-project` command is run, it should run the `postCreateProject` static function. Looking at the the framework source code, we see that this file is referenced in the `yii2-composer` package (refer to `https://github.com/yiisoft/yii2-composer/blob/master/Installer.php#L232`). This command then runs several post-project creation actions, namely setting the local disk permissions, generating a unique cookie validation key, and setting some asset installer paths for composer-asset-plugin.

Next, we have the `"extra"` block:

```
"extra": {
    "yii\\composer\\Installer::postCreateProject": {
        "setPermission": [
            {
                "runtime": "0777",
                "web/assets": "0777",
                "yii": "0755"
            }
        ],
        "generateCookieValidationKey": [
```

```
            "config/web.php"
        ]
    },
    "asset-installer-paths": {
        "npm-asset-library": "vendor/npm",
        "bower-asset-library": "vendor/bower"
    }
}
```

This section tells Composer to use these options when it runs the postCreateProject command. These preconfigured options give us a good starting point to create our applications.

Configuration

With our basic application now installed, let's take a look at a few basic configuration and bootstrap files that Yii2 automatically generated for us.

Requirements checker

Projects created from yii2-app-basic now come with a built-in requirements script called requirements.php. This script checks several different values in order to ensure that Yii2 can run on our application server. Before running our application, let's run the requirements checker:

php requirements.php

You'll get output similar to the following:

```
Yii Application Requirement Checker

This script checks if your server configuration meets the requirements
for running Yii application.

It checks if the server is running the right version of PHP,  if
appropriate PHP extensions have been loaded, and if php.ini file settings
are correct.

Check conclusion:

-----------------

PHP version: OK

[... more checks here ...]

-----------------------------------------

Errors: 0   Warnings: 6   Total checks: 21
```

In general, as long as the error count is set to 0, we'll be good to move forward. If the requirements checker notices an error, it will report it in the Check conclusion section for you to rectify.

> As part of your deployment process, it is recommended that your deployment tool runs the requirements checker. This helps ensure that your application server meets all the requirements for Yii2 and that your application doesn't get deployed to a server or environment that doesn't support it.

Entry scripts

Like its predecessor, Yii Framework 2 comes with two separate entry scripts: one for web applications and the other for console applications.

Web entry script

In Yii2, the entry script for web applications has been moved from the root (/) folder to the web/ folder. In Yii1, our PHP files were stored in the protected/ directory. By moving our entry scripts to the web/ directory, Yii2 has increased the security of our application by reducing the amount of web server configuration we need to run our application. Furthermore, all public asset (JavaScript and CSS) files are now completely isolated from our source code directories. If we open up web/index.php, our entry script now looks as follows:

```php
<?php

// comment out the following two lines when deployed to production
defined('YII_DEBUG') or define('YII_DEBUG', true);
defined('YII_ENV') or define('YII_ENV', 'dev');

require(__DIR__ . '/../vendor/autoload.php');
require(__DIR__ . '/../vendor/yiisoft/yii2/Yii.php');

$config = require(__DIR__ . '/../config/web.php');

(new yii\web\Application($config))->run();
```

While suitable for basic applications, the default entry script requires us to manually comment out and change the code when moving to different environments. Since changing the code in a nondevelopment environment doesn't follow best practices, we should change this code block so that we don't have to touch our code to move it to a different environment.

We'll start by creating a new application-wide constant called `APPLICATION_ENV`. This variable will be defined by either our web server or our console environment and will allow us to dynamically load different configuration files depending upon the environment that we're working in:

1. After the opening `<?php` tag in `web/index.php`, add the following code block:

    ```php
    // Define our application_env variable as provided by nginx/
    apache/console
    if (!defined('APPLICATION_ENV'))
    {
        if (getenv('APPLICATION_ENV') != false)
            define('APPLICATION_ENV',
            getenv('APPLICATION_ENV'));
        else
            define('APPLICATION_ENV', 'prod');
    }
    ```

    Our application now knows how to read the `APPLCATTION_ENV` variable from the environment variable, which will be passed either though our command line or our web server configuration. By default, if no environment is set, the `APPLICATION_ENV` variable will be set to prod.

    Next, we'll want to load a separate environment file that contains several environmental constants that we'll use to dynamically change how our application runs in different environments:

    ```php
    $env = require(__DIR__ . '/../config/env.php');
    ```

    Next, we'll configure Yii to set the `YII_DEBUG` and `YII_ENV` variables according to our application:

    ```php
    defined('YII_DEBUG') or define('YII_DEBUG', $env['debug']);
    defined('YII_ENV') or define('YII_ENV', APPLICATION_ENV);
    ```

2. Then, follow the rest of our `index.php` file under `web/`:

    ```php
    require(__DIR__ . '/../vendor/autoload.php');
    require(__DIR__ . '/../vendor/yiisoft/yii2/Yii.php');
    (new yii\web\Application($config))->run();
    ```

With these changes, our web application is now configured to be aware of its environment and load the appropriate configuration files.

 Don't worry; later in the chapter, we'll cover how to define the `APPLICATION_ENV` variable for both our web server (either Apache or NGINX) and our command line.

Configuration files

In Yii2, configuration files are still split into console- and web-specific configurations. As there are many commonalities between these two files (such as our database and environment configuration), we'll store common elements in their own files and include those files in both our web and console configurations. This will help us follow the DRY standard, and reduce duplicate code within our application.

 The **DRY** (**don't repeat yourself**) principle in software development states that we should avoid having the same code block appear in multiple places in our application. By keeping our application DRY, we can ensure that our application is performant and can reduce bugs in our application. By moving our database and parameters' configuration to their own file, we can reuse that same code in both our web and console configuration files.

Web and console configuration files

Yii2 supports two different kinds of configuration files: one for web applications and another for console applications. In Yii2, our web configuration file is stored in `config/web.php` and our console configuration file is stored in `config/console.php`. If you're familiar with Yii1, you'll see that the basic structure of both of these files hasn't changed all that much.

Database configuration

The next file we'll want to look at is our database configuration file stored in `config/db.php`. This file contains all the information our web and console applications will need in order to connect to the database.

In our basic application, this file looks as follows:

```php
<?php

return [
    'class' => 'yii\db\Connection',
```

```
        'dsn' => 'mysql:host=localhost;dbname=yii2basic',
        'username' => 'root',
        'password' => '',
        'charset' => 'utf8',
    ];
```

For an application that is aware of its environment, however, we should replace this file with a configuration that will use the APPLICATION_ENV variable that we defined earlier:

```
<?php return require __DIR__ . '/env/' . APPLICATION_ENV .
'/db.php';
```

 Right now, we're just setting things up. We'll cover how to set up our directories in the next section.

With this change, our application now knows that it needs to look in a file called db.php under config/env/<APPLICATION_ENV>/ to pull the correct configuration environment for that file.

Parameter configuration

In a manner similar to our database configuration file, Yii also lets us use a parameter file where we can store all of the noncomponent parameters for our application. This file is located at config/params.php. Since the basic app doesn't make this file aware of its environment, we'll change it to do that as follows:

```
<?php return require __DIR__ . '/env/' . APPLICATION_ENV .
'/params.php';
```

Environment configuration

Finally, we have the environment configuration that we defined earlier when working with our entry scripts. We'll store this file in config/env.php, and it should be written as follows:

```
<?php return require __DIR__ . '/env/' . APPLICATION_ENV .
'/env.php';
```

Most modern applications have several different environments depending upon their requirements. Typically, we'd break them down into four distinct environments:

- The first environment we typically have is called **DEV**. This environment is where all of our local development occurs. Typically, developers have complete control over this environment and can change it, as required, to build their applications.

- The second environment that we typically have is a testing environment called **TEST**. Normally, we'd deploy our application to this environment in order to make sure that our code works in a production-like setting; however, we normally would still have high log levels and debug information available to us when using this environment.

- The third environment we typically have is called **UAT**, or the User Acceptance Testing environment. This is a separate environment that we'd provide to our client or business stakeholders for them to test the application to verify that it does what they want it to do.

- Finally, in our typical setup, we'd have our **PROD** or production environment. This is where our code finally gets deployed to and where all of our users ultimately interact with our application.

As outlined in the previous sections, we've been pointing all of our environment configuration files to the config/env/<env> folder. Since our local environment is going to be called DEV, we'll create it first:

1. We'll start by creating our DEV environment folder from the command line:

   ```
   mkdir -p config/env/dev
   ```

2. Next, we'll create our dev database configuration file in db.php under config/env/dev/. For now, we'll stick with a basic SQLite database:

   ```php
   <?php return [
       'dsn' => 'sqlite:/' . __DIR__ .
       '/../../../runtime/db.sqlite',
         'class' => 'yii\db\Connection',
       'charset' => 'utf8'
   ];
   ```

3. Next, we'll create our environment configuration file in env.php under config/env/dev. If you recall from earlier in the chapter, this is where our debug flag was stored, so this file will look as follows:

   ```php
   <?php return [
       'debug' => true
   ];
   ```

4. Finally, we'll create our `params.php` file under `config/env/dev/`. As of now, this file will simply return an empty array:

```
<?php return [];
```

Now, for simplicity, let's copy over this configuration to our other environments. From the command line, we can do that as follows:

```
cp -R config/env/dev config/env/test
cp -R config/env/dev config/env/uat
cp -R config/env/dev config/env/prod
```

Setting up our application environment

Now that we've told Yii what files and configurations it needs to use for each environment, we need to tell it what environment to use. To do this, we'll set custom variables in our web server configuration that will pass this option to Yii.

Setting the web environment for NGINX

With our console application properly configured, we now need to configure our web server to pass the `APPLICATION_ENV` variable to our application. In a typical NGINX configuration, we have a location block that looks as follows:

```
location ~ \.php$ {
        include fastcgi_params;
        fastcgi_param SCRIPT_FILENAME $document_root/
        $fastcgi_script_name;
        fastcgi_pass   127.0.0.1:9000;
        #fastcgi_pass unix:/var/run/php5-fpm.sock;
        try_files $uri =404;
    }
```

To pass the `APPLICATION_ENV` variable to our application, all we need to do is define a new `fastcgi_param` as follows:

```
fastcgi_param   APPLICATION_ENV "dev";
```

After making this change, simply restart NGINX.

Setting the web environment for Apache

We can also easily configure Apache to pass the APPLICATION_ENV variable to our application. With Apache, we typically have a VirtualHost block that looks as follows:

```
# Set document root to be "basic/web"
DocumentRoot "path/to/basic/web"

<Directory "path/to/basic/web">
    # use mod_rewrite for pretty URL support
    RewriteEngine on
    # If a directory or a file exists, use the request directly
    RewriteCond %{REQUEST_FILENAME} !-f
    RewriteCond %{REQUEST_FILENAME} !-d
    # Otherwise forward the request to index.php
    RewriteRule . index.php

    # ...other settings...
</Directory>
```

To pass the APPLICATION_ENV variable to our application, all we need to do is use the SetEnv command as follows, which can be placed anywhere in our VirtualHost block:

```
SetEnv    APPLICATION_ENV dev
```

After making this change, simply restart Apache and navigate to your application.

At the most basic level, our application isn't doing anything different from what it was when we first ran the composer create-project command. Despite not doing anything different, our application is now significantly more powerful and flexible than it was before our changes. Later on in the book, we'll take a look at how these changes in particular can make automated deployments of our application a seamless and simple process.

Components and objects

There are two base classes that almost everything in Yii2 extends from: the Component class and the Object class.

Components

In Yii2, the `Component` class has replaced the `CComponent` class from Yii1. In Yii1, components act as service locators that host a specific set of application components that provide different services for the processing of requests. Each component in Yii2 can be accessed using the following syntax:

```
Yii::$app->componentID
```

For example, the database component can be accessed using this:

```
Yii::$app->db
```

The cache component can be accessed using this:

```
Yii::$app->cache
```

Yii2 automatically registers each component at runtime via the application configuration that we mentioned in the previous section by name.

To improve performance in Yii2 applications, components are lazy-loaded or only instantiated the first time they are accessed. This means that if the cache component is never used in your application code, the cache component will never be loaded. At times, however, this can be nonideal, so to force load a component, you can bootstrap it by adding it to the bootstrap configuration option in either `config/web.php` or `config/console.php`. For instance, if we want to bootstrap the log component, we can do that as follows:

```php
<?php return [
    'bootstrap' => [
        'log'
    ],
    [...]
]
```

The `bootstrap` option behaves in a manner similar to the preload option in Yii1 — any component that you want or need to be instantiated on bootstrap will be loaded if it is in the `bootstrap` section of your configuration file.

For more information on service locators and components, ensure that you read the *Definitive Guide to Yii* guide located at http://www.yiiframework.com/doc-2.0/guide-concept-service-locator.html and http://www.yiiframework.com/doc-2.0/guide-structure-application-components.html.

Objects

In Yii2, almost every class that doesn't extend from the Component class extends from the Object class. The Object class is the base class that implements the property feature. In Yii2, the property feature allows you to access a lot of information about an object, such as the __get and __set magic methods, as well as other utility functions, such as hasProperty(), canGetProperty(), and canSetProperty(). Combined, this makes objects in Yii2 extremely powerful.

> The object class is extremely powerful, and many classes in Yii extend from it. Despite this, using the magic methods __get and __set yourself is not considered best practice as it is slower than a native PHP method and doesn't integrate well with your IDE's autocomplete tool and documentation tools.

Path aliases

In Yii2, path aliases are used to represent file paths or URL paths so that we don't hardcode paths or URLs directly into our application. In Yii2, aliases always start with the @ symbol so that Yii knows how to differentiate it from a file path or URL.

Aliases can be defined in several ways. The most basic way to define a new alias is to call \Yii::setAlias():

```
\Yii::setAlias('@path', '/path/to/example');
\Yii::setAlias('@example, 'https://www.example.com');
```

Aliases can also be defined in the application configuration file by setting the alias option as follows:

```
return [
    // ...
    'aliases' => [
        '@path => '/path/to/example,
        '@example' => 'https://www.example.com',
    ],
];
```

Also, aliases can be easily retrieved using \Yii::getAlias():

```
\Yii::getAlias('@path') // returns /path/to/example
\Yii::getAlias('@example') // returns https://www.example.com
```

Several places in Yii are alias-aware and will accept aliases as inputs. For example, `yii\caching\FileCache` accepts a file alias as an alias for the `$cachePath` parameter:

```
$cache = new FileCache([
    'cachePath' => '@runtime/cache',
]);
```

 For more information on path aliases, check out the Yii documentation at `http://www.yiiframework.com/doc-2.0/guide-concept-aliases.html`.

Summary

In this chapter, we went over how to create new Yii2 applications via composer. We also went over the basic configuration files that come with Yii2 as well as how to configure our web application to load environment-specific configuration files. Finally, we also covered components, objects, and path aliases, which are fundamental to gaining mastery over Yii.

In the next chapter, we'll cover everything you need to know in order to become a master of console commands and applications.

2
Console Commands and Applications

Often when building modern web applications, we need to write background and maintenance tasks to support our main application. These tasks may include things such as generating reports, sending e-mails via a queuing system, or even running data analysis that would cause a web-based endpoint to timeout. With Yii2, we can build these tools and scripts directly into our application by writing console commands or even complete console applications.

Configuration and usage

The basic structure of Yii2 console applications is very similar to the structure used in web applications. In Yii2, console commands that extend from `yii\console\Controller` are nearly identical to `yii\web\Controller`.

Entry script

Before moving on to the configuration files themselves, let's take a look at the console entry script, which is part of the file called `yii`. This entry script serves as the bootstrapper for all our console commands, and in general, they can be run by calling this:

```
$ ./yii
```

This command will output all the currently available commands for the system. Like the web/index.php entry script, though, it isn't aware of its environment yet. We can change this by replacing yii with the following code block:

```php
#!/usr/bin/env php
<?php
/**
 * Yii console bootstrap file.
 */

// Define our application_env variable as provided by nginx/apache
if (!defined('APPLICATION_ENV'))
{
    if (getenv('APPLICATION_ENV') != false)
        define('APPLICATION_ENV', getenv('APPLICATION_ENV'));
    else
        define('APPLICATION_ENV', 'prod');
}

$env = require(__DIR__ . '/config/env.php');

defined('YII_DEBUG') or define('YII_DEBUG', $env['debug']);

// fcgi doesn't have STDIN and STDOUT defined by default
defined('STDIN') or define('STDIN', fopen('php://stdin', 'r'));
defined('STDOUT') or define('STDOUT', fopen('php://stdout', 'w'));

require(__DIR__ . '/vendor/autoload.php');
require(__DIR__ . '/vendor/yiisoft/yii2/Yii.php');

$config = require(__DIR__ . '/config/console.php');

$application = new yii\console\Application($config);
$exitCode = $application->run();
exit($exitCode);
```

 This script is intended for Linux-like environments. Yii2 also provides a yii.bat file that can be run on Windows. If you're following along on a Windows computer, ensure that you change yii.bat in addition to the yii file.

With our entry script files configured, we're ready to take a look at our application configuration files.

You may also notice that in the web/ folder, there is a separate entry script called index-test.php. This script is used by Codeception, a testing framework that is used to run unit, functional, and acceptance tests in Yii2. We'll cover how to configure and use this entry script and Codeception in *Chapter 10, Testing with Codeception*.

Configuration

In Yii2, the console configuration file is located at config/console.php and is nearly identical to our web configuration file:

```php
<?php

Yii::setAlias('@tests', dirname(__DIR__) . '/tests');

return [
    'id' => 'basic-console',
    'basePath' => dirname(__DIR__),
    'bootstrap' => ['log'],
    'controllerNamespace' => 'app\commands',
    'components' => [
        'cache' => [
            'class' => 'yii\caching\FileCache',
        ],
        'log' => [
            'targets' => [
                [
                    'class' => 'yii\log\FileTarget',
                    'levels' => ['error', 'warning'],
                ],
            ],
        ],
        'db' => require(__DIR__ . '/db.php'),
    ],
    'params' => require(__DIR__ . '/params.php'),
];
```

Like our web configuration file, we can include our database and parameters' configuration files using the environment-aware configurations we wrote in *Chapter 1, Composer, Configuration, Classes, and Path Aliases*. In fact, the only major difference between our web and console configuration is the explicit declaration of our console command namespace and the explicit declaration of the @test alias, which defines where our test files will be located.

Thanks to Yii's extremely flexible structure, we can reorganize our bootstrap and entry script files to be in many different physical locations on our file system. Because of this flexibility, the console configuration file expects us to declare the @test alias explicitly so that we can run our console tests.

Setting the console environment

Following the same convention we set up for our web application, we now need to instruct our console to pass the APPLICATION_ENV variable to our console application. From the command line, we can easily change the environment by exporting a variable:

```
export APPLICATION_ENV="dev"
```

If we want to make this change permanent for the server we are working on, we can store this variable in our ~/.bash_profile file, or we can store it globally for all users at /etc/profile. By adding this command to either of these files, the next time we log in to our shell, this variable will automatically be exported. Note that if you're using Windows, you'll need to export this variable to your %path% variable.

Go ahead and give it a try! Log out and log in to your shell again and run the following:

```
echo $APPLICATION_ENV
```

If your computer is configured correctly, you should see the environment outputted to your screen.

```
dev
```

Running console commands

With our console application now configured, we can easily run our console commands by running the following command:

```
$ ./yii
```

On Windows, this command is yii.bat.

If you are familiar with Yii1, this command has now replaced the `/yiic` command.

Without any arguments, this is the same as running `/yii help` and will output the help menu, which lists all the built-in console commands for our application:

```
$ ./yii
```

```
This is Yii version 2.0.6.

The following commands are available:

- asset                        Allows you to combine and compress your JavaScript
                               and CSS files.
    asset/compress (default)   Combines and compresses the asset files according
                               to the given configuration.
    asset/template             Creates template of configuration file for
                               [[actionCompress]].

- basic                        A basic controller for our Yii2 Application

- cache                        Allows you to flush cache.
    cache/flush                Flushes given cache components.
    cache/flush-all            Flushes all caches registered in the system.
    cache/flush-schema         Clears DB schema cache for a given connection
                               component.
    cache/index (default)      Lists the caches that can be flushed.

- fixture                      Manages fixture data loading and unloading.
    fixture/load (default)     Loads the specified fixture data.
    fixture/unload             Unloads the specified fixtures.

- gii                          This is the command line version of Gii - a code
                               generator.
    gii/controller             Controller Generator
    gii/crud                   CRUD Generator
    gii/extension              Extension Generator
    gii/form                   Form Generator
    gii/index (default)
    gii/model                  Model Generator
    gii/module                 Module Generator

- help                         Provides help information about console commands.
    help/index (default)       Displays available commands or the detailed
                               information

- message                      Extracts messages to be translated from source
                               files.
    message/config             Creates a configuration file for the "extract"
                               command.
    message/extract (default)  Extracts messages to be translated from source
                               code.

- migrate                      Manages application migrations.
    migrate/create             Creates a new migration.
    migrate/down               Downgrades the application by reverting old
                               migrations.
    migrate/history            Displays the migration history.
    migrate/mark               Modifies the migration history to the specified
                               version.
    migrate/new                Displays the un-applied new migrations.
    migrate/redo               Redoes the last few migrations.
    migrate/to                 Upgrades or downgrades till the specified version.
    migrate/up (default)       Upgrades the application by applying new
                               migrations.
```

Yii provides additional help information for each of the default commands. For example, if we want to see what subcommands exist for the cache command, we can run the following:

```
$ ./yii help cache
```

```
DESCRIPTION

Allows you to flush cache.

see list of available components to flush:

yii cache

flush particular components specified by their names:

yii cache/flush first second third

flush all cache components that can be found in the system

yii cache/flush-all

Note that the command uses cache components defined in your console application co
nfiguration file. If components
configured are different from web application, web application cache won't be clea
red. In order to fix it please
duplicate web application cache components in console config. You can use any comp
onent names.


SUB-COMMANDS

- cache/flush            Flushes given cache components.
- cache/flush-all        Flushes all caches registered in the system.
- cache/flush-schema     Clears DB schema cache for a given connection component.
- cache/index (default)  Lists the caches that can be flushed.

To see the detailed information about individual sub-commands, enter:

  yii help <sub-command>
```

In general, we can reduce the usage of the Yii console to the following pattern:

```
$ ./yii <route> [--option1=value1 --option2=value2 ... \
argument1 argument2 ...]
```

Here, `<route>` refers to the specific controller and action that we want to run. For example, if we wanted to flush the entire cache for our application from the console, we could run the following command:

```
$ ./yii cache/flush-all
```

This is the output we receive:

```
The following cache components were processed:
        * cache (yii\caching\FileCache)
```

The `./yii` command also enables you to use alternative console configuration files from the same command:

```
$ ./yii <route> --appconfig=path/to/config.php
```

Without having to change anything in our code, we can simply instruct Yii to use an alternate configuration file, which can contain anything, ranging from something as simple as a reference to another database or cache to something more complex such as an entirely different controller namespace. This option is especially useful when creating applications that have both a frontend and a backend that may contain different caches or database components.

Built-in console commands

Now that we know how to run console commands, let's take a look at the built-in commands to see how they work. As shown previously, Yii2 has seven built-in console commands: `help`, `asset`, `cache`, `fixtures`, `gii`, `message`, and `migrate`. During the development of our application, we're likely to use all seven in order to make our application more robust. Let's take a look at each one in more detail.

The help command

The first command built in to Yii2 is the `help` command. Often when running console commands, you may not know what options a certain command needs. Rather than referencing the Yii2 documentation, you can use the `help` command to provide you with all the core information you need.

At the most basic level, the `help` command will output all the currently available console commands:

```
$ ./yii help
```

Some commands contain additional subcommands that can be run. To view a list of all the available subcommands for a given command, you can run this:

```
$ ./yii help <command>
```

Some subcommands, such as those found in the Gii tool, require additional options to be passed to them in order for them to function. To see a list of all the required and optional flags for a given subcommand, you can run the following:

```
$ ./yii help <command/sub>
```

As we move through the next sections, ensure that you use the `help` command to see all the possible options and requirements for each command.

The asset command

The second default set of commands in our toolbox is the set of `asset` commands, which include `asset/template` and `asset/compress`.

The first command, `asset/template`, is used to generate a configuration file to automate the compression and minification of JavaScript and CSS assets, and it is used as follows:

```
$ ./yii asset/template path/to/asset.php
```

Running this command will generate a new file at `path/to/asset.php`, containing build instructions that are used by the next command, `asset/compress`. This file outlines which CSS and JavaScript compressor to use, a list of asset bundles to be compressed, a set of targets that the compressed assets will be outputted to, and any custom configuration for our `assetManager`.

The next command, `asset/compress`, reads our generated configuration file and builds the compressed asset files and a referable asset bundle configuration that we can load into our layouts and/or views. This command is called using the following:

```
$ ./yii asset/compress path/to/asset.php path/to/asset-bundle.php
```

 In *Chapter 6, Asset Management,* we will take an in-depth look at how we can use these commands in addition to the `assetManager` class in order to manage our assets in more detail.

The cache command

The third built-in command in our toolbox is the `cache` command. The `cache` command provides the functionality to flush caches that are generated by our application. These commands are `cache`, `cache/flush`, `cache/flush-all`, and `cache/flush-schema`.

The first command, `cache`, returns a named list of all the available caches defined in our configuration file and can be run using the following command:

```
$ ./yii cache
```

Here's the output:

```
The following caches were found in the system:
        * cache (yii\caching\FileCache)
```

The output of this command takes the following format so that we can identify which caches are in use. In our default application, only one cache is predefined: our file cache.

```
    <cache_name> (<cache_type>)
```

Once we know what caches are in use, we can then use the `cache/flush` command to flush that cache by name. Using the output of the previous command, we can clear the cache component by name by running this:

```
./yii cache/flush cache
```

Here's the output:

```
The following cache components will be flushed:
        * cache
The following cache components were processed:
        * cache (yii\caching\FileCache)
```

 Some commands in Yii2 are interactive and prompt for confirmation before running. This may be problematic when you need to automate the use of a command, such as on deployment. You can bypass this behavior by appending `--interactive=0` to the command. When running commands noninteractively, additional arguments may be required. Ensure that you reference the `help` command to determine what arguments you need to pass when running noninteractive commands.

Alternatively, if we want to flush the entire cache for our application, we can use the `cache/flush-all` option:

```
$ ./yii cache/flush-all
```

In our production environments, we'll want to reduce the load on our database server by caching our database schema. Yii2 will maintain a cache of the currently active db component (the database) and the database schema when instructed to. When making schema changes, such as when applying new migrations, we need to clear this cache so that Yii2 becomes aware of our updated database structure. We can clear the database schema cache by running this:

```
$ ./yii cache/flush-schema
```

 We'll cover how to enable the schema cache and improve the performance of our database in the next chapter.

The fixture command

When testing our application, we'll often want to set up our database such that our tests always run in a predictable and repeatable way. One way in which we can do this is by creating **fixtures**, which will represent database objects in our application for testing. Yii2 provides a set of commands to both load and unload fixtures; these commands are `fixture/load` and `fixture/unload`, and they do exactly what you expect them to do.

When using fixtures, our typical test flow is as follows:

1. Apply database migrations.
2. Execute our test cases in the following manner:
    1. Load our database fixtures.
    2. Execute a specific test.
    3. Unload our database fixtures.
3. Repeat as required until all tests have run.

The `fixture/load` and `fixture/unload` commands are called in the same way from the command line:

```
$ ./yii fixture/load <FixtureName>
$ ./yii fixture/unload <FixtureName>
```

Fixtures are a powerful way to create repeatable tests for our applications. Additionally, the yii2-codeception package provides additional support for the loading and unloading of fixtures when our tests run. In *Chapter 10, Testing with Codeception*, we'll cover how to creature new fixtures and how to integrate them with Codeception.

The Gii command

The next set of commands in our toolbox is the Gii command. If you are familiar with Yii1, Gii provides the functionality to generate controllers, models, forms, and even basic CRUD functionality. In Yii2, Gii has been extended from a web application module to both a web and console application and has been enhanced to include additional features as well.

The Gii module in Yii2 provides these console commands to automatically generate code: gii/controller, gii/model, gii/crud, gii/form, gii/extension, and gii/module. Each of these commands, when supplied with the right options, will generate the respective item identified by the subcommand. For a complete list of requirements and options, ensure that you use the help command on the Gii subcommands.

As a development tool, Gii has the ability to arbitrarily generate and override existing code in your application. For security purposes, you should conditionally load the Gii module only in your development environment. Moreover, the Gii module itself should never be deployed to your production environment. For this reason, it is advised that you only load the Gii module in the require-dev section of your composer.json file.

The require-dev section is a special section within our composer.json file, which allows us to separate our development dependencies from our production dependencies. By default, running Composer will install all packages in our require and require-dev sections. In production environments, we will want to exclude our development environments by passing the --no-dev flag to our Composer installation command. For more information on the Composer CLI, ensure that you reference the Composer documentation at https://getcomposer.org/doc/03-cli.md.

The message command

The next set of commands is the `message` commands, which provide functionalities to automatically generate message translations for our application in a variety of different formats.

The first subcommand is the `message/config` command, which generates a configuration file that the `message/extract` command will then use to output the translation files. Before generating any translations, we must run the `message/config` command as follows:

```
$ ./yii message/config /path/to/translation/config.php
```

This command generates a configuration file at `/path/to/translation/config.php` that contains all the information `message/extract` will need in order to generate the message output files.

After configuring your message configuration file to your liking, you can then run the `message/extract` command as follows:

```
$ ./yii message /path/to/translation/config.php
```

Depending upon your configuration file and the use of `\Yii::t()`, the built-in Yii translation tool in your application, this command will generate either a PHP file containing a list of messages, a `.po` file, and a command translation file format, or it will populate the specified table in your database with the necessary message lists.

> In *Chapter 11, Internationalization and Localization*, we'll go into more depth about how to use these commands to generate PHP message files and `.po` files and how to populate our database. We'll also cover the use of the `Yii::t()` method in detail.

The migration command

The final built-in command set with Yii2 is the `migration` command. The `migration` commands provide functionalities to generate, apply, revert, and review database migrations. This tool provides these subcommands: `migrate/create`, `migrate/history`, `migrate/mark`, `migrate/up`, `migrate/down`, `migrate/to`, `migrate/new`, and `migrate/redo`.

We'll cover how to completely use this tool and work with databases in general in more detail in *Chapter 3, Migrations, DAO, and Query Building*. For now, use the `./yii help migrate` command to view more information on the migration tool.

Creating console commands

Now that we know what built-in commands Yii2 provides, let's start adding our own commands. In Yii2, any custom commands we write are going to be stored in the / commands subfolder of our application. If this folder doesn't exist yet, go ahead and create it:

```
mkdir commands
```

Now, let's write a basic console command that just outputs some text:

1. First, we'll create a new file called `BasicController.php` in the commands folder:

    ```
    touch commands/BasicController.php
    ```

2. Now, let's write some PHP code. First, we need to declare the namespace that our `BasicController` lives in. This namespace directly corresponds to the `controllerNamespace` parameter we defined in `config/console.php`:

    ```php
    <?php

    namespace app\commands;
    ```

3. Then, we'll want to declare that we want to use the `\yii\console\Controller` class in our new controller:

    ```php
    use \yii\console\Controller;
    ```

4. Next, we'll declare our controller class as follows:

    ```php
    class BasicController extends Controller { }
    ```

5. Finally, inside our class, we'll create an `actionIndex()` method that will simply output `HelloWorld` and then gracefully return with a successful error code. By default, the `actionIndex()` method is the method that is called when an action is not specified to a controller:

```
public function actionIndex()
{
  echo "HelloWorld";
  return 0;
}
```

We have our first console command! Now, if we run the `help` command, you can see that our command appears in the list of available commands:

```
$ ./yii help
```

```
- basic                      A basic controller for our Yii2 Application
    basic/index (default)    Outputs HelloWorld
```

Moreover, we can now execute our command to verify that it functions properly:

```
$ ./yii basic
```

This is the output:

```
HelloWorld
```

Generating help information

While we can now run our commands, the `help` command for both the global help menu and the action help menu currently doesn't provide any useful information. In Yii2, this information is extracted directly from the document block comments (also known as `DocBlock` comments) that are used before our `BasicController` class and our `actionIndex()` method. For instance, consider that we add the following before our class declaration:

```
/**
 * A basic controller for our Yii2 Application
 */
class BasicController extends \yii\console\Controller {}
```

We could also provide more information to our `actionIndex()` method by specifying a `DocBlock` comment before the method:

```
/**
 * Outputs HelloWorld
 */
public function actionIndex() {}
```

Running the `help` command on the basic controller would then display the following:

$ ./yii help basic

```
DESCRIPTION

Outputs HelloWorld


USAGE

yii basic [...options...]


OPTIONS

--appconfig: string
  custom application configuration file path.
  If not set, default application configuration is used.

--color: boolean, 0 or 1
  whether to enable ANSI color in the output.
  If not set, ANSI color will only be enabled for terminals that support it.

--interactive: boolean, 0 or 1 (defaults to 1)
  whether to run the command interactively.
```

Passing command-line arguments

Like our web controllers (`yii\web\Controller`), we can also pass arguments through the command line to our console commands. Rather than using `$_GET` parameters to determine the arguments in use, Yii2 will pull the arguments directly from the command-line interface. Take, for instance, the following method of our `BasicController`:

```
/**
 * Outputs "$name lives in $city"
 * @param string $name   The name of the person
 * @param string $city  The city $name lives in
```

```
 * @return 0
 */
public function actionLivesIn($name, $city="Chicago")
{
  echo "$name lives in $city.\n";
  return 0;
}
```

The `help` command now shows us what arguments are required and what arguments are optional for this new method:

`$ ./yii help basic/lives-in`

```
DESCRIPTION

Outputs "$name lives in $city"


USAGE

yii basic/lives-in <name> [city] [...options...]

- name (required): string
  The name of the person

- city: string (defaults to 'Chicago')
  The city $name lives in


OPTIONS

--appconfig: string
  custom application configuration file path.
  If not set, default application configuration is used.

--color: boolean, 0 or 1
  whether to enable ANSI color in the output.
  If not set, ANSI color will only be enabled for terminals that support it.

--interactive: boolean, 0 or 1 (defaults to 1)
  whether to run the command interactively.
```

By now, you may have noticed that console commands can accept two types of input: arguments, (in this example, name and city), and options. Arguments serve as the data that we provide to your actions. On the other hand, options allow us to specify additional configuration for our controller in general. For instance, as previously shown, we can run our commands noninteractively by passing the --interactve=0 flag option. Each console application we create and use may have separate options that we can set. Ensure that you reference the Yii2 documentation for that class and use the help command to determine what options are available for each command.

Without any arguments, this command will throw the following error, indicating that the name parameter is required:

```
Error: Missing required arguments: name
```

Once we provide the name, the console outputs the result as expected:

```
$ ./yii basic/lives-in Alice
```

This is the output:

```
Alice lives in Chicago.
```

By providing a default value to the city parameter, that option is not required for our command to be executed. However, if we passed a value as the second parameter, it would override our default value as expected:

```
$ ./yii basic/lives-in Alice California
```

Here's the output:

```
Alice lives in California.
```

Depending upon how your shell is configured, you may not be able to pass certain characters (such as $ or *) from the command line. Ensure that you wrap any strings that use special characters in quotes to ensure that the full argument is passed to your application.

In addition to simple strings, Yii2 will also accept arrays in the form of comma-separated lists. Take, for instance, the following method:

```
/**
 * Outputs each element of the input $array on a new line
 * @param array $array A comma separated list of elements
 * @return 0
 */
public function actionListElements(array $array)
{
    foreach ($array as $$k)
        echo "$$k\n";

    return 0;
}
```

By type-hinting the first parameter using the array `type-hint`, we can notify Yii to convert the command-line arguments into a usable PHP array. From the command line, we can specify an element as an array by representing it as a comma-separated list:

`$ ./yii basic/list-elements these,are,separate,items`

This is the output that will appear:

these

are

separate

items

> Yii2 does not support the use of multidimensional arrays from the command line. If you need to pass a multidimensional array of data from the command line, you can pass a path to a configuration file instead and then load that file inside your controller action.
>
> The options to store this data range from a PHP file, which returns an array of data, to a JSON- or YAML-formatted file, which would be loaded and converted to a PHP array within your controller action.

Exit codes

As shown in our previous examples, each action we've written thus far has a return value of 0. While returning from our controller action isn't strictly necessary, it's considered a best practice so that our shell can be notified whether our console command has been executed successfully or not. By convention, an exit code of 0 indicates that our command ran without errors, whereas any positive integer greater than zero would indicate that a specific error occurred. The number returned will be the error code that is returned to the shell, and it can be used by our end users to reference our application documentation or support forum to identify what went wrong.

Suppose, for instance, that we wanted to validate one of our inputs without diving into custom forms and validators. In this example, we want our input of $shouldRun to be a positive nonzero integer. If that integer is less than zero, we could return an error code that our documentation would be able to reference:

```
/**
 * Returns successfully IFF $shouldRun is set to any
 * positive integer greater than 0
 *
 * @param integer $shouldRun
 * @return integer
 */
public function actionConditionalExit($shouldRun=0)
{
  if ((int)$shouldRun < 0)
  {
    echo 'The $shouldRun argument must be an positive
    non-zero integer' . "\n";
    return 1;
  }

  return 0;
}
```

Additionally, Yii2 provides some predefined constants for us to work with: Controller::EXIT_CODE_NORMAL, which has a value of 0, and Controller::EXIT_CODE_ERROR, which has a value of 1. If you have more than one return code, it is considered a good practice to define meaningful constants in your controller to identify your error code.

Formatting

Yii2 provides support for the formatting of the output of our console commands. This is provided through the `yii\helpers\Console` helper. Before we can use this helper, we need to import it into our class:

```php
<?php

namespace app\commands;
use yii\helpers\Console;
```

With this helper loaded, we can now use either the `stdout()` method from `\yii\console\Controller` or the `ansiFormat()` method. While both methods will format text, the `ansiFormat()` method can be used to dynamically combine multiple strings with different formats:

```php
/**
 * Outputs text in bold and cyan
 * @return 0
 */
public function actionColors()
{
    $this->stdout("Waiting on important thing to happen...\n",
    Console::BOLD);

    $yay = $this->ansiFormat('Yay', Console::FG_CYAN);
    echo "$yay! We're done!\n";
    return 0;
}
```

Then, if we run our new console command, we can see how our output text changes:

```
$ ./yii basic/colors
```

```
Waiting on important thing to happen...
Yay! We're done!
```

 A complete list of available constants is available in the Yii2 documentation at `http://www.yiiframework.com/doc-2.0/yii-helpers-baseconsole.html`.

Summary

In this chapter, we covered how to configure Yii to run console commands in a manner consistent with our web applications. We also covered the seven built-in console commands in brief. Additionally, we covered how to create our own console commands, how to pass parameters to our command, how to return values properly from within our code, and how to format the output of our commands.

In the next chapter, we'll expand our mastery of Yii by learning how to use and write migrations, how to use **database access objects** (**DAO**), and how to use Yii's built-in Query Builder.

3
Migrations, DAO, and Query Building

One of the most fundamental aspects of writing modern web application is working with databases. Through PHP's PDO driver, Yii2, can work with many different kinds of relational databases. In this chapter, we'll cover how to connect to different databases, write database migrations to instantiate our databases, use **database access objects (DAO)**, and use Yii2's built-in Query Builder. We'll also cover the basics of powerful tools such as data providers and data widgets as well as how to use Yii2 to replicate and load balance access to our databases.

Connecting to databases

The primary component required in order to work with databases is the yii\db\Connection class. Through this class, we can connect to a variety of different database types, ranging from local SQLite databases to clustered MySQL databases. The simplest way to establish a connection to a database is to create a SQLite database connection, as follows:

```
$connection = new \yii\db\Connection([
    'dsn' => 'sqlite:/' . \Yii::getAlias('@app') .
    '/runtime/db.sqlite',
    'charset' => 'utf8'
]);

$connection->open();
```

Normally, however, we'll want to use a single database connection across our entire application. We can keep our application *DRY* by putting our database configuration into the db component of our web or console configuration file. Following the examples laid out in the previous chapters, this component will reference the config/env/<ENV>/db.php file. As an example, establishing a SQLite connection in this file will be done as follows:

```php
<?php return [
    'dsn' => 'sqlite:/' . \Yii::getAlias('@app') .
    '/runtime/db.sqlite',
    'class' => 'yii\db\Connection',
    'charset' => 'utf8'
];
```

By storing our database configuration in the db component of our application, it can easily be shared between both our web and console applications without any additional effort on our part. Furthermore, since Yii2 loads components only when required, it can keep our application lean and performant.

In Yii2, components are only loaded when required. This process is often called **lazy loading**. Unless a component is preloaded, Yii2 will not create an instance of that component until it is first used. After being initially instantiated, Yii will then reuse the same component across your application rather than creating multiple instances of that component. Lazy loading is one of the primary reasons Yii is so performant.

With our database configuration stored within our configuration file, we can now access the database connection, as follows:

```
\Yii::$app->db;
```

This connection will also be shared to any Active Record models used in our application, which we'll discuss in *Chapter 4, Active Record, Models, and Forms*.

As stated earlier, Yii2 can connect to several different database types. As Yii2 binds on top of PHP's PDO library, it can connect to the same sources a native PDO driver can connect to. A few examples of the **data source names** (**DSNs**) that Yii2 supports are listed here:

Database Type	DSN Scheme
MySQL, Percona, MariaDB, and so on	`mysql:host=localhost;dbname=mydatabase`
SQLite	`sqlite:/path/to/database/file.sqlite`

Database Type	DSN Scheme
PostgreSQL	`pgsql:host=localhost;port=5432;dbname=mydatabase`
CUBRID	`cubrid:dbname=demodb;host=localhost;port=33000`
MS SQL Server (via the sqlsrv driver)	`sqlsrv:Server=localhost;Database=mydatabase`
MS SQL Server (via the dblib driver)	`dblib:host=localhost;dbname=mydatabase`
MS SQL Server (via the mssql driver)	`mssql:host=localhost;dbname=mydatabase`
Oracle	`oci:dbname=//localhost:1521/mydatabase`

If you're connecting to a MS SQL server, you'll need to have either the sqlsrv, dblib or mssql PHP drivers installed on your system. More information on these base drivers can be found within the PHP manual at `https://php.net/manual/en/pdo.drivers.php`.

Additionally, Oracle connections will require the installation of Oracle's OCI8 driver. More information on this driver can be found in the PHP manual at `https://php.net/manual/en/book.oci8.php`.

Note that Yii2 will not be able to connect to any database unless the appropriate PHP drivers are properly installed and configured. If you aren't certain which drivers you have installed, the native `phpinfo()` function can output a list of all the currently installed PHP extensions.

In addition to the base drivers listed earlier, Yii2 can also connect to databases over **Open Database Connectivity (ODBC)**. When connecting to a database via ODBC, you'll need to specify the `$driverName` property within your db connection component so that Yii2 can properly connect to your database:

```
'components' => [
    // [...]
    'db' => [
        'class' => 'yii\db\Connection',
        'driverName' => 'mysql', 'dsn' => 'odbc:Driver={MySQL};
        Server=localhost;Database=test',
        'username' => 'username',
    'password' => 'password',
    ]
]
```

As shown previously, some database configurations may require you to specify a username or password to connect to them. Within the db component, simply specify the username and password attributes that are appropriate for your database.

Additional configuration options

In addition to the basic db component options listed previously, Yii2 also provides several additional options that can be used to either enhance the performance of your application or deal with a known issue within the native PHP drivers. While many of these options can be found in the Yii guide and the API documentation, some of them will most likely be used more often than others. These properties are $emulatePrepare, $enableQueryCache, and $enableSchemaCache.

 A complete list of the available methods and properties for the yii\db\ Connection class can be found at http://www.yiiframework.com/ doc-2.0/yii-db-connection.html.

The first common attribute, $emulatePrepare, can be used to alleviate common issues identified by the Yii team when preparing database statements. By default, Yii2 will try to use the native prepare support built into the native PDO driver. To help alleviate issues with a few of the native PDO drivers (mainly, the MS SQL drivers), the $emulatePrepare attribute may need to be set to true in order to allow Yii2 to handle the prepare statements.

The next common property often enabled in our db component is $enableQueryCache. To improve the performance of our application, we can set this value to true and allow Yii to cache commonly executed queries. In an application that mostly performs read actions, enabling this attribute can greatly increase the performance of your application.

To completely enable this component, however, the additional properties we'll mention now must be set as well. The first property, $queryCache, specifies the named cache object that the query cache should use. If unset, this will simply default to the cache component in our application. The second property is $queryCacheDuration, and it determines how long any database query result will be cached for. By default, the query cache will be valid for 3,600 seconds, or 60 minutes:

```
'components' => [
  //[...
  'db' => [
```

```
        'dsn' => 'sqlite:/' . \Yii::getAlias('@app') .
        '/runtime/db.sqlite',
        'class' => 'yii\db\Connection',
        'charset' => 'utf8',
        'enableQueryCache' => true,
        'queryCache' => 'filecache',
        'queryCacheDuration' => 60
    ],
    'filecache' => [
        'class' => 'yii\caching\FileCache',
    ],
]
```

The final common property that often will be added to our db component is
$enableSchemaCache. Before Yii accesses the database, it will often need to
determine the database schema. This schema information is used to assist Yii
when running validators and working with relational models, such as related
Active Record models. Rather than having Yii try to determine our database
schema on every request, we can tell it that our schema isn't changing by setting
$enableSchemaCache to true.

Similar to the $enableCache parameter outlined previously, we'll also need to define
the $schemaCache parameter, which will tell Yii what cache component to use. We'll
also need to define the $schemaCacheDuration parameter so that Yii2 knows how
long the schema cache is valid for in seconds:

```
'components' => [
  // [...]
  'db' => [
        'dsn' => 'sqlite:/' . \Yii::getAlias('@app') .
        '/runtime/db.sqlite',
        'class' => 'yii\db\Connection',
        'charset' => 'utf8',
        'enableSchemaCache' => true,
        'schemaCache' => 'filecache',
        'schemaCacheDuration' => 3600
    ],
    'filecache' => [
        'class' => 'yii\caching\FileCache',
    ],
]
```

As the majority of our controller actions will most likely result in a database
operation, enabling these properties can greatly improve the performance of
our application.

Remember that because $enableSchemaCache and
$enableQueryCache are enabled, Yii2 will not perform common checks
against the database. Any change to the underlying data or schema in
your database may cause your application to return bad data or crash
entirely. If you change the data in your database directly rather than
through Yii2, or if you change the database schema, ensure that you flush
the relevant cache components defined by $enableSchemaCache or
$enableQueryCache to ensure that your application functions correctly.

Writing database migrations

When building and maintaining modern web applications, the underlying structure
of our database may need to change to account for changes in requirements or
scopes. To ensure that our database schema can evolve in tandem with our source
code, Yii2 provides built-in support to manage database migrations. Using database
migrations, we can treat our database as an extension of the source code and easily
change it when our source code changes.

An overview of schema

When working with database migrations, we'll often be working with the `yii\db\`
`Schema` class. When paired properly, we can often write our migrations in a way
that enables them to be run across a variety of database types. For example, when
working locally, we might need to use a local SQLite database even if our application
will ultimately run on a MySQL database.

At the heart of this class is a variety of different schema types that Yii2 will be able to
properly map to the appropriate data type within our database. These include data
types such as INT, DATETIME, and TEXT.

For a complete list of the available constants made available by the
Schema class, ensure that you refer to the Yii2 guide at http://www.
yiiframework.com/doc-2.0/yii-db-schema.html#constants.

Within our migrations, we can call any of these constants by running this:

```
Schema::<CONSTANT>
```

In the example of an integer, we can use this:

```
Schema::TYPE_INTEGER
```

Using these constants in our migration, we can ensure that our migrations map to the appropriate data type within our database and work across a variety of database types.

Writing migrations

As shown in the previous chapter, we can create a new migration by invoking the `migrate/create` command from the `yii` command-line tool. Using the source code from the previous chapter as a starting point, we'll do this by running the following from the command line:

```
./yii migrate/create init
```

```
Yii Migration Tool (based on Yii v2.0.4)

Create new migration '/var/www/ch3/migrations/m150523_194158_init.php'? (yes|no)
 [no]:yes
New migration created successfully.
```

Running this command will create a new migration in the `migrations` folder of our application.

> Depending upon the file permissions on your system, Yii2 may not be able to create the `migrations` folder if it does not exist. If the `migrations` folder doesn't exist yet, ensure that you create it before running the `migrate/create` command.

When running migrations, Yii2 will execute them in the order in which they were created. To determine this order, Yii2 will look at the filename or the migration that contains the name of the migration specified from the `migrate/create` command as well as the exact timestamp the migration was created at.

In our case, the filename is `m150523_194158_init.php`, which means that this migration was created on May 23, 2015 at 7:41:58 PM UTC.

> Because of this naming convention, any migration that you create will have a distinct and unique filename. If you're following along, ensure that you're working in the file that was created from the `./yii` command.

After running the `migrate/create` command, Yii2 provides us with a skeleton migration that will look similar to the following code block:

```php
<?php

use yii\db\Schema;
use yii\db\Migration;

class m150523_194158_init extends Migration
{
    public function up() {}

    public function down()
    {
        echo "m150523_194158_init cannot be reverted.\n";
        return false;
    }

    /*
    // Use safeUp/safeDown to run migration code within a
    transaction
    public function safeUp() {}

    public function safeDown() {}
    */
}
```

Migrations in Yii2 can operate in one of these two ways: we can either bring a migration up, or we can bring it down. These two operations correspond to one of four functions: `up()`, `safeUp()`, `down()`, and `safeDown()`. The `up()` and `down()` methods are the base methods required to run migrations and will execute any database command issued inside them even if there is an error. Alternatively, we can use the `safeUp()` and `safeDown()` methods, which are functionally identical to the `up()` and `down()` methods, with the exception that the entire operation is wrapped within a transaction. If our database supports transactions, running our migrations from the safe methods can help us catch migration errors at runtime before an error can cause problems with our entire database.

 Because of the additional safety they offer, `safeUp()` and `safeDown()` should be our go-to methods when writing migrations. Additionally, if `safeUp()` or `safeDown()` are used, the unsafe methods cannot be used.

Let's start by adding a simple table to our database in order to store our users. We'll start by simply storing an ID, an email address, a password, the username, and some timestamp metadata indicating when our user was created and last updated. Within our migration, we can write this as follows:

```
class m150523_194158_init extends Migration
{
    public function safeUp()
    {
        return $this->createTable('user', [
            'id'            => Schema::TYPE_PK,
            // $this->primaryKey()
            'email'         => Schema::TYPE_STRING,
            // $this->string(255) // String with 255 characters
            'password'      => Schema::TYPE_STRING,
            'name'          => Schema::TYPE_STRING,
            'created_at'    => Schema::TYPE_INTEGER,
            // $this->integer()
            'updated_at'    => Schema::TYPE_INTEGER
        ]);
    }

    public function safeDown()
    {
        return $this->dropTable('user');
    }
}
```

As illustrated previously, Yii2 supports two different ways to declare schema types for columns. We can either directly use the constants defined by the Schema class, or we can use the native migration methods, such as primaryKey(), integer(), string(), and text(). Using the migration methods is preferred because it permits us to add additional attributes to our column, such as the column size and length. For a complete list of methods offered by the migration class, refer to the Yii2 guide at http://www.yiiframework.com/doc-2.0/yii-db-migration.html.

In the previous example, we outlined two methods: createTable(), which will create a new database table within our application, and dropTable(), which will drop the table from our database.

A common convention when working with a database is to write field names with underscores and use singular names for table and column names. While Yii2 is smart enough to work with any field names you specify, following this convention will make your code more readable and working with your databases less complicated. While you don't have to explicitly follow this convention, following a convention can save you a lot of time in the future.

Running migrations

Running our migrations can be done through the `yii` command, as shown in the previous chapter:

```
./yii migrate/up
```

```
Yii Migration Tool (based on Yii v2.0.4)

Total 1 new migration to be applied:
    m150523_194158_init

Apply the above migration? (yes|no) [no]:yes
*** applying m150523_194158_init
    > create table user ... done (time: 0.001s)
*** applied m150523_194158_init (time: 0.019s)

Migrated up successfully.
```

Since we're using a SQLite database in our example, we can easily explore what just happened when we ran the `migrate/up` command. Using the `sqlite` command-line tool, we can explore our SQLite database:

```
sqlite3 /path/to/runtime/db.sqlite
```

If your package manager does not provide sqlite3, you can download the binary executables from https://www.sqlite.org/download.html.

By running the `.tables` command from our SQLite prompt, we can see that two tables were created when we ran the `migrate/up` command, `migration` and `user`:

```
sqlite> .tables
```

```
sqlite> .tables
migration   user
```

The first table, `migration`, contains a list of all the applied migrations as well as the time at which they were applied.

```
sqlite> .schema migration
CREATE TABLE `migration` (
        `version` varchar(180) NOT NULL PRIMARY KEY,
        `apply_time` integer
);
sqlite> SELECT * FROM migration;
m000000_000000_base|1432411913
m150523_194158_init|1432411919
```

The second table, `user`, shows the resulting schema that was created by Yii from our migration class.

```
sqlite> .schema user
CREATE TABLE `user` (
        `id` integer PRIMARY KEY AUTOINCREMENT NOT NULL,
        `email` varchar(255),
        `password` varchar(255),
        `name` varchar(255),
        `created_at` integer,
        `updated_at` integer
);
```

For instance, by specifying the `TYPE_PK` schema for our `ID` attribute, Yii2 knew that it needed to add `AUTOINCRIMENT` and `NOT NULL` attributes to our SQLite schema.

While database migrations are suited for most database changes, running them against large datasets may result in your database being unavailable to your application, resulting in downtime. Make sure that before you run a database migration through Yii2, your application should be able to handle temporary downtime. If even temporary downtime is not appropriate for your application, you may need to consider migrating your data to an updated schema in other ways.

Altering a database schema

When developing locally, we can simply use the `migrate/down` command to undo a specific migration (assuming we implemented a `down()` or `safeDown()` method). However, after committing and pushing our code to our DCVS system, such as Git or SVN, others may be using or working with our code. In this instance, we want to change our migrations without causing harm to their local instance; we can create new migrations that users of our code can apply in order to bring their applications up to date.

Take, for instance, the user schema that was created for us:

```
CREATE TABLE `user` (
        `id` integer PRIMARY KEY AUTOINCREMENT NOT NULL,
        `email` varchar(255),
        `password` varchar(255),
        `name` varchar(255),
        `created_at` integer,
        `updated_at` integer
);
```

Rather than having a single field for our username, we may want to have two fields: one for their first name and one for their last name. We may also want to make a few changes to other fields, such as our email field, to prevent them from being NULL. We can do this by writing a new migration and altering the schema of the database itself.

We'll start by creating a new migration:

./yii migrate/create name_change --interactive=0

 Remember, the --interactive=0 flag tells Yii to run our console command without prompts.

Within our new migrations/...name_change.php migration, we can write a safeUp() method to alter these columns for us:

```
public function safeUp()
{
    $this->renameColumn('user', 'name', 'first_name');
    $this->alterColumn('user', 'first_name', SCHEMA::TYPE_STRING);
    $this->addColumn('user', 'last_name', SCHEMA::TYPE_STRING);
    $this->alterColumn('user', 'email', SCHEMA::TYPE_STRING . '
    NOT NULL');
    $this->createIndex('user_unique_email', 'user', 'email',
    true);
}
```

In Yii2, migration commands are self-explanatory in what they do. For instance, the first method, renameColumn(), will simply rename the name column to first_name. In the same vein, addColumn() will add a new column with the specified name and schema to our database, alterColumn() will alter the schema for the named column, and createIndex() will create a unique index on the email field in our database, which will ensure that no two users will share the same email address.

A complete list of commands that can be run within the migration calls can be found in the Yii2 guide at http://www.yiiframework.com/doc-2.0/yii-db-migration.html.

If we try to run these migrations against our SQLite database, however, we would be presented with an error similar to the following, indicating that SQLite doesn't have support for these methods:

./yii migrate/up

Here's the output:

```
*** applying m150523_203944_name_change
    > rename column name in table user to first_name \
...Exception: yii\db\sqlite\QueryBuilder::renameColumn is not \
    supported by SQLite. \
(/var/www/ch3/vendor/yiisoft/yii2/db/sqlite/QueryBuilder.php:201)
```

While the previously listed migration would work on MySQL or PostgreSQL, our SQLite driver doesn't provide support for these commands. Since we're using SQLite, however, we'd have to rewrite our initial migration command and notify users of our application about the change. For SQLite, we can rewrite our newly created migrations/...name_change.php migration as follows:

```
public function safeUp()
{
    $this->dropTable('user');

    $this->createTable('user', [
        'id'          => Schema::TYPE_PK,
        'email'       => Schema::TYPE_STRING . ' NOT NULL',
        'password'    => Schema::TYPE_STRING . ' NOT NULL',
        'first_name'  => Schema::TYPE_STRING,
        'last_name'   => Schema::TYPE_STRING,
        'created_at'  => Schema::TYPE_INTEGER,
        'updated_at'  => Schema::TYPE_INTEGER
    ]);

    $this->createIndex('user_unique_email', 'user', 'email',
    true);
}
```

```
public function safeDown()
{
    return true;
}
```

 yii\db\Migration does not have a query() method that we can use to retrieve data. Consequently, if we need to query data within a migration, we will need to use Yii2's Query Builder to do this, which we'll cover later in this chapter. If our application has widespread adoption, it might be better to query for all of our users with Query Builder and store them temporarily in the memory (or a temporary store if we have a large number of records). Then, after creating our new table schema for our users table, we could then reinsert them into our database using the insert() method.

After updating our new migration, we can rerun our migration command. Since our first migration was already applied, that migration will be skipped when the migrate/up command is executed, and only our migrations/m150523_203944_change.php migration will be run:

./yii migrate/up

```
Yii Migration Tool (based on Yii v2.0.4)

Total 1 new migration to be applied:
    m150523_203944_name_change

*** applying m150523_203944_name_change
    > drop table user ... done (time: 0.001s)
    > create table user ... done (time: 0.001s)
    > create unique index user_unique_email on user (email) ... done (time: 0.00
1s)
*** applied m150523_203944_name_change (time: 0.013s)

Migrated up successfully.
```

After running our migration, we can query our database to see what our full schema looks like within SQLite:

sqlite3 /path/to/runtime/db.sqlite

```
sqlite> .schema user
CREATE TABLE `user` (
        `id` integer PRIMARY KEY AUTOINCREMENT NOT NULL,
        `email` varchar(255) NOT NULL,
        `password` varchar(255) NOT NULL,
        `first_name` varchar(255) NOT NULL,
        `last_name ` varchar(255) NOT NULL,
        `created_at` integer,
        `updated_at` integer
);
CREATE UNIQUE INDEX `user_unique_email` ON `user` (`email`);
```

 Migrations in Yii2 are extremely powerful. Take a look at the Yii2 documentation at http://www.yiiframework.com/doc-2.0/yii-db-migration.html to see everything that you can do with yii\db\Migration.

Database access objects

Yii database access objects, commonly referred to as DAO, provide a powerful object-oriented API to work with a relational database. As the foundation for more complex database access, such as Query Builder and Active Record, DAO enables us to work directly with our database through SQL statements and PHP arrays. Consequently, it is significantly more performant to work with DAO statements than it is to work with either Active Record or Query Builder.

At the core of DAO is our yii\db\Connection class, or more commonly, our db component \Yii::$app->db. Since our db component is already properly configured for SQLite, we'll use it moving forward. With DAO, there are two general types of queries that we can run: queries that return data, such as SELECT queries, and queries that execute data, such as DELETE or UPDATE.

 If you use the yii\db\Connection class directly, you'll need to explicitly call the open() method before you can run any queries against that connection.

Querying for data

The first way in which we can use DAO is to query for data. There are four main methods that are used to query for data: queryAll(), queryOne(), queryScalar(), and queryColumn().

The first method, `queryAll()`, is used to query for all the data in a specific table based upon the SQL statement used within the `createCommand()` method. Using our user table as an example, we can query for all the users in our database by running the following command:

```
$users = \Yii::$app->db
        ->createCommand('SELECT * FROM user;')
        ->queryAll();
```

After running this command, our `$users` variable will be populated with an array of users:

```
Array
(
    [0] => Array
    (
        [id] => 1
        [email] => test@example.com
        [password] => test123
        [first_name] => test
        [last_name] => user
        [created_at] => 0
        [updated_at] => 0
    )
)
```

The next method, `queryOne()`, is used to fetch a single record from the database.

```
$user = \Yii::$app->db
        ->createCommand('SELECT * FROM user WHERE id = 1;')
        ->queryOne();
```

The `queryOne()` method returns an array of data for a single element. In the event that no data is found, this method will return `false`:

```
Array
(
    [id] => 1
    [email] => test@example.com
    [password] => test123
    [first_name] => test
    [last_name] => user
    [created_at] => 0
    [updated_at] => 0
)
```

The third method, `queryScalar()`, is used to return the result of a SELECT query that returns a single value. For instance, if we want to count the number of users in our database, we can use `queryScalar()` to get the value:

```
$count = \Yii::$app->db
        ->createCommand('SELECT COUNT(*) FROM user;')
        ->queryScalar();
```

After running this command, our `$count` variable will be populated with the number of users in our database.

The final method, `queryColumn()`, is used to query a specific column in our database. For instance, if we want to know the email addresses of all the users in our database, we can use `queryAll()` to fetch all that data, or we can use `queryColumn()`, which would be significantly more efficient to use as it would query for less data:

```
$user = \Yii::$app->db
        ->createCommand('SELECT email FROM user;')
        ->queryColumn();
```

Like `queryAll()`, `queryColumn()` will return an array of results:

```
Array
(
    [0] => test@example.com
)
```

In the event that no results are found, `queryColumn()` will return an empty array.

With our knowledge of these methods, as an exercise, let's go back to our previous migrations and rewrite them to preserve our users across our schema change:

1. First, let's roll back our migrations to properly simulate the scenario:

    ./yii migrate/down

2. Then, we'll migrate our initial migration using the `migrate/to` command:

    ./yii migrate/to m150523_194158_init

3. Next, let's seed our database with some test data:

    ```
    sqlite3 /path/to/runtime/db.sqlite
    INSERT INTO user (email, password, name) VALUES
    ('test@example.com', 'test1', 'test user');

    INSERT INTO user (email, password, name) VALUES
    ('test2@example.com', 'test2', 'test user 2');
    ```

4. If we take a look at our database, we'll see that the initial schema and data is now in place.

```
sqlite> .schema user
CREATE TABLE `user` (
        `id` integer PRIMARY KEY AUTOINCREMENT NOT NULL,
        `email` varchar(255),
        `password` varchar(255),
        `name` varchar(255),
        `created_at` integer,
        `updated_at` integer
);
sqlite> SELECT * FROM user;
1|test@example.com|test1|test user||
2|test2@example.com|test2|test user 2||
```

5. Then, let's rewrite our `migrations/...name_change.php` migration to fetch our users from the database before running the initial migration that we created, and then reinsert our users back into our database. We'll do this using the `queryAll()` DAO method to fetch the data and the `insert()` method of `yii\db\Migration` to put it back into the database. The new code blocks have been highlighted for easy viewing:

```php
public function safeUp()
{
    $users = \Yii::$app->db
            ->createCommand('SELECT * FROM user')
            ->queryAll();

    $this->dropTable('user');

    $this->createTable('user', [
        'id'            => Schema::TYPE_PK,
        'email'         => Schema::TYPE_STRING . ' NOT
        NULL',
        'password'      => Schema::TYPE_STRING . ' NOT
        NULL',
        'first_name'    => Schema::TYPE_STRING,
        'last_name'     => Schema::TYPE_STRING,
        'created_at'    => Schema::TYPE_INTEGER,
        'updated_at'    => Schema::TYPE_INTEGER
    ]);

    $this->createIndex('user_unique_email', 'user',
    'email', true);
```

```
        foreach ($users as $user)
        {
            $this->insert('user', [
                'id'         => $user['id'],
                'email'      => $user['email'],
                'password'   => $user['password'],
                'first_name' => $user['name'],
                'created_at' => $user['created_at'],
                'updated_at' => $user['updated_at']
            ]);
        }
    }
```

6. Now we can rerun our migration. If successful, we should see our original migration run and an insert call executed for each user in our database.

```
./yii migrate/up -interactive=0
```

```
Yii Migration Tool (based on Yii v2.0.4)

Total 1 new migration to be applied:
      m150523_203944_name_change

Apply the above migration? (yes|no) [no]:yes
*** applying m150523_203944_name_change
    > drop table user ... done (time: 0.001s)
    > create table user ... done (time: 0.001s)
    > create unique index user_unique_email on user (email) ... done (time: 0.00
1s)
    > insert into user ... done (time: 0.004s)
    > insert into user ... done (time: 0.001s)
*** applied m150523_203944_name_change (time: 0.058s)

Migrated up successfully.
```

7. Finally, we can query our SQLite database to preview the updated schema and see our updated users:

```
sqlite3 /path/to/runtime/db.sqlite
```

```
sqlite> .schema user
CREATE TABLE `user` (
        `id` integer PRIMARY KEY AUTOINCREMENT NOT NULL,
        `email` varchar(255) NOT NULL,
        `password` varchar(255) NOT NULL,
        `first_name` varchar(255),
        `last_name ` varchar(255),
        `created_at` integer,
        `updated_at` integer
);
CREATE UNIQUE INDEX `user_unique_email` ON `user` (`email`);
sqlite> SELECT * FROM user;
1|test@example.com|test1|test user|||
2|test2@example.com|test2|test user 2|||
```

As you can see, DAO's query method provides us with the ability to quickly and efficiently fetch data from our database.

Quoting table and column names

When writing database-agnostic SQL queries, properly quoting field names can be problematic. To avoid this problem, Yii2 provides the ability to automatically quote table and column names for you using the correct quoting rule for the specific database in use.

To automatically quote a column name, simply enclose the column name in square brackets:

```
[[column name]]
```

To automatically quote a table, simply enclose the table name in curly brackets:

```
{{table name}}
```

An example of both of these tools in action is shown as follows:

```
$result = \Yii::$app->db
        ->createCommand("SELECT COUNT([[id]]) FROM {{user}}")
        ->queryScalar();
```

Executing queries

While the query methods provide the ability to select data from our database, we often need to execute UPDATE or DELETE commands, which do not return data. To execute these commands, we can use the execute() method in general:

```
\Yii::$app->db
    ->createCommand('INSERT INTO user (email, password) VALUES
    ("test3@example.com", "test3");')
    ->execute();
```

If successful, the execute() method will return with true, whereas if it fails, it will return false.

Yii2 also provides convenient wrappers for insert(), update(), and delete(), which enables us to write commands without having to write raw SQL. These methods properly escape and quote table and column names and bind parameters on your behalf.

For instance, we can insert a new user into a database as follows:

```
// INSERT ( tablename, [ attributes => attr ] )
\Yii::$app->db
    ->createCommand()
    ->insert('user', [
      'email'      => 'test4@example.com',
      'password'   => 'changeme7',
      'first_name' => 'Test',
      'last_name'  => 'User',
      'created_at' => time(),
      'updated_at' => time()
    ])
    ->execute();
```

We can update all the users in our database using the update() method:

```
// UPDATE (tablename, [ attributes => attr ], condition )
\Yii::$app->db
    ->createCommand()
    ->update('user', [
        'updated_at' => time()
    ], '1 = 1')
    ->execute();
```

The last argument listed in our update command defines the `where` condition of our query command, which we'll cover in more detail later in the chapter. `1=1` is a common SQL idiom to update all records.

We can also delete a user in our database using the `delete()` method:

```
// DELETE ( tablename, condition )
\Yii::$app->db
    ->createCommand()
    ->delete('user', 'id = 3')
    ->execute();
```

Additionally, if you need to insert several rows at the same time, you can use the `batchInsert()` method, which can be significantly more efficient than inserting a single row at a time:

```
// batchInsert( tablename, [ properties ], [ rows ] )
\Yii::$app->db
    ->createCommand()
    ->batchInsert('user', ['email', 'password', 'first_name',
    'last_name', 'created_at', 'updated_at'],
    [
        ['james.franklin@example.com', 'changeme7', 'James',
        'Franklin', time(), time()],
        ['linda.marks@example.com', 'changeme7', 'Linda',
        'Marks', time(), time()]
        ['roger.martin@example.com', 'changeme7',
        'Roger', 'Martin', time(), time()]
    ])
    ->execute();
```

 Yii2 does not provide a `batchUpdate()` or `batchDelete()` method as bulk updates and deletes can be handled by the `update()` and `delete()` methods using a normal SQL.

Parameter binding

The number one rule when working with user-submitted data is to never trust user-submitted data. Any data that passes through our databases and has come from an end user needs to be validated, sanitized, and properly bound to our statements before they are executed against our database.

Take, for instance, the following query:

```
\Yii::$app->db
    ->createCommand("UPDATE user SET first_name = 'Tom' WHERE id
    = " . $_GET['id'])
    ->execute();
```

Under normal circumstances, Yii would generate the following SQL, assuming `$_GET['id']` had a value of 1:

```
UPDATE user SET first_name = 'Tom' WHERE id = 1;
```

While this is innocent enough, any user who can manipulate the `$_GET['id']` variable can rewrite our query to something much more dangerous. For instance, they could drop our entire user table simply by substituting `$_GET['id']` with `1; DROP TABLE user; --`:

```
UPDATE user SET first_name = 'Tom' WHERE id = 1; DROP TABLE user; --
```

This kind of attack is called SQL injection. To help protect against SQL injection, Yii2 offers several different ways to bind parameters to our queries in a way that will filter our injected SQL. These three methods are `bindValue()`, `bindValues()`, and `bindParam()`.

The first method, `bindValue()`, is used to bind a single parameter to a token within our SQL statement. For example, we can rewrite the previous query as follows:

```
\Yii::$app->db
    ->createCommand("UPDATE user SET first_name = :name
    WHERE id  = :id)
    ->bindValue(':name', 'Tom')
    ->bindValue(':id', $_GET['id'])
    ->execute();
```

Alternatively, we can use the `bindValues()` method to bind several parameters into a single call:

```
\Yii::$app->db
    ->createCommand("UPDATE user SET first_name = :name
    WHERE id  = :id)
    ->bindValues([ ':name' => 'Tom', ':id' => $_GET['id'] ])
    ->execute();
```

For convenience, the previous query can be rewritten so that the parameters are in line with the `createCommand()` method:

```
$params = [ ':name' => 'Tom', ':id' => $_GET['id'] ];
\Yii::$app->db
    ->createCommand("UPDATE user SET first_name =
    :name WHERE id  = :id, $params)
    ->execute();
```

The final method, `bindParam()`, is valued to bind parameters by reference rather than by value:

```
$id = 1;
$name = 'Tom';
$q = \Yii::$app->db
    ->createCommand("UPDATE user SET first_name =
    :name WHERE id  = :id)
    ->bindParam(':name', $name)
    ->bindParam(':id', $id);
```

Because `bindParam()` binds parameters by reference, we can change the bounded values to execute multiple queries. Following the previous example, we can write the following to update multiple users without having to rewrite our query each time:

```
$q->execute();
$id = 2;
$name = 'Kevin';
$q->execute();
```

> Remember, the most important rule of working with user data is to never trust user-submitted data. Even in cases where you're 100% certain that SQL injection cannot happen, it's recommended that you use parameter binding rather than writing in line SQL. This will protect you against future changes to your code.

Transactions

When running multiple queries in a sequence, we often want to ensure that our database state remains consistent across these queries. Most modern databases support the use of transactions to accomplish this. In a transaction, changes are written to the database in such a way that they can be committed if everything went well or rolled back without consequence if any given query within the transaction failed. In Yii2, this looks as follows:

```
$transaction = \Yii::$app->db->beginTransaction();

try {
    \Yii::$app->db->createCommand($sql)->execute();
    \Yii::$app->db->createCommand($sql)->execute();
    //[ ... more queries ...]
    $transaction->commit();
} catch (\Exception $e) {
    $transaction->rollBack();
}
```

Query Builder

Building on top of the foundations laid by DAO is Yii's Query Builder. Yii's Query Builder allows us to write database-agnostic queries in a programmatic way. Consequently, queries written through the Query Builder are significantly more readable than their DAO counterparts.

The basics of Query Builder involve the creation an instance of yii\db\Query, the construction of a statement, and then the execution of that query statement. For example, we could simply query for all the users in our database in Query Builder using the following code:

```
$users = (new \yii\db\Query())
    ->select(['id', 'email'])
    ->from('user')
    ->all();
```

When working with Query Builder, we're actually using the yii\db\Query class rather than yii\db\QueryBuilder. While yii\db\QueryBuilder can generate SQL statements similar to those generated by yii\db\Query, yii\db\Query enables these statements to be database-agnostic. In general, you'll want to work with yii\db\Query when using Query Builder.

Query construction methods

The basics of Query Builder involve the chaining of multiple query methods together. These method names directly correspond with the SQL segment that they are named after. When working with Query Builder, the most common methods that you'll use will be the select(), from(), and where() methods.

Moving forward, we'll use the following variable to represent our query builder object:

```
$query = (new \yii\db\Query());
```

The select method

The `select()` method directly corresponds to the `SELECT` segment of our SQL query and accepts either a string of column names or an array of columns to specify the columns that we would want to select from our database. For instance, the following queries are identical:

```
$query->select('id, first_name)->from('user');
$query->select(['id', 'last_name'])->from('user');
```

 When using the `select()` method, the array format is generally easy to read and work with. If you choose to list the column names as a string, ensure that you do that consistently throughout your application. In the following examples, we'll use the array format.

The `select()` method also supports column aliases and table prefixes, as shown in the next example:

```
$query->select([
    'id' => 'user_id',
    'user.first_name' => 'fName']
)->from('user');
```

In addition to column names, the `select` method also provides support for expressions. For instance, if we want to retrieve the user's complete name as a single field, we can execute the following query:

```
$query->select([
    "id",
    "CONCACT(first_name, ' ', last_name)" => 'full_name'
])->from('user');
```

The `select` method can also be used to execute subqueries, such as `COUNT()`:

```
$query->select('COUNT(*)')->from('user');
```

Finally, the `select` statement can be chained with the `distinct()` method to retrieve unique records. For instance, if we want to list all the first names of our user's database, we can execute the following query:

```
$query->select('first_name')->distinct()->from('user');
```

Omitting the `select()` method from your query will result in a SELECT
* query being performed.

The from method

Our previous examples have already illustrated the basic usage of the `from()`
method. The `from()` method can also be used to specify a table alias, as shown
in the following example:

```
$query->select('first_name')->from(['u' => 'users']);
```

 Like the `select()` method, the `from()` method can also accept strings
as an input rather than an array. The preceding query can be rewritten as
`$query->select('first_name')->from(['users u']);`.

The where method

The `where()` method specifies the `where` segment of our SQL query and can be used
either in a string format, hash format, or operator format.

The string format

The string format of the `where()` method should always be chained with the
`addParams()` method in order to prevent SQL injection:

```
$query->select(['first_name', 'last_name'])
        ->from('user')
    ->where('id = :id')
    ->addParams([':id' => 1]);
```

Alternatively, the parameters can be rewritten as the second argument to the
`where()` method:

```
$query->select(['first_name', 'last_name'])
        ->from('user')
    ->where('id = :id', [':id' => 1]);
```

 Remember to avoid adding PHP variables inline in your `where()`
method in order to avoid SQL injection.

The hash format

The hash format provides an even better way to chain multiple AND conditions together in the where statement. Rather than passing a string as a parameter, we can instead pass an array of key values representing the column name and value. When using the hash format, the selected fields will be joined together with the SQL AND.

For example, we can find all the users in our database with the first name of John who were in their 20s and who didn't have a listed pet name by running the following query:

```
$query->from('user')
      ->where([
      'first_name' => 'John',
      'pets_name' => NULL,
      'age' => [20, 21, 22, 23, 24, 25, 26, 27, 28, 29],
      ]);
```

 Our database currently doesn't have an age or pets_name field. We will have to adjust our schema with a migration to add these fields to our database.

This would result in the following query:

```
SELECT *
FROM user
WHERE first_name = "John" AND
      pets_name IS NULL AND
      age IN (20, 21, 22, 23, 24, 25, 26, 27, 28, 29);
```

 As illustrated previously, the hash format allows you to generate more complex WHERE queries, such as those that use IN when specifying an array of values and IS NULL when passing null as the array value.

The operator format

The last way to use the where() method is to use the operator format. The operator format allows us to build more complex SQL queries containing conditionals such as LIKE, OR, BETWEEN, and EXISTS, just to name a few examples.

In general, the operator format takes the following format:

```
where([ operator, condition1, condition2 ]);
```

For example, if we want to fetch all users from our database who had the first name of John or Jill, we can execute this:

```
$query->where(['or', 'John', 'Jill']);
```

 For a complete list of all the available operators that the operator format supports, check out the Yii2 API documentation at http://www. yiiframework.com/doc-2.0/yii-db-query.html#where()-detail.

As you can imagine, the where() method can quickly become very bulky and complicated. Rather than using the operator, you may find your code more readable by using the andWhere() or orWhere() methods to chain multiple conditions together:

```
$query->andWhere(['in', 'id', [1,2,3,4,5]]);
```

Ordering results

Query builder can also sort results by a given field using the orderBy() method. For example, to sort all of our users in our database by age, we can construct the following query:

```
$query->from('user')
      ->orderBy('age ASC');
```

Limiting and offsetting data

Commonly used with the where() method are the limit() and offset() methods, which are used to limit the number of results and offset our results by a given number of results. When properly used together, these two methods form the basics of paginating through results:

```
$query->from('user')
      ->limit(5)
      ->offset(5);
```

Grouping and having

Often when working with diverse datasets, we'll need to perform some analysis on our data. Aggregate functions such as GROUP BY and HAVING can greatly assist in extracting additional information from our data. Yii2 supports these methods via the groupBy() and having() methods.

For example, if we want to list the number of users in our database in each age group, we can execute the following query:

```
$query->select(['age', 'COUNT(*)' => 'users'])
      ->from('user')
      ->groupBy('age');
```

This will generate the following SQL statement:

```
SELECT age, COUNT(*) AS users FROM user GROUP BY age;
```

The `groupBy()` method behaves similar to the `select()` method in that it accepts either an array or a string as an argument; however, when using database expressions, you'll need to use the array syntax.

After grouping our results with `groupBy()`, we can then filter our results with the `having()` method, which behaves the same as the `where()` method. The following example will only show the number of users in our dataset who are over a specified age:

```
$query->select(['age', 'COUNT(*)' => 'users'])
      ->from('user')
      ->groupBy('age')
      ->having('>', 'age', 30');
```

Joins and unions

When working across multiple tables, you may often need to perform a join or union on your datasets. Joins and unions can be performed through query builder using the `join()` and `union()` methods.

The join method has the following method syntax:

```
$query->join( $type, $table, $on, $params );
```

The first parameter, `$type`, specifies the join type you'd like to execute (for example, `INNER JOIN`, `LEFT JOIN`, or `OUTER JOIN`). The `$table` parameter specifies the table to be joined. The third parameter, `$on`, specifies the conditions on which the table should be joined and takes the syntax of the `where()` method, and the `$params` parameter specifies optional parameters to be bound to the join.

For example, suppose we had a posts and users table. We could join them as follows using the `join()` method:

```
$query->join('LEFT JOIN', 'post', 'post.user_id = user.id');
```

Assuming our database had both a user and post table, this would return a return containing a join of all users and their posts. The result would include all users joined with all the posts that they owned.

Joins can also be performed by type using the shortcut methods `rightJoin()`, `leftJoin()`, and `innerJoin()`.

In the same vein, unions of two different queries can be constructed by first building two separate `yii\db\Query` objects and then using the `union()` method on them, as follows:

```
$query1->union($query2);
```

Executing queries

After constructing our query with Query Builder, we'll need to specify the execution of our query. Yii2 provides the following query methods to execute queries built with Query Builder. The query methods are simply chained to the existing `$query` object, which will immediately result in their execution.

Most of the times when working with Query Builder, we'll want to fetch all the records in our database. This can be done by chaining the `all()` methods to our query object, which will retrieve all the records that fulfill the requirements of our `$query` object:

```
$results = $query->all();
```

The `$result` variable will then be populated with an array of rows, with each row containing an associated array of name-value key pairs for the resulting data.

Carefully consider using the `all()` method if you have a large dataset, as the resulting query execution could take a long time to complete, and it could either hang or cause an error in your application.

In other instances, it may be more beneficial just to fetch the first row of a query. To fetch the first row, we can use the `one()` method:

```
$row = $query->one();
```

At other times, we may just want to know whether a query would result in any data. To achieve this, we can use the `exists()` method, which will return either `true` or `false`, indicating that data would be returned from the resulting query.

For example, if we want to know whether we have any users in our database, we can use the `exists()` query to check whether we had users before we performed any more complex queries:

```
$areUsersInDb = (new \yii\db\Query)
                    ->from('user')
                    ->exists();
```

Alternatively, we can use the `count()` method to determine how many users exist in our database before running our query. The `count()` method will execute a `COUNT(*)` method within the `SELECT` fragment, and it will return a scalar value:

```
$count = (new \yii\db\Query)
            ->from('user')
            ->count();
```

When working with database expressions, such as `MIN()` and `MAX()`, or even more complex queries, you may find it useful to retrieve scalar values from query builder rather than an associative array. To fetch scalar values with query builder, we can use the `scalar()` method. For instance, if we want to know how old the oldest user is in our database using the `MAX()` SQL method, we can use the following code to return an integer representing their age:

```
$age = (new \yii\db\Query)
            ->select('MAX(age)')
            ->from('user')
            ->scalar();
```

Finally, we may find it beneficial to retrieve the first column of our database results, such as in the instance of using the `groupBy()` or `having()` methods. To fetch the first row of our results, we can use the `column()` method:

```
$result = (new \yii\db\Query)
            ->from('user')
            ->column();
```

In the previous example, the first column of our user table is the `ID` field. Consequently, an array of all IDs in our database will be returned.

> Selecting all columns (*) will result in all records being loaded into the memory, which, depending upon the size of the table, could result in performance degradation. It's important to remember when querying for data that you only query for the data you need. If you need all data, you query for it in iterative way such as to limit the memory required for each query.

Examining queries

After building a query, you may want to examine the resulting query. To achieve this, the `createCommand()` method can be used to convert the Query Builder object into a DAO command:

```
$command = $query->select(['first_name', 'last_name'])
                 ->from('user')
                 ->where('id = :id', [':id' => 1])
                 ->createCommand();

// Show the generated SQL statement
echo $command->sql;

// Show the bound parameters
var_dump($command->params);

// Execute the query via normal DAO commands
$rows = $command->queryAll();
```

Iterating over query results

Often when working with large datasets, the resulting datasets may be too large to load into the memory. To keep the memory consumption low and to prevent our application from hanging, we can use either the `batch()` or `each()` method. By default, both methods will fetch 100 rows from the database. To change the number of rows to be fetched, simply change the first parameter of each method:

```
$query->from('user');

// $users will ben an array of 100 or fewer rows from the database
foreach ($query->batch() as $users) {}

// Whereas the each() method allows you to iterate over the
// first 50 or fewer users one by one
foreach ($query->each(50) as $user) {}
```

A `batch()` method supports fetching the data in batches, which can keep the memory down. Think of this method as a query appended with a limit and an offset parameter, which will restrict the number of returned rows. Each iteration of the `batch()` query will contain multiple results. Like the `batch()` method, the `each()` method can be used to reduce memory consumption as well, but it will iterate over the query row-by-row instead, which means that each iteration of the method will result in a single instance of our data.

Data providers and data widgets

In Yii2, data providers are helper classes that are used to extract data via Query Builder to be passed to a data widget. The benefit of using data providers and data widgets over queries built via Query Builder is that they provide an interface to automatically deal with sorting and pagination.

The most common way to work with data providers is to use the yii\data\ ActiveDataProvider class. Typically, yii\data\ActiveDataProvider will be used with Active Record models:

```
$provider = new ActiveDataProvider([
    'query' => User::find(),
    'pagination' => [
        'pageSize' => 20,
    ],
]);
```

> We'll cover how to create and use Active Record and models in *Chapter 4, Active Record, Models, and Forms*.

Active data providers can also be populated through Query Builder, as shown in the following example:

```
$query = new yii\db\Query();
$provider = new ActiveDataProvider([
    'query' => $query->from('user'),
    'pagination' => [
        'pageSize' => 20,
    ],
]);
```

> Yii2 provides two additional data provider types: yii\data\ ActiveDataProvider and yii\data\SqlDataProvider. For more information on these data providers, check out the Yii2 guide at http://www.yiiframework.com/doc-2.0/guide-output-data-providers.html.

Once we have fetched our data with a data provider, we can pass the resulting data to a data widget. Data widgets in Yii2 are reusable building blocks used within views to create complex interfaces to interact with data. The most common data widgets are DetailView, ListView, and GridView, which behave similar to their Yii1 counterparts.

For instance, we can take our previous data provider and output it in `GridView`, as follows:

```
$query = new yii\db\Query();
$provider = new yii\data\ActiveDataProvider([
    'query' => $query->from('user'),
    'pagination' => [
        'pageSize' => 2,
    ],
]);

echo yii\grid\GridView::widget([
    'dataProvider' => $provider
]);
```

By itself, our resulting `GridView` widget will display all the fields in our database table. In some instances, there may be sensitive data that we don't want to display on this page. Alternatively, there could simply be too much data to display in `GridView`. To restrict the number of fields to display in our `GridView` widget, we can use the `columns` attribute:

```
echo yii\grid\GridView::widget([
    'dataProvider' => $provider,
    'columns' => [
        'id',
        'email',
        'first_name',
        'last_name',
        'created_at',
        'updated_at'
    ]
]);
```

Showing **1-2** of **3** items.

Id	Email	First Name	Last Name	Created At	Updated At
1	test@example.com	test user	(not set)	(not set)	1432420433
2	test2@example.com	test user 2	(not set)	(not set)	1432420433

« **1** 2 »

We can further enhance our data providers using the yii\data\Sort class, which provides sorting capabilities to our data providers. To add sorting to our data provider, we'll need to specify the sort parameter within yii\data\ ActiveDataProvider with an instance of yii\data\Sort, which specifies the attributes that can be sorted against:

```
$query = new yii\db\Query();
$provider = new yii\data\ActiveDataProvider([
    'query' => $query->from('user'),
    'sort' => new yii\data\Sort([
        'attributes' => [
            'email',
            'first_name',
            'last_name'
        ]
    ]),
    'pagination' => [
        'pageSize' => 2,
    ],
]);
```

Id	Email	First Name	Last Name	Created At	Updated At
1	test@example.com	test user	(not set)	(not set)	1432420433
2	test2@example.com	test user 2	(not set)	(not set)	1432420433

As illustrated, the listed attributes within the sort attribute are now clickable and sortable through our data provider.

 More information on output data widgets can be found in the Yii2 guide at http://www.yiiframework.com/doc-2.0/guide-output-data-widgets.html.

While some widgets, such as GridView, allow us to work with and display multiple rows, we can also use data providers and data widgets to display information for a single row. With the DetailView widget, we can dynamically configure a simple interface to display the information for a particular user in our database. The getModels() method of our data provider splits our data provider into individual models that our DetailView widget can understand:

```
echo yii\widgets\DetailView::widget([
    'model' => $user,
    'attributes' => [
        'id',
        'first_name',
        'last_name',
        'email',
        // Format the updated dates as datetime object
        // Rather than an integer
        'updated_at:datetime'
    ]
]);
```

 Typically when working with the DetailView widget, we'll supply it with an Active Record instance rather than a generated model from our data provider, which we'll cover in *Chapter 4, Active Record, Models, and Forms.*

This will be displayed on our screen:

Id	1
First Name	test user
Last Name	(not set)
Email	test@example.com
Updated At	May 23, 2015, 10:33:53 PM

In addition to simply displaying results from a database, the DetailView widget also supports the custom formatting of certain rows. In our previous example, we were able to format our Unix timestamp stored in the updated_at field as human-readable date and time fields by specifying the :datetime formatter in our updated field:

```
'attributes' => [
    [...],
    'updated_at:datetime'
]
```

 The formatter listed here is a powerful tool that allows us to quickly convert raw data into useful human-readable information. More information on the formatter can be found at http://www. yiiframework.com/doc-2.0/yii-i18n-formatter.html.

Data replication and load balancing

As we start working with larger and larger systems, we often find the need to build an additional redundancy into our system in order to enable high availability and protection against unexpected downtime. When working with large systems, we will split our database into a read-and-write master and a read-only slave of a set of slaves. Typically, our applications are unaware of our database architecture, which can introduce problems when required to migrate from a new master. With Yii2, we can configure our database connection to not only be aware of our master-slave database configuration, but also intelligently handle slave unavailability.

In Yii2, we can configure a single master and multiple slaves using the following database configuration. This will result in all writes going to our declared master and all reads going to one of our declared slaves:

```
$config = [
    'class' => 'yii\db\Connection',

    // configuration for the master
    'dsn' => '<master_dns>',
    'username' => 'master',
    'password' => '<master_password>',

    // common configuration for slaves
    'slaveConfig' => [
        'username' => 'slave',
        'password' => '<slave_password>',
        'attributes' => [
            // Use a small connection timeout
            PDO::ATTR_TIMEOUT => 10,
        ],
    ],

    // List of slave configurations.
    'slaves' => [
        ['dsn' => '<slave1_dsn>'],
        ['dsn' => '<slave2_dsn>'],
        ['dsn' => '<slave3_dsn>'],
    ]
];

$db = Yii::createObject($config);
```

```
// Would execute against an available slave
$users = $db->createCommand('SELECT * FROM user')->queryAll();

// Would execute against the master
$db->createCommand('UPDATE user SET updated_at =
NOW()')->execute();
```

 In general, queries executed with the execute() method will run against the master, whereas all other queries will run against one of the slaves.

In this configuration, Yii will execute write queries (such as UPDATE, INSERT, and DELETE) against the master and run a read query (such as SELECT) against one of the available slaves. When working with slaves, Yii will attempt to connect to slaves in the list until a slave responds and load balance queries against each of the available slaves. By setting PDO::ATTR_TIMEOUT equal to 10 seconds, Yii will abort trying to retrieve data from a slave if it receives no response within 10 seconds, and it will remember the state of the slave for the duration that the configuration is in effect.

Alternatively, using the following configuration, we can configure our application to work with both multiple masters and multiple slaves. When using multiple masters, Yii will execute writes against any available master and will load balance writes between the available masters:

```
$config = [
    'class' => 'yii\db\Connection',
    'masterConfig' => [
        'username' => 'master',
        'password' => '<master_password>',
        'attributes' => [
            // use a smaller connection timeout
            PDO::ATTR_TIMEOUT => 10,
        ],
    ],

    // list of master configurations
    'masters' => [
        ['dsn' => '<master1_dsn>'],
        ['dsn' => '<master2_dsn>'],
    ],

    'slaveConfig' => [...],
    'slaves' => [...]
];
```

If Yii2 is unable to connect to any of the available masters, an exception will be thrown.

When working with a master-slave topology, we may want to issue a read query against one of our masters. To do that, we would need to explicitly tell Yii2 to run our query against our master rather than our slaves:

```
$rows = $db->useMaster(function ($db) {
    return $db->createCommand('SELECT * FROM user')->queryAll();
});
```

When working with transactions, Yii2 will try to run transactions against our master by default. If we need to issue a transaction against a slave, we will need to explicitly begin the transaction on a slave, as follows:

```
$transaction = $db->slave->beginTransaction();
```

Summary

In this chapter, we covered the foundations of working with databases in Yii2. By working with database access objects, we showed how we can execute raw SQL statements to run against our database and how we can use transactions to protect our database integrity. We also illustrated the use of Query Builder, which can enable us to write database-agnostic queries in a programmatic way. We then discovered how we can use Query Builder to construct intelligent data providers, which are used to supply data to reusable data widgets. Finally, we learned how to configure Yii2 to be aware of master-slave and multi-master database cluster configurations and how to load balance between these connections.

In the next chapter, we discover the capstone of working with databases in Yii2 — Active Record — which is a powerful tool used to work with our data and model our database structure. We'll also dive into Active Records relatives, basic models, and forms, and we'll learn how we can use a powerful tool called Gii to automate the construction of much of the code our modern applications will work with.

4

Active Record, Models, and Forms

Like many modern web frameworks, Yii2 comes with several powerful classes to represent data both in and out of our database. These classes enable us to abstract our data management code away from DAO and Query Builder and into an easy-to-use programmatic interface. In this chapter, we'll cover the use and implementation of Active Record and learn how to create data models and custom forms. We'll also cover how to configure a powerful code generation tool called **Gii** to automate the creation of Active Record models and forms.

Configuring Gii

While Active Record models and forms can be generated by hand, in most cases, we'll want to automate the creation of this code. To achieve this, Yii2 provides a code generation tool called Gii, which can be executed both from the command line and from a web interface in order to create Active Record models that work with our database structure and forms that work with both our base models and Active Record models.

Unlike Yii1, Gii does not come prebundled with Yii2. In Yii2, nearly every module is available as a separate Composer package, which can be installed from the command-line interface. Consequently, we must use Composer to include Gii in our application. Since Gii is available as a composer package, we can include it in our application by running the following command from our command line:

```
$ composer require yiisoft/yii2-gii --dev
```

```
Using version ^2.0 for yiisoft/yii2-gii
./composer.json has been updated
Loading composer repositories with package information
Updating dependencies (including require-dev)
Nothing to install or update
Generating autoload files
```

Since Gii is a development tool and has the ability to write new code to our application, we should use the `--dev` flag so that Composer adds it to the `require-dev` section of our `composer.json` file. Typically, during our deployment process, we'll use the `--no-dev` flag to ensure that development packages are not deployed to our production environment.

With Gii installed, we now need to configure it to work with both the Yii2 console and within our web browser.

Gii for web applications

To enable the web interface for Gii, we'll need to specify a `module` section within our `config/web.php` configuration file and bootstrap the Gii module so that it loads properly:

```
return [
    'bootstrap' => ['gii'],
    'modules' => [
        'gii' => [
                'class'       => 'yii\gii\Module',
                'allowedIPs'  => ['*']
        ]
        // [...]
    ],
    // [...]
];
```

By default, Gii is only available on the loopback interface of your machine. If you're using a remote development server or a virtual machine, you'll need to either whitelist your host IP within the `allowedIPs` block or set the `allowedIPs` block to the wildcard character * in order to grant your computer access to Gii.

While this basic configuration will properly load the Gii module, it doesn't follow our convention of being aware of our environment. For instance, if we went to production with this configuration and deployed it with `composer install --no-dev`, as described earlier, our application would crash because Composer would not have installed the Gii module in our vendor folder.

Fortunately, since we previously defined our `APPLICATION_ENV` constant in our bootstrap file rather than returning a static array containing our configuration file, we can store our configuration as a variable and conditionally modify it to include the Gii module depending upon which environment we are working in:

```php
<?php

$config = [
    'id' => 'basic',
    'basePath' => dirname(__DIR__),
    'bootstrap' => ['log'],
    'components' => [
        'request' => [
            'cookieValidationKey' => '<random_key>',
        ],
        'cache' => [
            'class' => 'yii\caching\FileCache',
        ],
        'user' => [
            'identityClass' => 'app\models\User',
            'enableAutoLogin' => true,
        ],
        'errorHandler' => [
            'errorAction' => 'site/error',
        ],
        'log' => [
            'traceLevel' => YII_DEBUG ? 3 : 0,
            'targets' => [
                [
                    'class' => 'yii\log\FileTarget',
```

```
                       'levels' => ['error', 'warning'],
                ],
            ],
        ],
        'db' => require(__DIR__ . '/db.php'),
    ],
    'params' => require(__DIR__ . '/params.php'),
];

if (APPLICATION_ENV == "dev")
{
    $config['bootstrap'][] = 'gii';
    $config['modules'] = [
        'gii' => [
            'class' => 'yii\gii\Module',
            'allowedIPs' => ['*']
        ]
    ];
}

return $config;
```

As an alternative to APPLICATION_ENV, you can conditionally load Gii using the YII_ENV_DEV constant, which is typically defined in your bootstrap file:

```
if (YII_ENV_DEV) // YII_ENV_DEV = true. Define in ./yii
{                       // to enable this constant
    $config['bootstrap'][] = 'gii';
    $config['modules'] = [
        'gii' => 'yii\gii\Module'
    ];
}
```

For our configuration files, the use of either constant is appropriate. However, most developers find that allowing their web server or command line to define the APPLICATION_ENV constant requires less maintenance than manually managing the YII_ENV_DEV constant.

Gii can now be accessed by navigating our web browser to our application path and changing the URI to /index.php?r=gii.

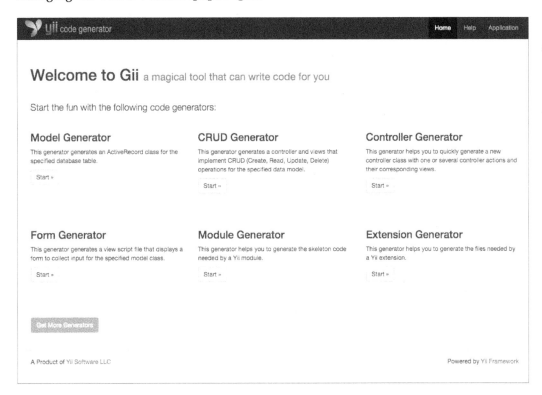

If you have already enabled pretty URLs for your application, Gii can be accessed by navigating to the /gii endpoint.

Gii for console applications

Unlike Yii1, Gii for Yii2 provides a new interface to work with Gii on the command line. With Yii2, we can now generate the source code for Active Record models, forms, and even extensions all from our command-line interface.

The simplest way to enable Gii for our console applications is to modify our `config/console.php` file to include the Gii module within the `module` section of our configuration file and then bootstrap the Gii module itself, as follows:

```
return [
    'bootstrap' => ['gii'],
    'modules' => [
        'gii' => 'yii\gii\Module',
        // [...]
    ],
    // [...]
];
```

Like our web application, this basic configuration doesn't enable our application function properly in every environment. We can reconfigure our `config/console.php` file in the same manner as our web configuration file in order to ensure that the Gii module is only loaded in our development environment:

```php
<?php

Yii::setAlias('@tests', dirname(__DIR__) . '/tests');

$config = [
    'id' => 'basic-console',
    'basePath' => dirname(__DIR__),
    'bootstrap' => ['log'],
    'controllerNamespace' => 'app\commands',
    'components' => [
        'cache' => [
            'class' => 'yii\caching\FileCache',
        ],
        'log' => [
            'targets' => [
                [
                    'class' => 'yii\log\FileTarget',
                    'levels' => ['error', 'warning'],
                ],
            ],
        ],
        'db' => require(__DIR__ . '/db.php'),
    ],
    'params' => require(__DIR__ . '/params.php'),
];
```

```
if (APPLICATION_ENV == "dev")
{
    $config['bootstrap'][] = 'gii';
    $config['modules'] = [
        'gii' => 'yii\gii\Module'
    ];
}


return $config;
```

As shown in the previous code block, the `module` section of our configuration file can be loaded using a shorter syntax if we don't need to register additional options with our module, which is generally the preferred way to load modules:

```
$config['modules'] = [
    'gii' => 'yii\gii\Module'
];
```

With our console environment configured, we can now run Gii from the command line by invoking the help command within the `./yii` command:

```
$ ./yii help gii
```

```
DESCRIPTION

This is the command line version of Gii - a code generator.

You can use this command to generate models, controllers, etc. For example,
to generate an ActiveRecord model based on a DB table, you can run:

$ ./yii gii/model --tableName=city --modelClass=City


SUB-COMMANDS

- gii/controller         Controller Generator
- gii/crud               CRUD Generator
- gii/extension          Extension Generator
- gii/form               Form Generator
- gii/index (default)
- gii/model              Model Generator
- gii/module             Module Generator

To see the detailed information about individual sub-commands, enter:

  yii help <sub-command>
```

With our console application configured to use Gii, we can now start using the Gii tool to create code. As we move through the rest of the chapter, we'll cover how to use Gii from the web interface as well as the console interface.

Active Record

One of the most important tasks when building rich web applications is ensuring that we properly model and represent our data in code. From a simple blog site to an application as big as Twitter, data modeling and representation are vital to ensuring that our application is easy to work with and can grow as required. To help us model our data, Yii2 implements the Active Record pattern, also known as Active Record within the `yii/db/ActiveRecord` class.

The Active Record pattern

Named by Martin Fowler in his 2003 book *Patterns of Enterprise Application Architecture*, the Active Record pattern is an **object-relational mapping (ORM)** pattern that's used to represent database rows and columns within an object. In the Active Record pattern, each database column is represented by a single Active Record class. Upon instantiation, that object then provides a simple interface to manage individual rows or a collection of rows within our code. New rows can be created, old ones can be deleted, and existing rows can be updated — all within a simple and consistent API. Active Record also enables us to programmatically reference and interact with related data, which is usually represented in our database by foreign key relations.

In Yii2, Active Record is implemented by the `yii/db/ActiveRecord` class and is often considered the go-to class to represent and work with the data within our database. While many frameworks and ORMs implement Active Record for relational databases only, Yii2 implements Active Record for search tools such as Sphinx and ElasticSearch as well as for NoSQL databases such as Redis and MongoDB. In this section, we'll cover how to create new Active Record classes, how to implement them within our code, and some common pitfalls of working with Active Record.

Before we start working with Active Record, we first need to create a couple of tables that we can work with. Included with the project resources for this chapter is a base migration that will create several new tables and populate them with some sample data:

```
$ ./yii migrate/up -interactive=0
```

```
Yii Migration Tool (based on Yii v2.0.4)

Creating migration history table "migration"...Done.
Total 1 new migration to be applied:
        m150523_203944_relational

*** applying m150523_203944_relational
    > create table user ... done (time: 0.001s)
    > create unique index user_unique_email on user (email) ... done (time: 0.00
1s)
    > create table role ... done (time: 0.000s)
    > create table post ... done (time: 0.001s)
    > insert into role ... done (time: 0.002s)
    > insert into user ... done (time: 0.003s)
    > insert into post ... done (time: 0.002s)
*** applied m150523_203944_relational (time: 2.971s)

Migrated up successfully.
```

After running the migration, you can verify that the following schema exists within our database by running the `.schema` command from the sqlite3 tool.

Creating Active Record classes

To get started with Active Record in Yii2, we first need to declare an instance of `yii/db/ActiveRecord` within our application. Since Active Record instances in Yii2 extend from the `yii/base/Model` class and are considered models, we will generally store them within the `models/` directory of our application and under the `app/models` namespace.

In Yii2, `@app` is a predefined alias that points to our application base path. Consequently, any namespace declared in our application will typically take the form of `app\<folder>`, which enables Yii2's built-in autoloader to automatically reference that namespace to our class found in `/<folder>/ClassName.php`. If we want to, we can declare additional aliases, such as `@frontend` and `@backend`, to divide our application into different sections, which would enable us to create multiple Active Record instances in different namespaces.

To keep things simple in this chapter, we'll declare only those Active Record classes that are within the `app\models` namespace.

To illustrate an example, let's create an Active Record class for the `user` table we created in *Chapter 3, Migrations, DAO, and Query Building*:

1. First, we need to create a new file in the `models/` directory of our application, called `User.php`:

```
touch models/User.php
```

2. Next, we need to declare the namespace our Active Record instance will live in and extend the `yii/db/ActiveRecord` class:

```php
<?php

namespace app\models;

use yii\db\ActiveRecord;

class User extends ActiveRecord {}
```

3. Finally, we need to implement the static method `tableName()` within our class, which defines the table name our Active Record model will use. Since our Active Record model will use the `user` table, we will define this method as follows:

```php
/**
 * @return string    the string name of the database table
 */
public static function tableName()
{
    return 'user';
}
```

Creating active record classes with Gii

While it's possible to create Active Record instances by hand, generally, we'll want to use Gii to create these classes for us. Using Gii to create our Active Record classes has several advantages: in addition to creating the class, it will also create attribute labels for our fields, create validation rules based upon our database schema, and generate model relationships to another Active Record classes based upon our databases' foreign key structure.

Using Gii's web interface

Like Yii1, Gii provides a friendly and easy-to-use web interface to create our Active Record instances. To get started with Gii, navigate to the /gii endpoint of our application and click on the **Start** button underneath the **Model Generator** section.

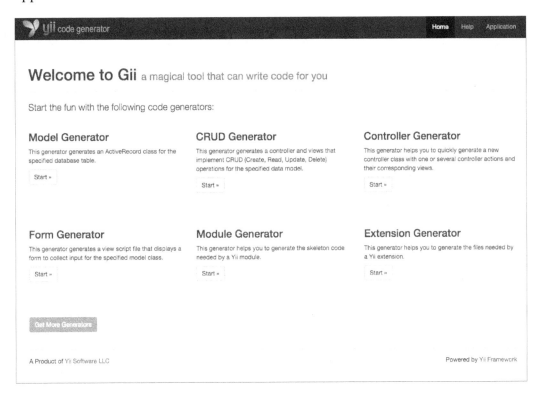

From this page, we can generate Active Record classes based upon our database schema. As an example, let's create an active record instance for our user table:

1. First, we need to populate the Table name field with user, the name of the user table in our database. As you type, Gii will try to show you possible database tables that match our text entry, which can be extremely beneficial when working with large databases.

2. Next, we need to either press the *Tab* key on our keyboard, or focus our mouse onto the Model name field, which should autopopulate the field with User, which will be the name of the class that Gii will generate.

3. Then, we need to ensure that the **Generate Relations** checkbox is selected. This will automatically add the required code to our class in order to generate our model relations for the Post and Role classes, which we'll create in the next section. After checking this box, our form should be filled as follows:

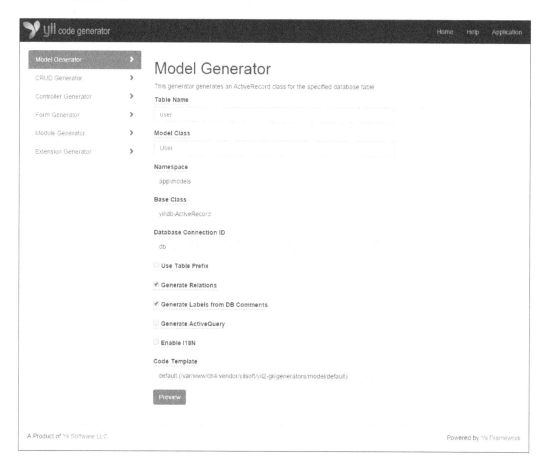

4. Then, we can click on the **Preview** button at the bottom of the page, which will enable us to preview the code that Gii will generate for us before we confirm the creation of our class.

5. After we preview the class, we can click on the **Generate** button to generate our User class, which will be located at models/User.php.

```
The code has been generated successfully.

Generating code using template "/var/www/ch4/vendor/yiisoft/yii2-gii/generators/model/default"...
generated models/User.php
done!
```

In order to create new classes for us, the web user that our server is running under needs write access to our models/ directory. If Gii returns an error indicating it cannot write to the models/ directory, you'll need to adjust the permissions on the directory. In our Linux environment, this can be done by adding the www-data group to the folder and adjusting the permissions so that the user can write to it:

```
chown -R <me>:www-data /path/to/models/
chmod -R 764 /path/to/models/
```

As an alternative, you can use the chmod tool to adjust the permissions in the models/ directory to 777. Just ensure that you readjust the permissions to something more reasonable after using Gii to create the model.

By default, Gii is configured to add new models to the models/ folder in our application and create the models under the app/models namespace. Additionally, the yii/db/ActiveRecord class is configured to automatically use the db component of our application. All of these fields are configurable within the Gii web interface for us to change.

Using Gii's console interface

As an alternative to Gii's web interface, Gii can generate Active Record classes from the command line. When running Gii from the command line, we simply need to provide two attributes: the table name that we are working with and the name of the model. This takes the following form:

```
./yii gii/model --tableName=<tablename> --modelClass=<ModelName>
```

As an example, we can create a class for our post table by running the following command:

```
./yii gii/model --tableName=post --modelClass=Post
```

```
Running 'Model Generator'...

The following files will be generated:
        [new] models/Post.php

Ready to generate the selected files? (yes|no) [yes]:yes

Files were generated successfully!
Generating code using template "/var/www/ch4/vendor/yiisoft/yii2-gii/generators/
model/default"...
 generated models/Post.php
done!
```

While we're here, let's also create a class for our `role` table:

```
./yii gii/model --tableName=role --modelClass=Role
```

Working with Active Record

Now that our models have been generated, let's take a look at what Gii actually wrote to the disk. We'll start by opening up `models/User.php`, which should be identical to the following code block:

```php
<?php

namespace app\models;

use Yii;

/**
 * This is the model class for table "user".
 *
 * @property integer $id
 * @property string  $email
 * @property string  $password
 * @property string  $first_name
 * @property string  $last_name
 * @property integer $role_id
 * @property integer $created_at
 * @property integer $updated_at
 *
```

```php
 * @property Post[] $posts
 * @property Role $role
 */
class User extends \yii\db\ActiveRecord
{
    /**
     * @inheritdoc
     */
    public static function tableName()
    {
        return 'user';
    }

    /**
     * @inheritdoc
     */
    public function rules()
    {
        return [
            [['email', 'password'], 'required'],
            [['role_id', 'created_at', 'updated_at'], 'integer'],
            [['email', 'password', 'first_name', 'last_name'],
            'string', 'max' => 255],
            [['email'], 'unique']
        ];
    }

    /**
     * @inheritdoc
     */
    public function attributeLabels()
    {
        return [
            'id'          => 'ID',
            'email'       => 'Email',
            'password'    => 'Password',
            'first_name'  => 'First Name',
            'last_name'   => 'Last Name',
            'role_id'     => 'Role ID',
            'created_at'  => 'Created At',
            'updated_at'  => 'Updated At',
        ];
    }
}
```

```
/**
 * @return \yii\db\ActiveQuery
 */
public function getPosts()
{
    return $this->hasMany(Post::className(),
    ['author_id' => 'id']);
}

/**
 * @return \yii\db\ActiveQuery
 */
public function getRole()
{
    return $this->hasOne(Role::className(), ['id'
    => 'role_id']);
}
}
```

Model validation rules

The first section we should notice in our generated active record class is the `rules()` method, which Gii generated for us. Since `yii/db/ActiveRecord` extends `yii/base/Model`, it inherits all the validation logic and tools that `yii/base/Model` has:

```
public function rules()
{
    return [
        [['email', 'password'], 'required'],
        [['role_id', 'created_at', 'updated_at'], 'integer'],
        [['email', 'password', 'first_name', 'last_name'],
        'string', 'max' => 255],
        [['email'], 'unique']
    ];
}
```

When Gii created our model, it scanned our database schema to determine any necessary validation rules it thought we would need to have by default. As shown in the previous code block, it has marked both the `email` and `password` attributes as `required` and the `email` field as `unique`, and it has correctly identified the appropriate data types for our name fields as well as timestamps.

The `rules()` method in Yii consists of an array of validation rules that take the following format:

```
[
    // Specifies which attributes should be validated, REQUIRED
    ['attr', 'attr2', ...],

    // Specifies the validator to be used, REQUIRED
    // Can be either a built in core validator,
    // a custom validator method name, or a validator alias
    'validator',

    // Specifies the scenarios that the validator should
    // run on, OPTIONAL
    'on' => ['scenario1', 'scenario2', ...],

    // Specifies additional properties to be passed
    // to the validator, OPTIONAL
    'property1' => 'value1', 'property2' => 'value2'
]
```

A complete list of built-in validators can be found in the Yii2 guide at `http://www.yiiframework.com/doc-2.0/guide-tutorial-core-validators.html`.

Adding custom validators

In addition to the many built-in core validators Yii2 has, we may need to write our own custom validators for our classes. Custom validators can either be written inline using anonymous functions, or they can be written as a separate method within our class.

For instance, suppose we only want to permit changes to our user information between certain core hours of our business. As an anonymous function, this can be written as follows:

```
public function rules()
{
    return [
        // [... other validators ..],

        // an inline validator defined as an anonymous function
        ['email', function ($attribute, $params) {
                $currentTime = strtotime('now');
```

```
            $openTime    = strtotime('9:00');
            $closeTime   = strtotime('17:00');

            if ($currentTime > $openTime && $currentTime <
            $closeTime)
                return true;
            else
                $this->addError('email', 'The user\'s email
                address can only be changed between 9 AM
                and 5 PM');
        }],
    ];
}
```

Alternatively, we can write this as a separate method by providing a name for our validator and then use that name as a method within our class:

```
public function rules()
{
    return [
        // [... other validators ..],

        // a custom validator
        ['email', 'validateTime']
    ];
}


public function validateTime($attributes, $params)
{
    $currentTime = strtotime('now');
    $openTime = strtotime('9:00');
    $closeTime = strtotime('17:00');

    if ($currentTime > $openTime && $currentTime < $closeTime)
        return true;
    else
        $this->addError('email', 'The user\'s email address can
        only be changed between 9 AM and 5 PM');
}
```

Additionally, custom validators can be written by creating and extending the `yii\validators\Validator` class and implementing the `validateAttribute($model, $attribute)` method within that class:

```php
// app/models/User.php::rules()
public function rules()
{
    return [
        // [... other validators ..],

        // a custom validator
        ['email', 'EditableTime']
    ];
}

// app/components/EditableTimeValidator.php
<?php

namespace app\components;

use yii\validators\Validator;

class EditableTimeValidator extends Validator
{
    public function validateAttribute($model, $attribute)
    {
        $currentTime = strtotime('now');
        $openTime = strtotime('9:00');
        $closeTime = strtotime('17:00');

        if ($currentTime > $openTime && $currentTime < $closeTime)
            return true;
        else
            $this->addError($model, $attribute, 'The user\'s email
            address can only be changed between 9 AM and 5 PM');
    }
}
```

Customizing validator error messages

Nearly all validators in Yii2 come with built-in error messages. However, if we want to alter the error message for a certain property, we can do that by specifying the message parameter for a specific validator. For instance, we can adjust the error message for our unique validator by changing the last line of our validator to the following:

```
[['email'], 'unique', 'That email address is already in
use by another user!']
```

Working with validation errors

Yii2 provides several ways to interact with and customize errors as and when they happen. As you may have noticed in the previous example, we can use the `yii/base/Model` method and `addError()` to add new errors to our model attributes during our workflow. As shown in the previous example, this takes the following form:

```
$this->addError($attribute, $message);
```

Additionally, we can use the `getError()` method to retrieve either all the errors for our model or just the errors for a particular attribute. This method will return an array of errors containing an array of error messages applicable for each attribute:

```
[
    'email' => [
        'Email address is invalid.',
        'The user\'s email address can only be changed between
        9 AM and 5 PM'
    ],
    'password' => [
        'Password is required.'
    ],
]
```

Manually executing validation rules

In Yii2, validation rules are executed when the `validate()` method on `yii/db/ActiveRecord` is called. While this can be done manually in our controller, it is typically executed before the `save()` method is executed. The validator method will return either `true` or `false`, indicating whether the validation was successful or not.

The `validate()` method can also be extended by either overriding the `beforeValidate()` and `afterValidate()` methods or by listening to the `yii\base\Model::EVENT_BEFORE_VALIDATE` or `yii\base\Model::EVENT_AFTER_VALIDATE` events.

We'll cover events in more detail in *Chapter 8, Routing, Responses, and Events.*

Model attribute labels

The next method that Gii automatically implements for us is the `attributeLabels()` method. The `attributesLabels()` method enables us to name our model attributes with more descriptive names that we can use as form labels. By default, Gii will automatically generate labels for us based upon our column names. Furthermore, by following the convention of using underscores in our column names in our `user` table, Gii has automatically created titleized and readable attribute labels for us:

```
public function attributeLabels()
{
    return [
        'id'            => 'ID',
        'email'         => 'Email',
        'password'      => 'Password',
        'first_name'    => 'First Name',
        'last_name'     => 'Last Name',
        'role_id'       => 'Role ID',
        'created_at'    => 'Created At',
        'updated_at'    => 'Updated At',
    ];
}
```

Since our `attributeLabels()` method just returns an array of key-value pairs, we can enhance our application by translating our attribute labels into multiple languages using the `\Yii::t()` method:

```
public function attributeLabels()
{
    return [
        'id'            => 'ID',
        'email'         => \Yii::t('app', 'Email'),
        // [ ... other attribute labels ... ]
    ];
}
```

Assuming that our application was properly configured to use translations, we can fetch the translated text for our attribute labels using the `getAttributeLabel()` method for our `email` attribute:

```
$user->getAttributeLabel('email'); // returns "Email"
```

If our application was configured for the English locale, it would simply return the string `"Email"`; however, if our application was running in a different language, say Spanish, this method would return the string `"Correo"` instead of `"Email"`.

> We'll cover the `Yii::t()` method as well as general internationalization and localization in *Chapter 11, Internationalization and Localization*.

Active Record relationships

Assuming that we configured our database schema properly with primary and foreign keys, Yii2 will also generate model relationships for us. Unlike Yii1, Yii2 has done away with the `relations()` methods and replaced them with magic `__getter()` methods. Our `User` model illustrates this for the `Post` and `Role` relationships:

```
/**
 * @return \yii\db\ActiveQuery
 */
public function getPosts()
{
    return $this->hasMany(Post::className(), ['author_id' =>
    'id']);
}

/**
 * @return \yii\db\ActiveQuery
 */
public function getRole()
{
    return $this->hasOne(Role::className(), ['id' => 'role_id']);
}
```

Yii2 also simplified the relationships method, and now, it only supports two types of relationships: has-one, as used by the `hasOne()` method, and has-many, as defined by the `hasMany()` method. Like Yii1, though, related data can be accessed simply by calling the `__getter()` method. For instance, if we want to retrieve the name of the role for a user we are working with, we can simply execute the following:

```
$user = new User::findOne(4);  // Fetch a user in our db
echo $user->role->name;     // "Admin"
```

Gii makes several inferences based upon your database schema to create model relationships. Check whether your relationships map to the correct classes and have the correct relationship types before executing your code.

Using multiple database connections with Active Record

By default, all active record instances will use the db component to connect to our database. In the instance where we have multiple databases connected to our application, we can configure active record to work with an alternate database by defining the static method getDb() within our Active Record class:

```
public static function getDb()
{
    // the "db2" component
    return \Yii::$app->db2;
}
```

Behaviors in Active Record

Yii2 supports several behaviors, which can be used to automatically handle some of the more tedious tasks of model management, such as managing the created and updated times, automatically creating URL slugs for our application, and logging which user created and modified a specific record.

To use a behavior with an Active Record class in Yii2, we simply need to specify that we want to use the behavior class at the top of our PHP file and then add the behavior to the behaviors() method of our model. For instance, since both our User and Post classes have the created_at and updated_at attributes, we can add the following to let Yii2 manage these attributes for us:

```
<?php

use Yii;
use yii\behaviors\TimestampBehavior
class User extends yii\db\ActiveRecord
{
    /**
     * Allow yii to handle population of
     * created_at and updated_at time
     */
    public function behaviors()
```

```
        {
            return [
                TimestampBehavior::className(),
            ];
        }
        // [... other methods ...]
    }
```

By default, the `yii\behaviors\TimestampBehavior` class will populate the `created_at` and `updated_at` attributes with the current time, as extracted from the native PHP `time()` function. Like most things in Yii2, this is completely configurable. For instance, if our database has created and updated fields that use the MySQL TIMESTAMP column type, we can adjust the behavior as follows:

```
public function behaviors()
{
    return [
        [
            'class' => TimestampBehavior::className(),
            'createdAtAttribute' => 'created',
            'updatedAtAttribute' => 'updated',
            'value' => new \yii\db\Expression('NOW()'),
        ],
    ];
}
```

 More information on behaviors can be found from the Yii2 guide located at http://www.yiiframework.com/doc-2.0/guide-concept-behaviors.html.

Working with Active Record

Now that we have learned what Gii automatically provides for us when creating new Active Record classes and what additional options we can add to our classes to enhance them, let's take a look at how we can use active record instances to perform basic create, read, update, and delete (CRUD) actions.

Querying data

To query data with Active Record, we can query for data using the yii/db/
ActiveRecord::find() method, which will return an instance of yii/db/
ActiveQuery. Since yii/db/ActiveQuery extends yii/db/Query, we can take
advantage of nearly all the methods and query objects we learned in *Chapter 3,
Migrations, DAO, and Query Building*. Let's take a look at several different examples
of using the yii/db/ActiveRecord::find() method.

```
// Find the user in our database with the ID of 1.
// one() returns an instance of User model, for the user with id=1
$user = User::find()->where(['id' => 1])
                     ->one();

// Find all users in our database and order them by ID
// Returns an array of User objects
$users = User::find()->orderBy('id'])
                      ->all();

// Returns the number of users in our database
$userCount = User::find()->count();
```

As an alternative to yii/db/ActiveQuery, yii/db/ActiveRecord also provides
two additional methods to query for data, findOne(), which will return the first
Active Record instance from a query, and findAll(), which will return an array of
Active Record instances. Both methods accept a scalar argument, an array of scalar
arguments, or an array of associative pairs to query data:

```
// Fetches user with the ID of 1
User::findOne(1);

// Fetches users with the ID of 1, 2, 3, and 4
User::findAll([1, 2, 3, 4]);

// Fetches admin users (role_id = 2 from migration)
// with the last name of Doe
User::findOne([
    'role_id' => 2,
    'last_name' => 'Doe'
]);
```

```
// Retrieves users with the last name of Doe
User::findAll([
    'last_name' => 'Doe'
]);
```

 The yii/db/ActiveRecord::findOne() method will not add
LIMIT 1 to the generated SQL query, which may result in longer
running queries as yii/db/ActiveRecord::findOne() will
simply fetch the first row from the query result. If you encounter
performance issues using yii/db/ActiveRecord::findOne(),
try to use the yii/db/Activequery::find() method paired
with the limit() and one() methods instead, as follows:

```
User::find()->limit(1)->one();
```

Using yii/db/ActiveQuery can be extremely memory-intensive at times, depending
upon how many records are being accessed. One way to get around this limitation is
to convert our resulting data into an array format using the asArray() method:

```
$users = User::find()->asArray()
                ->all();
```

Rather than returning an array of Active Record instances, the asArray() method
will return an array of arrays containing Active Record data attributes.

 While the asArray() method can be used to increase the performance of
large queries, it has several downsides. The data returned will not be an
instance of Active Record, and thus, it will not have any of the methods
or helpful attributes associated with it. Moreover, since data is being
returned directly from PDO, the data will not be typecast automatically
and will be returned as a string instead.

Data access

When using Active Record, each row from our database query will generate a single
Active Record instance. The column values from our Active Record instance can be
accessed via the model attributes for that Active Record instance:

```
$user = User::findOne(1);
echo $user->first_name; // "Jane"
echo $user->last_name; // "Doe"
```

Moreover, relational information can be accessed through the related object's attributes. For instance, to retrieve the author's name from a given post, we can run the following code:

```
$post = Post::findOne(1);
echo $post->id; // "1"

// "Site Administrator"
echo $post->author->first_name . ' ' . $post->author->last_name;
```

> Active Record attributes are named after the column names. If having Active Record attributes with underscores doesn't match your coding style, you should rename your column names.

Our data can also be manipulated by creating a custom getter and setter method within our Active Record class. For instance, if we want to display the user's complete name without changing our database schema, we can add the following method to our User Active Record class:

```
/**
 * Returns the user's full name
 * @return string
 */
public function getFullName()
{
    return $this->first_name . ' ' . $this->last_name;
}
```

This data can then be accessed directly either through the getFullName() method or as a pseudo attribute:

```
$user = User::findOne(1);
echo $user->fullName;       // "Jane Doe"
echo $user->getFullName(); // "Jane Doe"
```

Along the same vein, we can also create custom setters. For instance, the following method takes the user's complete name as input and populates the first_name and last_name attributes for us:

```
/**
 * Set the users first and last name from a single variable
 * @param boolean
 */
```

```
public function setFullName($name)
{
    list($firstName, $lastName) = explode(" ", $name);
    $this->first_name = $firstName;
    $this->last_name = $lastName;

    return true;
}
```

Our setter then enables us to treat the user's complete name as a settable attribute:

```
$user = User::findOne(1);
$user->fullName = 'Janice Doe'; // or $user->setfullName('Janice
Doe');
echo $user->first_name; // "Janice"
echo $user->last_name;  // "Doe"
```

Saving data

Once we've made changes to our Active Record instance, we can save these changes to our database by calling the `save()` method on our instance, which will return `true` if the model was successfully saved to the database, or it'll return `false` if there was an error.

```
$user = User::findOne(1);
$user->first_name = "Janice";
$user->last_name = "Doe";
$user->save();
```

 If an error occurred during either the save or validation process, you can retrieve the errors through the `yii/db/ActiveRecord::getErrors()` method.

If we retrieved our user information from the database again, we would see that the results were stored:

```
$user = User::findOne(1);
echo $user->first_name; // "Janice"
echo $user->last_name;  // "Doe"
```

Data can also be assigned in bulk through the `yii/db/ActiveRecord::load()` method. Typically when using the `load()` method, we'll provide data from a form submission, which we'll cover later in this chapter.

```
$user = User::findOne(1);
$user->load(\Yii::$app->request->post());
$user->save();
```

 \Yii::$app->request represents the request object and is configured in our `config/web.php` file. The `post()` method represents any data submitted via a POST request.

Creating new records

Creating new records in our database can be done by instantiating a new instance of an active record class using the `new` keyword, populating the model with data, and then calling the `save()` method on the model.

```
$user = new User;
$user->load(\Yii::$app->request->post());
/**
    $user->attributes = [
        'first_name' => 'Janice',
        'last_name'  => 'Doe',
        // ... and so forth
    ];
*/
$user->save();
```

Deleting data

Data can also be deleted from our database via Active Record by calling the `delete()` method on our model. The `delete()` method will permanently delete data from the database and will return `true` if the deletion was successful or `false` if an error occurred.

```
$user = User::findOne(1);
$user->delete(); // return true;
```

Multiple data rows can be deleted by calling the `yii/db/ActiveRecord::deleteAll()` static method:

```
Post::deleteAll(['author_id' => 4]);
```

Be careful when using the deleteAll() method as it will permanently delete any data that the condition statement specifies. A mistake in the conditional can result in an entire table being truncated.

Active Record events

As an alternative to creating before and after method handlers such as beforeSave() and afterDelete(), Yii2 supports several different events that our application can listen to. The events that Active Record supports are outlined in the following table:

Event	Description
EVENT_INIT	An event that is triggered when an Active Record instance is initialized via the init() method
EVENT_BEFORE_UPDATE	An event that is triggered before a record is updated
EVENT_BEFORE_INSERT	An event that is triggered before a record is inserted
EVENT_BEFORE_DELETE	An event that is triggered before a record is deleted
EVENT_AFTER_UPDATE	An event that is triggered after a record is modified
EVENT_AFTER_INSERT	An event that is triggered after a record is inserted
EVENT_AFTER_DELETE	An event that is triggered after a record is deleted
EVENT_AFTER_FIND	An event that is triggered after a record is created and populated with a query result

We'll cover what exactly events are and how to use them in *Chapter 8, Routing, Responses, and Events.*

Models

In Yii1, base models and form models were two separated classes (CModel and CFormModel). In Yii2, these two classes have been consolidated into a single class, yii/base/Model. This class is used throughout Yii2 for data representation and should be our go-to class when representing data we can't represent with yii/db/ActiveRecord.

Since yii/db/ActiveRecord extends yii/base/Model, we're already familiar with the majority of methods and properties that yii/base/Model offers, such as getAttributes(), rules(), attributeLabels(), and getErrors(). Refer to the Yii2 API documentation for a complete list of all the methods supported by yii/base/Model at http://www.yiiframework.com/doc-2.0/yii-base-model.html.

Model attributes

In yii/db/ActiveRecord, data attributes and attribute names are pulled directly from our database column names. In yii/base/Model, data attributes and attribute names are defined as public properties within our model class. For instance, if we want to create a model called UserForm to collect user information, we can write the following class:

```php
<?php

use Yii;

class UserForm extends yii/base/Model
{
    public $email;
    public $password;
    public $name;
}
```

Unlike Active Record instances, information stored in base models is not persisted. Calling unset() on the class or creating a new instance of the class will not grant user the access to the data stored in other instance of the model. Since our model attributes are public properties of our PHP class, we can access them like any public property.

Scenarios

When working with models or active record classes, we may want to reuse the same model for different situations, such as logging in a user or registering a user. To help us write less code, Yii2 provides the scenarios() method to define what business logic and validation rules should be executed for each scenario. By default, scenarios are determined by our validation rules using the on property in our validation rules:

```php
public function rules()
{
    return [
```

```
            [['email', 'password'], 'required'],
            [['email'], 'email'],
            [['email', 'password', 'name'], 'string', 'max' => 255],
            [['email', 'password'], 'required', 'on' => 'login'],
            [['email', 'password', 'name'], 'required', 'on' =>
               'register'],
        ];
    }
```

This behavior can be customized by overriding the `scenarios()` method with our custom logic:

```
    public function scenarios()
    {
        return [
            'login'    => ['email', 'password'],
            'register' => ['email', 'password', 'name']
        ];
    }
```

Alternatively, if we want to add new scenarios to our model without altering the current scenarios defined in our model validation rules, we can simply add them by fetching the classes' parent scenarios, adding the new scenarios we want to add, and then returning our updated scenarios' array:

```
    public function scenarios()
    {
        $scenarios = parent::scenarios();
        $scenarios['login'] = ['email', 'password'];
        $scenarios['register'] = ['email', 'password', 'name'];
        return $scenarios;
    }
```

We can then control which scenario is active when we instantiate our model or when we define the scenario property of our model at runtime:

```
    // Instantiate a model with a specific scenario
    $model = new UserForm(['scenario' => 'login']);

    // Set scenario at runtime
    $model = new UserForm;
    $model->scenario = 'register';
```

 When a scenario is not specified either at runtime or during model instantiation, the default scenario is used. The default scenario marks all model attributes as active for both mass assignment and model validation.

Forms

In Yii2, we can dynamically generate rich HTML5 forms based upon our model using the `yii/widgets/ActiveForm` class. The `yii/widgets/ActiveForm` class has several advantages over managing forms manually. In addition to providing several useful helper methods and pairing well with the HTML helper `yii/helpers/Html`, forms can be generated from the Gii tool using our model data. When working with models and active record instances, this is the preferred way to generate forms.

Generating forms with Gii

Like Active Record classes, forms can be generated automatically for us from both the web Gii tool and the console Gii tool. Let's take a look at generating a form for authentication, which we'll call `LoginForm`, and a form to handle registration, which we'll call `RegisterForm`.

Generating forms with Gii's web interface

For our `LoginForm` form, let's start by opening up the Gii web tool by navigating to the `/gii` endpoint of our application and then clicking on the **Start** button underneath the **Form Generator** section.

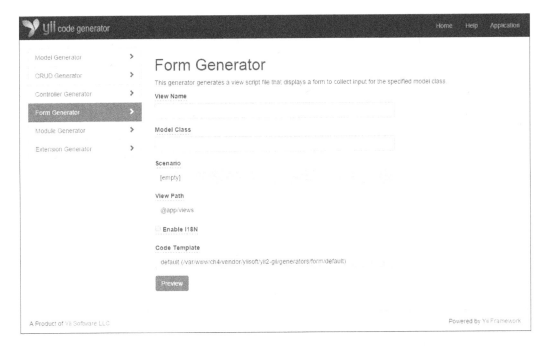

Like our model generator, to generate a form, we only need to provide a few fields. For forms, we only need to know the view name (which will translate to the filename) and the model class. For our view name, let's use site/forms/LoginForm, and for our model class, we may want to use the UserForm class that we generated previously. Since we want to use our form just to log in, we should also specify that we want to use the *login* scenario.

When specifying the model class, we need to specify both the namespace and the class so that Yii can find our class. For our UserForm class, we will need to provide app\models\UserForm.

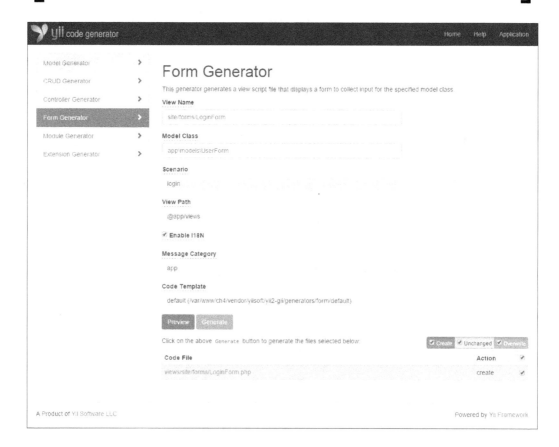

Once we have specified all the necessary attributes, we can click on the **Preview** button to preview our form, and then we can click on the **Generate** button to generate the source code.

```
The form has been generated successfully.
You may add the following code in an appropriate controller class to invoke the view:

<?php

public function actionLoginForm()
{
    $model = new app\models\UserForm(['scenario' => 'login']);

    if ($model->load(Yii::$app->request->post())) {
        if ($model->validate()) {
            // form inputs are valid, do something here
            return;
        }
    }

    return $this->render('LoginForm', [
        'model' => $model,
```

```
Generating code using template "/var/www/ch4/vendor/yiisoft/yii2-gii/generators/form/default"...
 generated views/LoginForm.php
done!
```

Unlike our model generator, after the generation, our form generator will also provide us with a template action that we can put into our controller:

```php
<?php

// app\controllers\SiteController.php::actionLogin()
public function actionLogin()
{
    $model = new \app\models\UserForm(['scenario' => 'login']);

    if ($model->load(Yii::$app->request->post())) {
        if ($model->validate()) {
            // form inputs are valid, do something here
            return;
        }
    }

    return $this->render('LoginForm', [
        'model' => $model,
    ]);
}
```

Generating forms with Gii's console interface

As an alternative to generating forms with Gii's web interface, we can also use Gii's console interface to generate basic forms for our model class. To generate forms with our console interface, we can run the `gii/form` tool, as shown in the following example:

```
./yii gii/form --modelClass=app\\models\\UserForm --viewName=site/forms/
RegisterForm --scenarioName=register --enableI18N=1
```

 Most console shells treat the backslash character as an escape character. To pass a backslash character to Gii, we need to escape the backslash character with a second backslash.

Here's the output:

```
Running 'Form Generator'...

The following files will be generated:
        [new] views/site/forms/RegisterForm.php

Ready to generate the selected files? (yes|no) [yes]:yes

Files were generated successfully!
Generating code using template "/var/www/ch4/vendor/yiisoft/yii2-gii/generators/
form/default"...
 generated views/site/forms/RegisterForm.php
done!
```

Our resulting `RegisterForm` view will look as follows:

```php
<?php

use yii\helpers\Html;
use yii\widgets\ActiveForm;

/* @var $this yii\web\View */
/* @var $model app\models\UserForm */
/* @var $form ActiveForm */
?>
<div class="site-forms-RegisterForm">

    <?php $form = ActiveForm::begin(); ?>
```

```
        <?= $form->field($model, 'email') ?>
        <?= $form->field($model, 'password') ?>
        <?= $form->field($model, 'name') ?>

        <div class="form-group">
            <?= Html::submitButton(Yii::t('app', 'Submit'),
            ['class' => 'btn btn-primary']) ?>
        </div>
    <?php ActiveForm::end(); ?>

</div><!-- site-forms-RegisterForm -->
```

> Remember, Gii's console interface only prompts you for the most
> basic information it needs in order to generate the class. Remember
> to use the `help` tool to discover other command-line arguments for
> additional customization.

Using forms

Now that we've created our forms, let's take a brief look at how exactly they work.
As shown earlier, our `yii/widgets/ActiveForm` class expects a model to work with.
In most cases, this is going to be defined in our controller and then passed down to
our view:

```
$model = new app\models\UserForm(['scenario' => 'login']);
```

One thing you may notice about our generated forms is that they only contain
core form logic and don't contain extra HTML, such as the `html`, `head`, and `body`
tags. In Yii2, generated forms are intended to be rendered as a partial view rather
than a complete view. Rather than specifying our form, `LoginForm`, directly in our
controller, we will pass our model down to a parent view, which will then render
our form. As an example, our login action within our controller will change to
the following:

```
// app\controllers\SiteController::actionLogin()
return $this->render('login', [
    'model' => $model,
]);
```

We will then create a new view file at `views/site/login.php`, which will render our `LoginForm`:

```
// views/site/login.php
<div class="site-login" style="margin-top: 100px";>
    <div class="body-content">
        <?php echo $this->render('forms/LoginForm', [ 'model'
        => $model ]); ?>
    </div>
</div>
```

> Unlike Yii1, Yii2 doesn't have a `renderPartial()` method to render partial views. Instead, it has two separate `render()` methods: one in `yii/base/Controller` and another in `yii/base/View`. The `render()` method called in our previous example is called from `yii/base/View` and is used to render any view file whether we consider it a partial view or a complete view.

The resulting view from our render chain would then look as follows if we navigate to the `site/login` endpoint of our application:

> *Chapter 8, Routing, Responses, and Events*, will help us gain a better understanding of how routing works in Yii2 and how we can easily figure out which controller actions match to which view actions.

ActiveForm and input types

Now that we know how to render our form, let's break down our form view. Since view files and controllers are separated in Yii2, we need to first make sure that we use our active form class in our view file:

```
<?php use yii\widgets\ActiveForm; ?>
```

Our active form elements are then contained within a static call in the `ActiveForm` class to the `begin()` and `end()` methods.

```php
<?php $form = ActiveForm::begin(); ?>
<?php ActiveForm::end(); ?>
```

By default, our `begin()` method will provide us with several built-in HTML defaults, such as an ID and class attribute. To customize these, we can provide an array of arguments to our `begin()` method to manually specify these attributes:

```php
$form = ActiveForm::begin([
    'id' => 'login-form',
    'options' => [
'class' => 'form-horizontal'
  ]
]) ?>
```

The next item to notice about our form is that model attributes are wrapped within a call to `$form->field()`:

```php
<?= $form->field($model, 'email') ?>
<?= $form->field($model, 'password') ?>
```

The `field()` method is a chainable method that specifies the `<input>` tag for our model attribute, adding some basic client-side validation (such as the `required` attribute) and populating the `form` field with data in the instance of a model validation error in our `POST` submission. Since the method is chainable, we can chain additional attributes onto our form. For instance, if we want to add client-side validation for our `email` field so that our browsers can verify our text field was an email address, we can chain the following:

```php
<?= $form->field($model, 'email')->input('email') ?>
```

In addition to our required validator, our view now verifies that our email is a valid email address.

Likewise, we can customize our `password` field to obstruct our password by specifying that the field should be a password input:

```
<?= $form->field($model, 'password')->passwordInput() ?>
```

With `ActiveForm`, we can also add an inline hint or modify the label for any attribute using the `hint()` method and the `label()` method:

```
<?= $form->field($model, 'name')->textInput()->hint('Please
enter your name')->label('Your Name') ?>
```

While the `$form` property is an instance of `yii/widgets/ActiveForm`, the `field()` method returns an instance of `yii/widgets/ActiveField`. For a list of all the available methods and options for `yii/widgets/ActiveField`, refer to the Yii2 documentation at `http://www.yiiframework.com/doc-2.0/yii-widgets-activefield.html`.

Summary

We covered a lot of information in this chapter! We covered how to properly set up and configure Gii, the code generation tool for Yii2. We then covered how we can automatically create Active Record classes based upon our database schema using both the web and console interface for Gii in addition to many of the common methods and properties we can bind to our Active Record classes, such as validation rules, attribute labels, and behaviors. Next, we covered how to create basic models that do not depend upon our database and how to add scenarios to our models and Active Record classes. We finally covered how we can use the Gii tool to create HTML forms based upon our models and explored some of the functionality that comes with the `ActiveForm` class.

In the next chapter, we are going to expand our knowledge of the available helpers and widgets that come with Yii2. We will also dive into modules in Yii2 and explore how we can use them to create reusable self-contained applications that we will keep building upon throughout the book.

As we move forward, we are going to build upon much of the knowledge we have gained thus far. Before moving forward, ensure that you review the classes and information we have learned about.

5
Modules, Widgets, and Helpers

Like its predecessor, Yii2 provides several useful tools and reusable code blocks to help us quickly develop our applications, known as widgets and helpers. Yii2 also provides us with the ability to build and include mini applications known as modules that can enable us to rapidly add new features to our application while maintaining a clear separation of concerns in our main application and any extended functionality. In this chapter, we'll cover the basics of building and working with modules within our application. We'll also cover several of Yii2's built-in widgets and helpers and learn how we can implement our own custom widgets.

Modules

In Yii2, modules are considered to be mini self-contained software packages containing the complete MVC stack. When paired with an application, modules provide a way to extend applications by adding new features and tools without adding code to our main code base. Consequently, modules are a great way to create and reuse code. When creating applications with Yii2, you'll most likely work with prebuilt models, such as Gii or the Yii2 dev module; however, modules can also be custom applications created specifically to build upon and separate code for a specific purpose. In this section, we'll go over the basic modules in Yii2 as well as cover how to create and implement them within our application.

Module components

Compared to Yii1, modules in Yii2 haven't changed much. At their core, they still consist of the same structure and share many of the same ideas. In Yii2, modules are stored in the `modules` directory of our application root and are registered with our application through our web or console configuration files. If we were to break down a basic module, its directory structure and core files would be as follows:

```
app/
    modules/
        mymodule/
            Module.php
            controllers/
                DefaultController.php
            models/
            views/
                layouts/
                default/
                    index.php
```

Each module registered with our application resides within its own dedicated module folder, which registers itself with its corresponding route with our URL manager by default (in this instance, the `mymodule` folder will correspond to the `/mymodule` URI route). Consequently, any controller within the module, unless otherwise registered with our URL manager, will be available as a dedicated controller route within the module itself. For example, the `DefaultController.php` controller will map to the root route of our module (`/mymodule`), while any other controller will map to the controller name within the `/mymodule` URI.

Additionally, modules provide full support for the basic MVC architecture within Yii2. Each module may have its own set of models, views, controllers, and even components. Like complete applications, modules also have support for their own views and layouts, allowing them to be styled and managed differently than our main application. As part of a Yii2 application, they also have complete access to the models and classes implemented within our main application.

The module class structure

The most important part of a module is the module class defined in the `Module.php` file in the root directory of our module. At its most basic level, a module must simply extend the `yii\base\Module` class:

```php
<?php

namespace app\modules\mymodule;

class Module extends \yii\base\Module {}
```

Like everything in Yii2, however, modules can define their custom initialization code and configuration files by overloading the public `init()` method of our class. At the minimum, when overloading this method, we'll want to ensure that the parent `init()` method from `yii\base\Module` is called.

```
public function init()
{
    parent::init();

    // Set custom parameters
    $this->params['a'] = 'b';

    // Register a custom Yii config for our module
    \Yii::configure($this, require __DIR__ .
    '/config/config.php');
}
```

We can also define additional custom parameters with our module by adding values to the `yii\base\Module::$params` array. Additionally, custom configurations can be registered to our module using the `Yii::configure()` static method. This configuration can be a simple key-value pair, or it can be a complete configuration file, such as those used in our web and console configuration files.

> The Yii2 configuration syntax can be explored in detail in the Yii2 guide located at `http://www.yiiframework.com/doc-2.0/guide-concept-configurations.html`.

Controllers

Within a module, controllers are placed within the `controllers/` directory of the main module, and as per the Yii2 convention, they live within the module's namespace. For example, to create the default controller for our `mymodule` module, we would add the following to `app/modules/mymodule/controllers/DefaultController.php`:

```php
<?php

namespace app\modules\mymodule\controllers;

class DefaultController extends \yii\web\Controller
{
    public function actionIndex()
    {
        return $this->render('index');
    }
}
```

Like other controllers within our project, the default action within our controller is the index action. Since controllers within our module extend `yii\web\controller`, we can adjust our default action by setting the `yii\web\controller::$defaultAction` parameter.

By default, Yii2 will route the `/mymodule` URI route to the `DefaultController` class. Should we wish to change this, however, we can adjust the `$defaultRoute` parameter of our `Module` class. For instance, if we have a controller to handle users called `UserController`, we can make our default route map to our controller, as follows:

```php
<?php

namespace app\modules\mymodule;

class Module extends \yii\base\Module
{
    public $defaultRoute = 'user'; // user maps to UserController
}
```

Consequently, navigating to `/mymodule` within our module will result in our `UserController` class being executed rather than `DefaultController`.

> Remember that unless otherwise specified, controllers will always be available in their named URI. In our example, both `/mymodule` and `/mymodule/user` will map to the same controller and perform similar actions. If you do not want the named controller route to be enabled after adjusting the `$defaultRoute` parameter, adjust your router accordingly.

Views and layouts

Since controllers within modules extend from `yii\web\controller`, we can take advantage of view and layout rendering within our module. To get started with rendering our view, we first need to define which layout we want to use. By default, modules will use whatever the parent modules layout file is until it reaches the main layout file, and then it will default to the layout file defined in `app/views/layouts`.

If we do not want to use our application's layout file, we can define a custom layout file for our module by setting the `yii\base\Module::$layout` property, as follows:

We will then define a layout file called `main.php` within the `app/modules/mymodules/views/layouts` folder:

```php
<?php use yii\helpers\Html; ?>

<?php $this->beginPage() ?>
<!DOCTYPE html>
<html lang="en">
    <head>
        <meta charset="UTF-8"/>
        <?php echo Html::csrfMetaTags() ?>
        <title><?php echo Html::encode($this->title) ?></title>
        <?php $this->head() ?>
    </head>
    <body>
        <?php $this->beginBody() ?>
        <?php echo $content ?>
        <?php $this->endBody() ?>
    </body>
</html>
<?php $this->endPage() ?>
```

> The only component needed in a layout file to render our view files is
> `<?php echo $content ?>`. When working with views, however,
> you may find many things you would expect to work in views will
> not however unless a full HTML document is defined with the
> `beginPage()`, `endPage()`, `beginBody()`, `endBody()`, and `head()`
> methods from `yii\base\view`. For more information on these methods,
> refer to the layout section of the Yii2 documentation at `http://`
> `www.yiiframework.com/doc-2.0/guide-structure-views.`
> `html#layouts` and the `yii\base\view` class at `http://`
> `www.yiiframework.com/doc-2.0/yii-base-view.html`.

After defining our layout, we'll need to define the view file for our `DefaultContro` `ller::actionIndex()` method, where we previously declared that we wanted to render the index view. Within modules, views are PHP files with the same name as the requested view within our `render()` method, and they map to the `app/modules/mymodule/views/<controller>` path. In our case, this view maps to `app/modules/mymodule/views/default/index.php`. For now, let's simply add the following to this view file:

```php
<?php echo "MyModule: Hello World!"; ?>
```

Registering modules

Once we have created our module, we need to register it with our configuration file by defining a `modules` section within our `app/config/web.php` file:

```
'modules' => [
    'mymodule' => 'app\modules\mymodule\Module'
],
```

Alternatively, if we want to pass additional parameters to our module, we can define our configuration as follows:

```
'modules' => [
    'mymodule' => [
        'class' => 'app\modules\mymodule\Module',
        'foo' => 'bar' // Maps to app\
        modules\mymodule\Module::$foo, assuming $foo is declared
    ]
]
```

 Like many configuration options in Yii2, modules can receive additional arguments using the previously mentioned configuration file. Any key-value pair will populate the public property of the specified class with the value listed in the array.

Dynamically registering modules

Often when working with large projects, several components will be broken down into modules that need to be registered with our application. Moreover, there may be circumstances where only certain modules need to be registered at a given time. One way to automate the process of registering many different modules at once is to create a dynamic configuration script and let our application scan our modules for us.

To do this, we first need to adjust the modules section of our `app/config/web.php` file to load a custom configuration for our modules, as follows:

```
'modules' => require(__DIR__ . '/module.php'),
```

Then, we'll define `app/config/module.php`, as follows:

1. First, we'll want to set the directory that we want to scan as well as try to load a precached configuration file, should one exist.

   ```
   <?php
   ```

```
// Set the scan directory
$directory = __DIR__ . DS . '..' . DS . 'modules';
$cachedConfig =
__DIR__.DS.'..'.DS.'runtime'.DS.'modules.config.php';
```

2. Then, we'll try to return our cached configuration file, should it exist.

```
// Attempt to load the cached file if it exists
if (file_exists($cachedConfig))
    return require_once($cachedConfig);
```

3. If we don't have a precached configuration file, we'll then want to iterate all the folders in our app/modules directory and then dynamically build a module configuration array. Additionally, we'll also attempt to load a module specific configuration file located at app/modules/<module>/config/main.php. This will enable us to package the configuration with our module without making changes to our app/config/web.php file:

```
else
{
    // Otherwise generate one, and return it
    $response = array();

    // Find all the modules currently installed, and
    preload them
    foreach (new IteratorIterator(new
    DirectoryIterator($directory)) as $filename)
    {
        // Don't import dot files
        if (!$filename->isDot() && strpos
        ($filename->getFileName(), ".") === false)
        {
            $path = $filename->getPathname();

            if (file_exists($path.DS
            .'config'.DS.'main.php'))
            {
                $config = require($path.
                DS.'config'.DS.'main.php');
                $module = [ 'class' => 'app\\modules\\'
                . $filename->getFilename() . '\Module' ];

                foreach ($config as $k=>$v)
                    $module[$k] = $v;

                $response[$filename->getFilename()] =
                $module;
```

```
            }
            else
                $response[$filename->getFilename()] = 'app
                \\modules\\' . $filename->getFilename()
                . '\Module';
        }
    }
```

4. Finally, we generate a cached version of our generated configuration file to eliminate duplicate work on each request. Now, when adding new modules to our application, we simply need to remove the runtime/modules.confg.php file rather than tediously update our web configuration file:

```
    $encoded = serialize($response);
    file_put_contents($cachedConfig, '<?php return
    unserialize(\''.$encoded.'\');');

    // return the response
    return $response;
}
```

Altogether, our dynamic configuration file will look as follows:

```
<?php

// Set the scan directory
$directory = __DIR__ . DS . '..' . DS . 'modules';
$cachedConfig = __DIR__.DS.'..'.DS.'runtime'.DS.'modules.config.php';

// Attempt to load the cached file if it exists
if (file_exists($cachedConfig))
    return require_once($cachedConfig);
else
{
    // Otherwise generate one, and return it
    $response = array();

    // Find all the modules currently installed, and preload them
    foreach (new IteratorIterator(new
    DirectoryIterator($directory)) as $filename)
    {
        // Don't import dot files
        if (!$filename->isDot() && strpos($filename
        ->getFileName(), ".") === false)
        {
```

```
    $path = $filename->getPathname();

    if (file_exists($path.DS.'config'.DS.'main.php'))
    {
        $config = require(
        $path.DS.'config'.DS.'main.php');
        $module = [ 'class' => 'app\\modules\\' .
        $filename->getFilename() . '\Module' ];

        foreach ($config as $k=>$v)
            $module[$k] = $v;

        $response[$filename->getFilename()] = $module;
    }
    else
        $response[$filename->getFilename()] = 'app
        \\modules\\' . $filename->getFilename() .
        '\Module';
    }
}

$encoded = serialize($response);
file_put_contents($cachedConfig, '<?php return
unserialize(\''.$encoded.'\');');

// return the response
return $response;
}
```

Using a configuration file and the module registration process, we can drastically reduce our configuration file management overhead and make our application extremely flexible, should we package features into separate modules that may or may not be installed at the same time.

Bootstrapping modules

Some modules, such as the debug module, need to be executed on every request when enabled. To ensure that these modules run on every request, we can Bootstrap them by adding them to the Bootstrap section of our configuration file. If you're familiar with Yii1, the bootstrap option is used in a manner similar to the Yii1 preload configuration option:

```
[
    'bootstrap' => [
        'debug',
```

```
        ],

        'modules' => [
            'debug' => 'yii\debug\Module',
        ],
    ]
```

Due to the way Yii2 lazily loads new objects, you may encounter race conditions between Yii2's autoloading of the class and the actual population of that object. The `Bootstrap` parameter of our configuration option will ensure that Yii2 will autoload and register the object early on in the execution flow rather than waiting until the class it requires.

Be careful with adding items to the `bootstrap` section, however, as forcing Yii2 to register objects before they're needed can introduce performance degradation into your application.

Accessing modules

When working with modules, you may need to get the instance of the currently running module to either access the module ID and parameters or components associated to the module. To retrieve the current active instance of a module, you can use the `getInstance()` method on the module class directly:

```
$module = \app\modules\mymodule\Module::getInstance();
```

Alternatively, if you know the name of the module, you can access it through the `\Yii` instance:

```
$module = \Yii::$app->getModule('mymodule');
```

Moreover, if you are working in a controller, you can access a module from within a running controller using the following method:

```
$module = \Yii::$app->controller->mymodule;
```

Once you have an instance of the module, you can access any public properties, parameters, and components associated with that module:

```
echo $module->foo;
var_dump($module->params);
```

Managing modules with Composer

When packaging projects, it's often beneficial to manage and version our modules independent of our main applications. Using Composer and semantic versioning, we can manage our modules such that they are versioned to specific points in time in our application while still enabling developers to work with us. Moreover, we can also configure our main project to automatically install modules for us on deployment, which can drastically reduce the overhead involved in managing modules:

1. To get started with managing our modules with Composer, we first need to move our module source code out of our main application and push it to our DCVS repository.

2. Next, we need to create a `composer.json` file within our new module's repository:

```json
{
    "name": "masteringyii/chapter5-mymodule",
    "description": "The mymodule module for Chapter 5
of the book Mastering Yii",
    "license": "MIT",
    "type": "drupal-module",
    "keywords": [
        "mastering yii",
        "book",
        "packt",
        "packt publishing",
        "chapter 5"
    ],
    "authors": [
        {
            "name": "Charles R. Portwood II",
            "homepage": "https://www.nasteringyii.com"
        }
    ],
    "support": {
        "source": "https://
github.com/masteringyii/chapter5-mymodule"
    },
    "homepage": "https://www.masteringyii.com"
}
```

The tool we are using to manage the installation of our modules is called composer-installers. To automatically install modules to our modules directory, we need to explicitly declare the type of our Composer package. The composer-installers project does not support Yii-specific modules currently; however, for our purpose, the `drupal-module` type does what we need.

3. Next, we'll need to make some changes to our main projects' `composer.json` file. The first change we need to make is the inclusion of the composer-installers dependency. We can do this by adding the following to the require block of our `composer.json` file:

```
"composer/installers": "v1.0.21"
```

4. The second change we need to make to our main project's `composer.json` file is reference our modules' DCVS repository. We can do this by creating a repositories block populated with the DCVS information for our module repository and then adding the module to our `require` block:

```
"repositories": [
        {
                "type": "vcs",
                "url": "https://github.com/masteringyii/chapter5-mymodule"
        },
    ],
"require": {
    "php": ">=5.4.0",
    "yiisoft/yii2": "*",
    "yiisoft/yii2-bootstrap": "*",
    "yiisoft/yii2-swiftmailer": "*",
    "composer/installers": "v1.0.21",
    "masteringyii/chapter5-mymodule": "dev-master"
},
```

5. Then, we need to add the installation information to the extras section of our `composer.json` file. This provides the required information to the composer-installers package:

```
"installer-paths": {
    "modules/mymodule/": [
        "masteringyii/chapter5-mymodule"
    ],
}
```

6. Then, we'll want to ensure that our module directory is excluded from our DCVS repository. We can do this adding a .gitignore file to our module directory with the following information:

   *

7. Finally, we can run Composer to update and automatically install our module:

   ```
   composer update -o
   ```

> Since we have specified that we wanted to use the dev-master branch of our mymodule repository, Composer will clone the project into our application, which will allow us to develop it independent of our main application, as usual. During deployments, however, you should semantically version your module so that the versioned copy of the module is downloaded rather than cloned.

Our module has now been installed from Composer.

Modules in summary

Modules are best used in large applications where certain features or reusable components need to be created. As we've shown in this section, modules are extremely powerful and can be used to extend our application.

Widgets

In Yii2, widgets are reuseable code blocks that are used in views to add configurable user interface logic to our application in an object-oriented way. Yii2 comes with several different types of reusable widgets, some of which we have already seen in previous chapters. Custom widgets can also be created to create tools that can be reused across multiple projects. In this section, we'll go over the basic types of widgets, how to use them, and how to implement our own within our applications.

Using widgets

As a presentation layer tool, widgets are most commonly used within our view files. In Yii2, widgets can be used in one of two distinct ways. The first way to use widgets is to call the `yii\base\Widget::widget()` method on a supported widget within a view. This method takes a configuration array as an option and returns a rendered widget as a result. For instance, to display a Twitter Bootstrap 3 style alert on our page, we can use the `yii\bootstrap\Alert` widget as follows:

```php
<?php use yii\bootstrap\Alert; ?>

<?php echo Alert::widget([
    'options' => [
        'class' => 'alert-info',
    ],
    'body' => 'This is a bootstrap alert widget using widget()',
]);
```

Alternatively, we can construct an instance of a specific widget using `yii\base\widget::begin()` and `yii\base\widget::end()` to construct our widget. Using our previous example, this will look as follows:

```php
<?php use yii\bootstrap\Alert; ?>

<?php $widget = Alert::begin([
    'options' => [
        'class' => 'alert-warning',
    ],
]);

echo 'This is an bootstrap3 alert widget warning using begin() and end()';

$widget->end();
```

What both Alert widgets will look like once rendered

As a view object, widgets are responsible for registering and loading their own assets to ensure that they are presented properly. This is why we can create an instance of `yii\bootstrap\Alert` and see an alert rendered with all the appropriate styles and functionalities.

Commonly used built-in widgets

To help quickly develop applications, Yii2 comes with several powerful widgets built in that we can use to jumpstart development.

Bootstrap widgets

One of the main widget types Yii2 provides is specific to Twitter Bootstrap 3 styles and provides a quick and easy way to add a functionality to our application. When working with Bootstrap widgets, Yii2 will inject the necessary HTML, CSS, and JavaScript objects into the DOM for us. However, this can be optimized by including the core Bootstrap assets within our application's asset manager, `AppAsset.php`, located in your `@app/assets` directory:

```
public $depends = [
    'yii\web\YiiAsset',
    'yii\bootstrap\BootstrapAsset', // this line
];
```

We'll cover `AssetManager` in more detail in *Chapter 6, Asset Management*.

All Bootstrap-specific widgets belong to the `\yii\bootstrap` namespace. These core widgets are as follows:

Widget	Result
ActiveForm	A styled ActiveForm instance
Alert	A style alert
Button	A styled button
Button Dropdown	A button drop-down group
Button Group	A button group
Carousel	An images or a text carousel
Collapse	An accordion collapse JavaScript widget
Dropdown	A drop-down menu
Model	A model
Nav	A navigation menu
NavBar	A navigation top bar
Progress	A styled process bar
Tabs	A styled tab

More information on Bootstrap-specific widgets can be found on the Yii guide at `http://www.yiiframework.com/doc-2.0/guide-widget-bootstrap.html`. More information on Twitter Bootstrap 3 can be found at `http://getbootstrap.com`.

jQuery UI widgets

Through an official Yii2 extension, Yii2 also provides several jQuery-UI-specific widgets. Support for jQuery UI widgets can be added to our application by including the `yii2-jui` Composer package in our application:

```
php composer.phar require --prefer-dist yiisoft/yii2-jui "*"
```

Once installed, the jQuery UI package provides support for the following widgets under the \yii\jui namespace:

Widget	Result
Accordion	An accordion element
AutoComplete	An autocomplete element
DatePicker	A date time picker object
Dialog	A dialog box
Draggable	A draggable element
Droppable	A droppable element
Menu	A menu
ProgressBar	A styled progress bar
Resizable	A resizable element
Selectable	A selectable element
Slider	A slider
SliderInput	An input slider
Sortable	A sortable element

> More information on jQuery-UI-specific widgets can be found in the Yii guide at http://www.yiiframework.com/doc-2.0/guide-widget-jui.html. More information on jQuery UI can be found at https://jqueryui.com.

Yii-specific widgets

Yii2 comes with support for familiar Yii1 widgets such as ActiveForm and GridView, both of which we explored in previous chapters. All widgets in Yii2 that are specific to Yii2 are namespaced under \yii\widget.

Widget	Result
ActiveForm	An ActiveForm instance used to display Yii2 forms
GridView	A view to display model and data provider data in a grid table view
DetailView	A view to display data for a specific modal
ListView	A list view to display multiple modals on a single page
AjaxForm	A widget to construct an Ajax form
LinkPager	A widget to display a pagination element for multiple records
LinkSorter	A widget to sort data from a data provider

Widget	Result
Pjax	An implementation of jQuery's pjax functionality in Yii2
Breadcrumb	A widget to display a breadcrumb trail
ContentDecorator	The content decorator widget is used to capture all output between the begin() and end() methods and pass it to the corresponding view in the $content variable.
FragmentCache	Used to cache view fragments
InputWidget	A widget used to display an input field.
MaskedInput	An input widget used to force users to enter properly formatted data
Menu	A widget used to display a Yii menu
Spaceless	A widget to remove whitespace characters between HTML tags

 Several online projects also exist to extend Yii2's widget collection. Before trying to implement your own widget, try to search Yii2's extensions to see whether someone might have already implemented what you need.

Creating custom widgets

In some instances, it may make more sense to create our own widget to handle a specific task. To create a custom widget in Yii2, we need to create a class that extends yii\base\Widget and implements either the init() or run() method. For instance, suppose we want to create a widget that displays a greeting with the user's name depending upon the time of the day. We can create that widget by implementing the following:

```php
<?php
namespace app\components;

use yii\base\Widget;
use yii\helpers\Html;

class GreetingWidget extends Widget
{
    public $name = null;

    public $greeting;

    public function init()
    {
```

```
        parent::init();

        $hour = date('G');

        if ( $hour >= 5 && $hour <= 11 )
            $this->greeting = "Good Morning";
        else if ( $hour >= 12 && $hour <= 18 )
            $this->greeting = "Good Afternoon";
        else if ( $hour >= 19 || $hours <= 4 )
            $this->greeting = "Good Evening";
    }

    public function run()
    {
        if ($this->name === null)
            return HTML::encode($this->greeting);
        else
            return HTML::encode($this->greeting . ',
            ' . $this->name);
    }
}
```

We can then implement our widget by adding the following to our view file:

```
<?php
use app\components\GreetingWidget;
echo GreetingWidget::widget([ 'name' => ' Charles' );
```

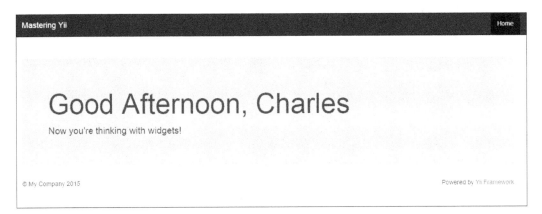

We can also write our widgets so that they use the `begin()` and `end()` format. As an illustration, let's create a widget that outputs whatever is wrapped within a `begin()` and `end()` tag in an HTML `div` element. We can write this class as follows:

```php
<?php

namespace app\components;

use yii\base\Widget;
use yii\helpers\Html;

class EchoWidget extends Widget
{
    public function init()
    {
        parent::init();
        ob_start();
    }

    public function run()
    {
        $content = ob_get_clean();
        echo Html::tag('div', $content, ['class' =>
        'echo-widget']);
    }

}
```

We can then use our widget as follows in our view:

```php
<?php use app\components\EchoWidget; ?>

<?php EchoWidget::begin(); ?>
    <?php echo "Echo this!"; ?>
<?php EchoWidget::end(); ?>
```

When using widgets, you may find it necessary to pass information to a view file to handle more complex view logic. In Yii2, widgets have native support for the `render()` method, allowing us to render view files.

```php
public function run()
{
    return $this->render('greeting');
}
```

By default, view files should be stored within the `WidgetPath\views` folder. In our example, since the `GreetingWidget` class is namespaced under `app\components`, our greeting view file will be located at `@app\components\views\greeting.php`.

A summary of widgets

Widgets are powerful object-oriented reusable code blocks that we can add to our views to quickly and easily add additional functionality to our application. As self-contained objects, widgets follow the MVC pattern and handle dependency management for any and all assets and external scripts required for the widget to function.

Helpers

Yii2 has several built-in helper classes to streamline common coding tasks, such as HTML, array, and JSON manipulation. These helper functions take the form of static classes (which means that they should be called statically rather than being instantiated) and live underneath the `\yii\helpers` namespace. In this section, we'll go over several of the more common helpers.

 Comprehensive documentation for all helpers Yii2 supports can be found on the Yii2 API documentation page underneath the helpers section at `http://www.yiiframework.com/doc-2.0/`.

The URL helper

The first helper commonly used in Yii2 is the URL helper. The URL helper helps us retrieve specific URLs, such as the base and home URL, and generate URL routes to specific paths. The URL helper lives under the `yii\helpers\Url` namespace.

To retrieve the home URL of your application, use the `home()` static method. Several different arguments can be passed to get different types of URLs:

```
$relativeHomeUrl = Url::home();
$absoluteHomeUrl = Url::home(true);
$httpsAbsoluteHomeUrl = Url::home('https');
```

Alternatively, you can use the `base()` method to retrieve the base URL of your application:

```
$relativeBaseUrl = Url::base();
$absoluteBaseUrl = Url::base(true);
$httpsAbsoluteBaseUrl = Url::base('https');
```

 The `home()` method returns the home route for our application, whereas the `base()` method returns the base URL for our application for internal use.

The URL helper can also be used to generate routes to other parts of your application using the `toRoute()` and `to()` method. In general, the `toRoute()` method takes the following form:

```
// Generate a relative URL to controller/action
$url = Url::toRoute(['controller/action', 'foo' => 'bar',
'let' => 'asl']);
```

Alternatively, `toRoute()` can generate absolute URLs by adding a preceding slash to the first array parameter:

```
// Generate an absolute URL to controller/action with
multiple params.
$url = Url::toRoute(['/controller/action', 'foo' => 'bar',
'let' => 'asl']);
```

Furthermore, the method can be reduced to a single string if we do not have the need for extra parameters:

```
// Navigate to controller/action
$url = Url::toRoute('controller/action');
```

As an alternative to the `toRoute()` method, the `to()` method can be used. The `to()` method is identical to the `toRoute()` method, except that it always expects an array rather than a string:

```
// Generates a URL to controller/action
echo Url::to(['controller/action']);

// Generates a URL to controller/action with params
// controller/action?foo=bar#name
echo Url::to(['controller/action', 'foo' => 'bar',
'#' => 'name']);

// the currently requested URL
echo Url::to();
```

Additionally, if we want to retrieve the current URL, we can use the current() method. When passed without arguments, the current URL will be returned. Any array arguments passed to the method will generate the current URL with its parameters:

```
// The current URL
echo Url::current();

// The current URL with params
echo Url::current([ 'foo' => 'bar' ]);
```

The HTML helper

Another common helper in Yii is the HTML helper. The HTML helper provides many different static methods to generate HTML safe tags. In general, HTML tags can be generated by calling the tag() method, as follows:

```
use \yii\helpers\Html; // HTML Helper namespace
// Generates an HTML encoded span tag with the class name,
and the users name HTML encoded.
// <span class="name">Charles</span>
Html::tag('span', Html::encode($user->name), ['class' => 'name']);
```

As shown in the previous example, data can also be HTML-encoded to make it safe for client viewing using the Html::encode() method.

 Any piece of data submitted by the end user should be wrapped within the encode() method to prevent XSS injection.

The CSS styles for our HTML tags can also be managed by our HTML helper via the removeCssClass() and addCssClass() methods. The addCssClass() method can work with either a string or an array definition of a class, and it will not add a class if it already exists:

```
$options = ['class' => 'btn btn-default'];

Html::removeCssClass($options, 'btn-default');
Html::addCssClass($options, 'btn-success');
Html::addCssClass($options, 'btn'); // Has no effect

Html::tag('span', Html::encode($user->name), $options);
```

The HTML helper can also be used to generate links:

```
// Generate a link to the user's profile
// <a href="profile/view/id/$id" class="profile">My Profile</a>
Html::a('My Profile', ['profile/view', 'id' => $id], ['class' =>
'profile']);

Html::mailto('Contact me', 'admin@masteringyii.com');
```

The helper can also be used to generate image tags:

```
// Generates an IMG tag
// <img src="https://www.masteringyii.com/images/logo.png"
alt="masteringyii logo" />
Html::img('@web/images/logo.png', ['alt' => 'masteringyii logo']);
```

Moreover, the HTML helper can be used to include inline CSS styles and JavaScript:

```
// <style>.greeting { color: #2d2d2d; }</style>
Html::style('.greeting { color: #2d2d2d; }');

//<script defer>alert("Hello World!");</script>
Html::script('alert("Hello World!");');
```

CSS files and JavaScript can also be included with the HTML helper:

```
//<link href="@web/css/styles.css" />
Html::cssFile('@web/css/styles.css');

// <!--[if IE 9]>
//     <link href="http://example.com/css/ie9.css" />
// <![endif]-->
Html::cssFile('@web/css/ie9.css', ['condition' => 'IE 9']);

// <script type="text/javascript" src="@web/js/main.js"></script>
Html::jsFile('@web/js/main.js');
```

 The HTML helper can also be used to generate many different types of HTML tags. A complete method list is available at http://www.yiiframework.com/doc-2.0/yii-helpers-html.html.

The JSON helper

Working with JSON objects can often be complicated. To help alleviate some of the problems with complex JSON objects, Yii2 provides the `yii\helpers\Json` class, which provides support for the encoding and decoding of complex JSON objects:

```
$data = [
    'foo' => 'bar,
    'a', => 'b',
    'param' => [
        'param2' => [ 'a' => 'b'],
        'foo' => 'bar'
    ]
];

// Encodes an array to JSON
$json = Json::encode($data);

// Decodes JSON to a PHP array
$decoded = Json::decode($json);
```

> The `yii\helpers\Json` class builds upon the native PHP `json_enocde()` and `json_decode()` classes to provide more robust support for complex JSON objects. It's recommended when using Yii that you use this class instead of the native PHP functions.

The Markdown helper

Markdown is a text to HTML conversion tool used to write on the Web. Meant to replace problematic WYSIWYG editors, Markdown has very quickly become the preferred writing method for professionals across the world. To help you work with Markdown, Yii2 provides the `yii\helpers\Markdown` helper with support for some of the most common markdown flavors, including GitHub Flavored Markdown and Markdown Extra.

```
use \yii\helpers\Markdown;
$html = Markdown::process($markdown); // use original
markdown flavor
$html = Markdown::process($markdown, 'gfm'); // use github
flavored markdown
$html = Markdown::process($markdown, 'extra'); // use
markdown extra
```

Variable dumping

Often when debugging, we need to explore a given array or object. Most developers will use the native PHP functions `var_dump()` or `print_r()`, both of which can be problematic with large arrays or objects. To help work with objects and arrays, Yii2 provides the VarDumper helper within the `yii\helpers\VarDumper` namespace.

While this class replicates much of the functionality of `var_dump()` and `print_r()`, it can identify recursive structures to avoid recursive display of the same object over and over again. VarDumper can be used as follows:

```
yii\helpers\VarDumper;
VarDumper::dump($var);
```

Inflector

Often when working with strings, we need to apply inflection to the string to get the appropriate tense or plural. The `yii\helpers\Inflector` class enables us to do this. Several examples of inflector are provided as follows:

```
use \yii\helpers\Inflector;

// WhoIsOnline
echo Inflector::camelize('who is online?');

// person => people
echo Inflector::classify('person');

// Who is online
echo Inflector::humanize('WhoIsOnline');

// 26 => 26th
echo Inflector::ordinalize(26);

// person => People
echo Inflector::pluralize('person');

// People => Person
echo Inflector::singularize('People');
```

```
// SendEmail => send_email
echo Inflector::underscore('SendEmail');

// SendEmail => Send Email
echo Inflector::titlize('SendEmail');
```

 The inflection class will work only with English words.

FileHelper

To help us work with files, Yii2 provides the yii\helpers\FileHelper class. To search for files in a given directory, we can use FileHelper, as follows:

```
use \yii\helpers\FileHelper;
$files = FileHelper::findFiles('/path/to/search/');
```

Now, you have all files listed in the $files variable as an array.

With the find files method, we can specify the file type we want to have or exclude:

```
// Only .php and .txt files
FileHelper::findFiles('.', ['only' => ['*.php', '*.txt']]);

// Exclude .php and .txt files
FileHelper::findFiles('.', ['except' => ['*.php', '*.txt']]);
```

By default, fileHelper() will perform a recursive search. To disable this behavior, we can set the recursive attribute to false:

```
FileHelper::findFiles('.', ['recursive' => false]);
```

FileHelper can also be used to determine the MIME type of a specific file or a file extension:

```
// image/jpeg
FileHelper::getMimeType('/path/to/img.jpeg');

// image/jpeg
FileHelper::getMimeTypeByExtension('jpeg');
```

Summary

In this chapter, we covered many of the different tools we can use to help us develop applications quicker in Yii2 and extend Yii2. We first covered the basics of a module, its MVC structure, and how to integrate it into our main application. We also covered how to use Composer to automate the inclusion of modules in our projects for development as well as deployment. We then covered widgets in Yii2 and learned how we can use them in our application. We also covered how to create our own widgets. Finally, we covered several of the built-in helpers in Yii2 and learned how to use them.

In the next chapter, we'll explore how assets are managed in Yii2 and how to use `yii\web\AssetManager` to optimize the usage of our assets. We'll also cover how we can integrate other tools, such as Grunt, Node, and Bower, to simplify the use of our assets in Yii2.

Asset Management

6

Modern web applications are made up of many different components. Second only to functionality, the presentation of our application might be considered the most important aspect of our application. Presentation of our user interface and the corresponding user experience is vital to building excellent web applications. In web applications, the presentation and experience is usually defined by **Cascading Style Sheets** (**CSS**), and JavaScript files. With raw HTML, we can include any necessary scripts and styles we need to, however often we need to handle our assets in a programmatic way (such as when using modules, components, or widgets). To help manage our assets, we can use a combination of third-party tools and Yii2's built-in asset manager. In this chapter, we'll cover how to use Yii2's asset management tools, as well as cover several third-party tools we can use to simplify management of our asset files.

Asset bundles

Assets in Yii2 are managed through an asset bundle. An asset bundle in Yii2 is simply a class that declares all the assets that we want to use in our application, and resides within the `assets/` directory of our application, usually within the `AppAsset.php` file that declares an `AppAsset` class that extends `yii\web\AssetBundle`. Since our default application comes within a pre-defined `AppAsset` class, let's take a look at what is already defined in that file.

```php
<?php

namespace app\assets;
use yii\web\AssetBundle;

class AppAsset extends AssetBundle
{
    public $basePath = '@webroot';
```

```
    public $baseUrl = '@web';

    public $css = [
        'css/site.css',
        '//ajax.googleapis.com/
        ajax/libs/jquery/2.1.1/jquery.min.js'
    ];

    public $js = [ ];

    public $depends = [
        'yii\web\YiiAsset',
        'yii\bootstrap\BootstrapAsset',
    ];
}
```

Our example asset bundle file declares several public properties. The first properties are the base path and base URL for our application which define where our assets should be loaded from. The second properties are an array of CSS and JavaScript files which define which assets should be registered with our asset bundle. Finally our asset bundle defines which asset bundles our current asset bundle depends upon. The details of the most common properties are outlined as follows:

Property	Explanation
basePath	The string or path alias to the public directory of our web server contains the asset files.
baseUrl	The base URL for the relative assets listed in the JS or CSS property.
css	An array of CSS files to include in the asset bundle.
cssOptions	An array of options and conditionals that will be rendered with the generated <link> tag.
depends	A array of asset bundles that this asset bundle depends upon.
js	An array of JavaScript files to be included in the asset bundle.
jsOptions	An array of options and conditionals that will be rendered with the generated <script> tag.
publishOptions	Options to be passed to the publish() method of yii\web\ AssetManager.
sourcePath	Defines the directory that contains the asset files we want to include in our bundle. Setting this property will override basePath and baseUrl.

Using asset bundles

After defining our asset bundles, we then need to include them in our layout files. We can do that by adding the following to the beginning of our main layout file (in our case this is `views/layouts/main.php`).

```php
<?php
use app\assets\AppAsset;
AppAsset::register($this);
```

On page load, our asset bundle will register all of its dependent asset bundles, and publish any and all non-web accessible files to a web-accessible directory. Then during the view rendering stage, it will generate all the necessary HTML markup to be included in our view.

> In the previous instance, `$this` is an instance of `yii\web\View`. When working in widgets or components, you can retrieve the view object within a component or widget by using `$this->view`.

Configuration

Internally, Yii2 manages asset bundles and their configuration through the `assetManager` application component, which is implemented by the `yii\web\AssetManager` class. By configuring the `$bundles` property of this component, we can customize how our asset bundles behave. Take for instance the `yii\web\JQueryAsset` bundle; by default, it provides a version of jQuery from **Bower** (a third-party asset dependency manager we'll cover later in the chapter) when our Yii2 project is installed. If we wanted this asset bundle to use a different version of jQuery, or wanted to improve performance by using a third-party CDN, we could override the jQuery asset bundle options as follows.

```php
// config/web.php
return [
    // [...],
    'components' => [
        // [...],
        'assetManager' => [
            'bundles' => [
                'yii\web\JqueryAsset' => [
                    // Prevents the asset bundle from publishing
                    this file
                    'sourcePath' => null,
                    'js' => [
```

```
                          'https://cdnjs.cloudflare.com/ajax/
                          libs/jquery/2.1.4/jquery.js',
                      ]
                  ],
              ],
          ],
      ],
  ];
```

In this instance, we're redefining the JavaScript files for the asset bundle by setting the `js` parameter to a CloudFlare CDN, and telling our `JQueryAsset` bundle to not push the asset as it is being rendered from a third-party CDN.

Alternatively, we can also conditionally redefine which files are rendering, say in the instance where we have a minified version of a script we want to display in production, but a non-minified version we'd like to use in other environments.

```
// config/web.php
return [
    // [...],
    'components' => [
        // [...],
        'assetManager' => [
            'bundles' => [
                'yii\web\JqueryAsset' => [
                    'js' => [
                        APPLICATION_ENV == 'prod' ?
                        'jquery.min.js' : 'jquery.js'
                    ]
                ],
            ],
        ],
    ],
];
```

 As a reminder, our `APPLICATION_ENV` constant is dependent upon our multi-environment setup we established in *Chapter 1, Composer, Configuration, Classes, and Path Aliases.*

Additionally, we can disable specific asset bundles by setting that bundle to `false`, as shown in the following example.

```
// config/web.php
return [
    // [...],
```

```
    'components' => [
        // [...],
        'assetManager' => [
            'bundles' => [
                'yii\web\BootstrapAsset' => false
            ],
        ],
    ],
];
```

Moreover, we can completely disable all included asset bundles within our application by setting the `bundles` property to `false`.

```
// config/web.php
return [
    // [...],
    'components' => [
        // [...],
        'assetManager' => [
            'bundles' => false
        ],
    ],
];
```

Asset mapping

In some instances, multiple asset bundles may define different versions of the same script. For example, one asset bundle may include jQuery version 2.1.3, and another may define 2.1.4. To resolve these conflicts, we can set the `assetMap` property of our configuration file to resolve any named instances of an asset file to a single dependency that will be included in our view.

```
// config/web.php
return [
    // [...],
    'components' => [
        // [...],
        'assetManager' => [
            'assetMap' => [
                'jquery.js' => 'https://cdnjs.cloudflare.com/
                ajax/libs/jquery/2.1.4/jquery.js',
                'jquery.min.js' => 'https://cdnjs.cloudflare.com/
                ajax/libs/jquery/2.1.4/jquery.min.js'
            ]
        ],
    ],
];
```

In this instance, any asset bundle that has an instance of `jquery.js` and `jquery.min.js` defined within the `js` section of the asset bundle will have that asset re-mapped to our CloudFlare CDN asset.

> The `assetMap` property matches on the last part of an asset file within bundles as a key-value pair.

Asset types and locations

Depending upon their location, Yii2 will classify an asset in one of three different ways. Assets will be classified as a source asset, a published asset, or an external asset. Source assets are asset files that are mixed in within our source code and are not in a web-accessible directory. Such assets are often included with modules, widgets, extensions, or components. Any assets that Yii2 defines as source assets will need to be published by Yii2 to a web-accessible directory. Published assets are source assets that have been published to a web-accessible directory. And finally, external assets are assets that are located in a web-accessible location, such as on our current server or on another server or CDN. Unlike published assets, Yii2 will not publish these assets to our assets directory, and will instead reference them directly as an external resource.

When working with asset bundles, if the `sourcePath` property is specified, Yii2 will consider any assets listed with a relative path as a source asset, and will attempt to publish those assets during runtime. If the `sourcePath` property is not specified, Yii2 will assume the listed assets are in a web-accessible directory and are published. In this case, it is necessary to specify either the `basePath` property, or the `baseUrl` property to tell Yii2 where the assets are located.

> Do not use the `@webroot/assets` alias for the `sourcePath` property, as this directory is used by asset manager to save the asset files published from their source location. Any data stored in this directory could be removed at any time by Yii2.

Asset options

Like the `yii\web\View` methods `registerJsFile()` and `registerCssFile()`, asset bundles can be rendered with a given set of options by setting the respective `$jsOptions` and `$cssOptions` properties of our asset bundle.

For example, we can have our asset bundle include our listed JavaScript files at the end of the `<body>` tag within our view.

```
public $jsOptions = ['position' => \yii\web\View::POS_END];
```

 The `yii\web\View` class also provides position methods for the beginning of the body (`yii\web\View::POS_BEGIN`), the end of the body (`yii\web\View::POS_END`), within a `jQuery(window).load()` event (`yii\web\View::POS_LOAD`), and within a `jQuery(window).ready()` event (`yii\web\View::POS_READY`).

With CSS, we can also define `<noscript>` blocks as follows:

```
public $cssOptions = ['noscript' => true];
```

Additionally, we can wrap our CSS blocks in conditionals:

```
public $cssOptions = ['condition' => 'IE 11'];
```

This will result in the following HTML being rendered:

```
<!--[if IE11]>
<link rel="stylesheet" href="path/to/ie11.css">
<![endif]-->
```

 Setting the `$jsOptions` or `$cssOptions` property will apply the specified options to all CSS and JavaScript files defined in the asset bundle. To apply different conditionals to each asset individually, you'll need to create a separate asset bundle defining those conditionals, or inline the assets within the view using the `registerCssFile()` or `registerJsFile()` methods.

Asset publication

As previously mentioned, if the assets referenced by an asset bundle are located in a directory that is not publicly accessible from a web browser (or has the `sourcePath` property set), its assets will be copied to `@webroot/assets` (which corresponds to the web path of `@web/assets`) as part of the automatic publication process the asset manager performs when the bundle is registered with the view. As previously mentioned, the publication path can be altered by setting the `baseUrl` and `basePath` properties of the asset bundle.

As you may expect, the process of copying over files on a web request can be rather expensive, and can cause performance-related issues in production environments if allowed to continually run. To help alleviate this problem, Yii2 provides two alternatives.

Rather than copying over files, Yii's asset manager can be configured to create a symbolic link between the origin asset files and the web-accessible directory by setting the `linkAssets` property of `assetManager` as follows:

```php
// config/web.php
return [
    // [...],
    'components' => [
        'assetManager' => [
            'linkAssets' => true,
        ],
    ],
    // [...],
];
```

 The publication process usually only occurs once. Once Yii2 has published our assets, it won't publish them again unless we remove our assets directory or tell Yii2 to republish our assets.

By default, Yii2 will run the publication process on every file listed in the `sourcePath` property, which means if you have a large directory then every file will be copied over regardless of whether it is actually used. To have Yii2's asset manager only copy over the files you need, you can modify the `publishOptions` property of the asset bundle.

Take for instance if we're using Yahoo's popular CSS library, `purecss`. To build `purecss` from source, we need to run Bower, NPM, and Grunt, which will leave behind build files we shouldn't publish to our web directory.

By setting the `publishOptions` property as shown in the following example, we can ensure only the build files are published, which can drastically improve performance during initial publication.

```php
<?php
namespace app\assets;

use yii\web\AssetBundle;

class PureCssAsset extends AssetBundle
{
    public $sourcePath = '@bower/purecss';
```

```
    public $css = [
        'build/base-min.css',
    ];

    public $publishOptions = [
        'only' => [
          'build/'
        ]
    ];
}
```

Client cache management with asset bundles

When running applications in production, we often set long-lived cache expiration dates on our JavaScript and CSS assets to improve performance. When pushing out new code, often our assets will change, but their file locations will not, which will prevent clients from receiving our updated assets when we make changes. The simplest way to overcome this issue is to append a version or timestamp to the end of our assets so that browsers can cache a specific version of our assets, and be able to re-cache new assets as we push to them.

With Yii2, we can configure our asset manager to automatically append the last modified timestamp to our assets by setting the `appendTimestamp` property of our `assetManager` as follows:

```
// config/web.php
return [
    // [...],
    'components' => [
        'assetManager' => [
            'appendTimestamp' => true,
        ],
    ],
    // [...],
];
```

Using preprocessor with asset bundles

To make asset development simpler and easy to manage, many developers have moved to extended syntax languages such as LESS and CoffeeScript, and rely on their corresponding tools to convert those assets into CSS and JavaScript files. Yii2 can help facilitate this process by enabling asset manager to take care of this build process for you. Using Yii2's asset bundles, you can list LESS, SCSS, Stylus, CoffeeScript, and TypeScript files directly in asset bundles and Yii2 will identify them and automatically run them through their corresponding preprocessor. Take for instance the following asset bundle:

```php
<?php
namespace app\assets;

use yii\web\AssetBundle;

class AppAsset extends AssetBundle
{
    public $basePath = '@webroot';

    public $baseUrl = '@web';

    public $css = [
        'css/app.less',
    ];

    public $js = [
        'js/app.ts'
    ];

    public $depends = [
        'yii\web\YiiAsset'
    ];
}
```

When our asset bundle is registered with our view, Yii2 will automatically run the appropriate pre-processor tool to convert the assets to CSS and JavaScript to include in our views.

 Yii2 is dependent upon the corresponding pre-processor software to be installed on your computer for this feature to work.

When working with pre-processors it may be necessary to specify additional arguments to the pre-processor for your assets to be generated correctly. To set this in Yii2, you can set the `converter` property of our `assetManager` instance as follows.

```
// config/web.php
return [
    // [...],
    'components' => [
        'assetManager' => [
            'converter' => [
                'class' => 'yii\web\AssetConverter',
                'commands' => [
                    'less' => ['css', 'lessc {from} {to}'],
                    'ts' => ['js', 'tsc --out {to} {from}'],
                ],
            ],
        ],
    ],
    // [...],
];
```

While convenient to use, it's generally not a good idea to let Yii2 build our asset files in production, as it introduces unnecessary software into production environments that may not match that in your development environment or have security vulnerabilities, and can seriously hinder application performance as Yii2 will need to build out the asset files on its initial run. When working in production, it's usually a better idea to build all of your asset files on a build server before pushing your application out to production. We'll cover how to build asset files with Grunt, NodeJS, and Bower later on in this chapter, and cover some basic deployment strategies in *Chapter 13, Debugging and Deploying*.

The asset command line tool

With HTTP/1.1 applications, to save bandwidth and requests, it's often better to combine and compress multiple asset files together. Yii2 can help facilitate this process through the `asset` command, which can help you use Yii2, and some third-party Java tools to compress and combine your asset files.

Due to changes in the HTTP/2 protocol, it's often more beneficial to serve asset files individually rather than combining them. As more web servers such as Nginx and Apache start supporting the HTTP/2 protocol, you should run your own experiments to determine if combining assets or not is the best choice for your application.

The asset command-line tool provides two options asset/template, which is used to generate an instruction file called asset.php for use by the second command asset/compress, which is used to compress files together. The first tool, asset/template, is invoked as follows:

./yii asset/template config/assets.php

After running this command, a file called assets.php will be generated in the config directory of our application, and by default will have the following output.

```php
<?php
/**
 * Configuration file for the "yii asset" console command.
 */

// In the console environment, some path aliases may not exist.
Please define these:
// Yii::setAlias('@webroot', __DIR__ . '/../web');
// Yii::setAlias('@web', '/');

return [
    // Adjust command/callback for JavaScript files compressing:
    'jsCompressor' => 'java -jar compiler.jar --js {from}
--js_output_file {to}',
    // Adjust command/callback for CSS files compressing:
    'cssCompressor' => 'java -jar yuicompressor.jar
--type css {from} -o {to}',
    // The list of asset bundles to compress:
    'bundles' => [
        // 'app\assets\AppAsset',
        // 'yii\web\YiiAsset',
        // 'yii\web\JqueryAsset',
    ],
```

```
    // Asset bundle for compression output:
    'targets' => [
        'all' => [
            'class' => 'yii\web\AssetBundle',
            'basePath' => '@webroot/assets',
            'baseUrl' => '@web/assets',
            'js' => 'js/all-{hash}.js',
            'css' => 'css/all-{hash}.css',
        ],
    ],

    // Asset manager configuration:
    'assetManager' => [
        //'basePath' => '@webroot/assets',
        //'baseUrl' => '@web/assets',
    ],
];
```

 To compress assets, Yii2 by default will try to use Closure Compiler (`https://developers.google.com/closure/compiler/`) and YUI Compressor (`https://github.com/yui/yuicompressor/`). You will need to install both of these tools for the `asset` command to function as intended.

This configuration file defines several different options. The first two options, `jsCompressor` and `cssCompressor`, define what commands should be run to compress both JavaScript and CSS files. By default, these tools will try to use Closure Compile and YUI Compressor; both can be configured as needed if you wish to use other tools.

The second option, `bundles`, defines the asset bundles that you wish to compress together. The third option, `assetManager`, defines some basic options that the asset manager component should use, such as the `basePath` and `baseUrl` for the compressed assets. Finally, the `targets` option defines the output asset bundles that will be generated. By default, Yii2 will create a target called `all`, and will generate compressed assets for all asset bundles listed.

In many cases, we often have assets split among several different asset bundles, such as a shared, frontend, and backend tool. As the frontend assets don't need to be included with our backend assets, we can define multiple targets, which will generate separate assets after compression, allowing us to include those assets specifically, thus saving bandwidth for our end user. An example is shown as follows:

```php
<?php
/**
 * Configuration file for the "yii asset" console command.
 */

// In the console environment, some path aliases may not exist.
Please define these:
// Yii::setAlias('@webroot', __DIR__ . '/../web');
// Yii::setAlias('@web', '/');

return [
    // [...],
    'targets' => [
        'shared' => [
            'js' => 'js/shared-{hash}.js',
            'css' => 'css/shared-{hash}.css',
            'depends' => [
                'yii\web\YiiAsset',
                'app\assets\AppAsset',
            ],
        ],
        'backend' => [
            'js' => 'js/backend-{hash}.js',
            'css' => 'css/backend-{hash}.css',
            'depends' => [
                'yii\web\YiiAsset',
                'app\assets\AdminAsset'
            ],
        ],
        'frontend' => [
            'js' => 'js/frontend-{hash}.js',
            'css' => 'css/frontend-{hash}.css',
            'depends' => [],
        ],
    ]
];
```

After writing our asset configuration file, we can then generate our compressed asset files by running the asset command, as follows:

```
./yii asset/compress config/asset.php
```

The asset configuration file is provided as convenience should desire to keep everything in Yii2 as much as possible. While Closure Compiler and YUI Compressor are good tools, tools like Grunt and NodeJS can often provide a solution that is easier to work with and develop for, while eliminating much of the configuration you need to do in Yii2 to compile and compress assets. When working with assets, be sure to find a tool that works best with your development workflow, team, and build process.

Third-party asset tools

When working with modern web applications, we often need to include many different types of asset from various sources. Including these assets directly in our application can cause several problems, namely:

- Licensing of third-party assets
- Management of versions and security
- Repository size
- Build processes

Rather than including assets directly in our application, we can utilize third-party asset management tools such as NodeJS and Bower, which can alleviate all of the issues outlined previously.

With Yii2, we can work directly with Node and Bower packages. For simple applications, we can include these packages directly in our `composer.json` file by including `bower-asset/PackageName` and `npm-asset/PackageName` within the `require` section. Yii2's post-scripts will automatically take care of including these assets within the `@bower` folder and the `@npm` folder, which we can then reference in our asset bundle. In a typical Yii2 instance, this will correspond to `vendor/bower` and `vendor/npm`, respectively.

With more complicated projects, it may make more sense to utilize those third-party tools directly in our application, and included the requisite CSS and JavaScript files later. In this next section, we'll take a look at three tools: NodeJS, Bower, and Grunt, and explore how we can use them in conjunction with Yii2.

NodeJS

The first and most important tool we'll often use to manage our assets is called **NodeJS**, and is a tool that we can use to install the other two packages, Bower and Grunt. To get started with node, we'll first need to download the software from `https://nodejs.org/download/` and install it on our system.

For our purposes, NodeJS will provide us with the tools and packages that we need to automatically download and build our asset files. To get started with NodeJS, we first need to include a `package.json` file within our application. This file will define all the dependencies we want to use. A typical NodeJS file for asset management will look as follows:

```
{
  "name": "masteringyii-ch6",
  "description": "Chapter 6 source code for the book
  'Mastering Yii'",
  "repository": {
    "type": "git",
    "url": "https://www.github.com/masteringyii/chapter6"
  },
  "dependencies": {
    "ansi-styles": "^1.1.0",
    "bower": "1.3.12",
    "grunt": "^0.4.4",
    "grunt-cli": "^0.1.13",
    "grunt-contrib-concat": "^0.4.0",
    "grunt-contrib-cssmin": "0.6.1",
    "grunt-contrib-uglify": "0.2.0"
  }
}
```

> There are two different ways of working with other packages such as Bower and Grunt within NodeJS. The first way is to include them as dependencies within our `package.json` file. This is advantageous as we can version lock our build tools to our application. Alternatively, we can globally install these tools so that we can run them directly through the command line. When working with many developers and teams, it's generally better to use the tools as defined in the `package.json` file.

In our `package.json` file, we defined a few details about our repository such as the name, description, and repository details, as well as several of the tools we want to use, such as Bower, Grunt, and a few Grunt tools to concatenate and minify our CSS and JavaScript files.

With our NodeJS configuration file setup; we can now use NodeJS to add these tools to our repository by running the following command:

```
npm install
```

This will install our build tools to the `node_modules` directory.

 Since this directory contains build tools, we should exclude it from our repository by adding it to our `.gitignore` file.

Bower

To manage CSS and JavaScript libraries, we can utilize an asset dependency management tool called Bower. To get started with Bower, we first need to create a `bower.json` file in the root directory of our application, and populate it with the libraries we want to include. As an example, let's include the popular CSS library PureCSS in our application. We can do that by writing out a basic `bower.json` file as follows:

```
{
    "name": "masteringyii-ch6",
    "dependencies": {
        "pure": "~0.6.0"
    }
}
```

 A full list of package names can be discovered at `http://bower.io/`.

To install these packages, we can then run Bower from our `node_modules` directory as follows:

```
./node_modules/.bin/bower install
```

This will add our libraries and CSS to the `vendor/bower` directory in the root of our application.

 By default, Bower will install itself to the `bower_components` directory. Since, however, Yii2 has already defined the installation directory, it is re-mapped to `vendor/bower`.

Grunt

Since we already know how to use YUI Compressor and Closure Compiler and the Yii2 `asset` command, one option we have at this point is to direct our asset bundle and asset configuration file to the `node_modules` and `bower_components` directory. While this eliminates many of the issues listed previously, we can alternatively use another third-party tool called Grunt to take care of compressing and concatenating our files together.

In short, Grunt is JavaScript task-runner, designed to help automate much of the trivial tasks that need to be repeated, such as building asset files. The main benefit of using a tool like Grunt is that you can automate your workflow both for development and for your build server.

To get started with Grunt, we first need to create a file called `Gruntfile.js`, which will contain all the build instructions for our app.

1. The first step in creating our `Gruntfile.js` file is to declare that we're using Grunt, and to specify the Grunt modules we want to use (the names of which we specified in our `package.json` file).

```
module.exports = function(grunt) {

    // Register the NPM tasks we want
    grunt.loadNpmTasks('grunt-contrib-concat');
    grunt.loadNpmTasks('grunt-contrib-cssmin');
    grunt.loadNpmTasks('grunt-contrib-uglify');

};
```

2. Within this section, we'll then want to declare our default task by specifying which tasks we want to run when we run Grunt. In our case, we want to concatenate our JavaScript and CSS files, then minify both our JavaScript and CSS files.

```
// Register the tasks we want to run
grunt.registerTask('default', [
    'concat',
    'cssmin:css',
    'uglify:js'
]);
```

3. We then begin configuring our Grunt tasks by telling Grunt where it can find our `package.json` file, and setting up some basic path aliases.

```
grunt.initConfig({
    pkg: grunt.file.readJSON('package.json'),

    paths: {
        assets: 'web',
        bower: 'vendor/bower',
        css : '<%= paths.assets %>/css',
        js: '<%= paths.assets %>/js',
        dist: '<%= paths.assets %>/dist',
    },
}
```

4. Within this section we then define our task to concatenate our JavaScript and CSS files.

```
concat: {
    css: {
        src: [
            '<%= paths.bower %>/pure/pure-min.css',
            '<%= paths.css %>/*'
        ],
        dest: '<%= paths.dist %>/app.css'
    },
    js : {
        src: [
            '<%= paths.js %>/*.js'
        ],
        dest: '<%= paths.dist %>/app.js'
    }
},
```

5. Our task to minify our CSS assets after concatenating them together.

```
cssmin : {
    css:{
        src: '<%= paths.dist %>/app.css',
        dest: '<%= paths.dist %>/app.min.css'
    }
},
```

6. And finally, the task to compress our JavaScript files.

```
uglify: {
    js: {
        files: {
            '<%= paths.dist %>/app.min.js' : ['<%= paths.dist %>/
app.js']
        }
    }
},
```

With our `Gruntfile.js` file now configured, we can then build our asset files by running Grunt as follows:

```
./node_modules/.bin/grunt
```

If everything ran well, we should see the following output:

```
Running "concat:css" (concat) task
File web/dist/app.css created.


Running "concat:js" (concat) task
File web/dist/app.js created.


Running "cssmin:css" (cssmin) task
File web/dist/app.min.css created.


Running "uglify:js" (uglify) task
File "web/dist/app.min.js" created.


Done, without errors.
```

As shown in the output of Grunt, we generated four files for us, a compressed and uncompressed JavaScript and CSS file containing all the assets we want to include in our website. From this point, we can then conditionally include our asset files in our asset bundle, and toggle off our APPLICATION_ENV or YII_ENV_<ENV> environment so that we use the minified versions in production, and the non-minified versions in our non-production environment.

> NodeJS, Bower, and Grunt each provide powerful tools to accomplish certain tasks automatically, and work well with Yii2. Before deciding on a specific technology to use however, be sure to consult your team to determine what works best for them.

Summary

In this chapter, we covered how assets work and are managed in Yii2. We explored the basics of asset bundle files and their integration with Yii2's asset manager. We also explored how we can use the asset command to build configuration files and to combine and compress our assets. Finally, we explored three third-party tools: NodeJS, Bower, and Grunt, and illustrated how we can use those tools in conjunction with our asset bundle to automate the building of our asset files.

Having explored the front-end aspect of Yii, in the next chapter, we're going to return to the backend to learn how we can handle user authentication and authorization within our application, as well as cover how we can set up access control filters and rule-based authentication within our app.

7
Authenticating and Authorizing Users

When working with modern web applications, we often need to authenticate our users to ensure that they are who they claim to be and that they have the appropriate permissions (authorization) required to access information. In this chapter, we'll cover the basics of authenticating users with Yii2 and granting them access to specific pages within our applications using basic access control filters and more complex role-based access control filters.

In this chapter, we'll be building upon the migration scripts and models we created in *Chapter 4, Active Record, Models, and Forms*. Before starting this chapter, make sure you have a good understanding of the models and migrations we created in that chapter.

Authentication of users

With nearly every sufficiently sized web application, we will ultimately need our application to support the storage and authentication of users in order to ensure that the users working with our application are who they claim to be. With web applications, we typically handle authentication through a public identity (such as an e-mail address) and a secret that the user knows (such as a password). Depending upon the sensitivity of our data and our threat model, we can also extend our authentication process to include a two-factor authentication code issued either through an SMS text message or a two-factor authentication application, such as Authy or Google Authenticator. In this section, we'll cover how to implement basic authentication with Yii2 and explore how we can enhance the security of our users through the authentication process.

In Yii2, authentication is managed through the user component and is defined in our config/web.php application configuration file. Before we can start authenticating users in our application, we first need to define this component in our configuration file. Specifically, we need to tell Yii2 where it can find the identity class we'll use to handle the authentication logic within our application. In the following code block, we've defined our identity class as our User model that we created in *Chapter 3, Migrations, DAO, and Query Building*:

```
return [
    // [...],

    'components' => [
        'user' => [
            'identityClass' => 'app\models\User',
        ],
    ],

    // [...],
];
```

In the upcoming sections, we'll go over how to extend our User class to support authentication.

Implementing the user identity interface

To implement our identity class with the required authentication logic, we must first have our identity class (app\models\User, defined in models\User.php) implement yii\web\IdentityInterface.

> Remember, in PHP 5+, interfaces are PHP constructs that define which methods the implemented class must contain.

In PHP 5+, we can enhance our User object with the required interface methods by first using the implements keyword in our class, as follows:

```
class User extends \yii\db\ActiveRecord implements
\yii\web\IdentityInterface
```

Then, we can implement the methods outlined in the `IdentityInterface` interface. These methods are `findIdentity($id)`, `findIdentityByAccessToken()`, `getId()`, `getAuthKey($token, $type)`, and `validateAuthKey($authKey)`:

1. The first method we need to implement is `findIdentity($id)`. This method is responsible for finding an instance of the `identity` class with the specified `$id` attribute, and is primarily used when Yii2 needs to authenticate the user from the session data.

2. To implement this method, we need to define the static method and return an instance of our `User` class, as shown in the following example:

    ```
    /**
     * @inheritdoc
     */
    public static function findIdentity($id)
    {
        return static::findOne($id);
    }
    ```

3. The next method defined in `yii\web\IdentityInterface` that we need to define is `findIdentityByAccessToken($token, $type)`. In Yii2, authentication can be handled through a frontend web form, a cookie (if we're using cookie-based authentication), or a RESTful API. The `findIdentityByAccessToken` method is used when we're using RESTful authentication. Since our application doesn't have a REST API yet, we can simply define this method with an empty body, as follows:

    ```
    /**
     * @inheritdoc
     */
    public static function findIdentityByAccessToken($token,
    $type=null) { }
    ```

If we want to add basic support for token-based authentication, we will need to perform the following steps:

1. Add a new migration to store an access token with our user data.

2. Create an API-based authentication method that generates an access token and store it alongside our user data

3. Implement the `findIdentityByAccessToken()` method, as follows:

```php
public static function
findIdentityByAccessToken($token, $type=null)
{
    return static::findOne(['access_token' =>
    $token]);
}
```

We'll cover RESTful API authentication in more detail in *Chapter 9, RESTful APIs.*

4. Next, we need to explicitly define the `getId()` method, which will return the ID of our user:

```php
/**
 * @inheritdoc
 */
public function getId()
{
    return $this->id;
}
```

While `yii\base\Object`, which `yii\base\ActiveRecord` extends from, defines a magic method __getter for all of our public properties defined in our `ActiveRecord` instance, interfaces in PHP 5+ require all methods listed in the interface to be explicitly defined.

5. Finally, we need to implement the `getAuthKey()` and `validateAuthKey()` methods within our application. As stated previously, these two methods are explicitly used for cookie-based authentication. Since we won't be using cookie-based authentication in this chapter, we can leave these two methods, as follows:

```php
/**
 * @return string current user auth key
 */
public function getAuthKey() {}

/**
```

```
 * @param string $authKey
 * @return boolean if auth key is valid for current
user
 */
public function validateAuthKey($authKey)
{
    return true;
}
```

Cookie-based authentication

When working with users, we often need to include a feature similar to the *Remember me* feature in our application so that our users can seamlessly log in to our application after they have been away for some time. To make cookie-based authentication work in Yii2, we need to make several changes to our application:

1. First, we need to set the enableAutoLogin property of our user component in our web configuration file to true. This will allow Yii2 to automatically log users in if they have the appropriate cookie set:

```
return [
    'components' => [
        // [...],
        'user' => [
            'identityClass' => 'app\models\User',
            'enableAutoLogin' => true,
        ],
        // [...],
    ]
];
```

2. Next, we'll need to define a location to store and persist our user's cookie-based authentication token. One way to achieve this would be to add an additional migration that adds an auth_key column to our user table. During the creation of our user, we can then seed this value, as follows:

```
public function beforeSave($insert)
{
    if (parent::beforeSave($insert))
    {
        if ($this->isNewRecord)
        {
            $this->auth_key = \Yii::
            $app->security->generateRandomString();
        }
        return true;
    }
    return false;
}
```

Alternatively, we can make this value persist into a secondary storage system, such as in Memcached or Redis. We'll cover how to use cache data using Redis and Memcached in *Chapter 12, Performance and Security*.

3. Finally, when we define our login form method that instantiates our `IdentityInterface` object, we'll need to log the user in with a duration, as follows:

```
Yii::$app->user->login($identity, 3600*24*30);
```

Yii2 will consequently create a cookie that it will use internally and that will automatically log the user in as long as the cookie is valid. If the duration is not set, session-based authentication will be used instead of a cookie-based one, which means that our user session will expire when the user closes their browser rather than when the user's cookie expires.

Working with user identities

Now that we've defined the methods required for our identity interface, let's take a look at the `yii\web\User` object in more detail.

Remember, the `yii\web\User` class is distinct from the `app\models\User` class.

The `yii\web\User` object is referenced in Yii2 through `\Yii::$app->user`, which contains information on the current user. Information about our user can be retrieved through the `\Yii::$app->user->identity` property. If a user isn't authenticated, this property will be NULL. However, if a user is authenticated, it will be populated with information about the current user. For instance, if we want to fetch the complete name of the user as defined in the `app\models\User` class we extended in *Chapter 4, Active Record, Models, and Forms*, we can do that as follows:

```
$name = \Yii::$app->user->identity->getFullName(); // "Jane Doe";
```

Alternatively, we can detect whether a user is logged in by checking the `isGuest` property of `yii\web\User`, as follows. This property will return `true` if the user is not authenticated and `false` if they are:

```
\Yii::$app->user->isGuest;
```

Moreover, if we want to retrieve the ID of the user, we can access it through the getId() method we defined in our User class:

```
\Yii::$app->user->getId();
```

Finally, we can log our user in and out of our application using the respective login() and logout() methods in Yii::$app->user. To log a user in, we first need to create an instance of the identity we established earlier. In the following example, we're fetching the identity information from the user's e-mail address. As mentioned previously, we can also supply a duration parameter as part of the login() method for cookie-based authentication:

```
$identity = User::findOne([ 'email' => $emailAddress ]);
Yii::$app->user->login($identity);
```

After we're authenticated, we can log users out of our application by calling \Yii::$app->user->logout(). By default, this parameter will destroy all the session data associated with the current user. If we want to preserve this data, we can pass false as the first parameter to the logout() method.

Authenticating users with forms

Now that we've implemented our identity interface and know the basics of the yii\web\User component, let's piece these components together with the user data we created in *Chapter 3, Migrations, DAO, and Query Building*, and the UserForm class and scenario we created in *Chapter 4, Active Record, Models, and Forms*. As a reminder, here is the UserForm class we started with in *Chapter 4, Active Record, Models, and Forms*:

```php
<?php

namespace app\models;
use Yii;

class UserForm extends \yii\base\Model
{
    public $email;
    public $password;
    public $name;

    public function rules()
    {
        return [
            [['email', 'password'], 'required'],
            [['email'], 'email'],
```

```
            [['email', 'password', 'name'], 'string', 'max' =>
            255],
            [['email', 'password'], 'required', 'on' => 'login'],
            [['email', 'password', 'name'], 'required', 'on' =>
            'register']
        ];
    }

    public function scenarios()
    {
        return [
            'login' => ['email', 'password'],
            'register' => ['email', 'password', 'name']
        ];
    }
}
```

To enhance our `UserForm` class to facilitate logging in, we need to make a couple of changes:

1. First, since we'll be working with our identity object in multiple places, we should create a private variable to store it. This will help reduce the number of queries we need to make to our database when working with our form. We'll also want to define a method to retrieve this property:

```
private $_user = false;

/**
 * Finds user by [[email]]
 * @return User|null
 */
    public function getUser()
    {
        if ($this->_user === false)
            $this->_user = User::findOne(['email' =>
            $this->email]);

        return $this->_user;
    }
```

2. Next, we'll need to implement a method to validate our user's password. As mentioned in *Chapter 3, Migrations, DAO, and Query Building*, we're hashing the user's password using the PHP 5 `password_hash` method. To validate passwords that are hashed this way, we can use the PHP 5 `password_verify` method. For our application, let's add a `verifyPassword()` method to our `app\models\User` class:

```
/**
 * Validates password
 *
 * @param  string   $password password to validate
 * @return boolean if password provided is valid for current user
 */
public function validatePassword($password)
{
    return password_verify($password, $this->password);
}
```

3. To call this method, we're going to add a new validator to the `rules()` method of our `UserForm` class that only executes on the login scenario we defined previously:

```
public function rules()
{
  return [
    // [...],
    [['password'], 'validatePassword', 'on' => 'login'],
  ];
}
```

4. Recalling the information we covered in *Chapter 4, Active Record, Models, and Forms*, we know that in the login scenario, the `validatePassword` method will be called to satisfy the new validation rule we added to our `rules()` method. We can define this method as follows:

```
/**
 * Validates the password.
 * This method serves as the inline validation for password.
 *
 * @param string $attribute the attribute currently
being validated
 * @param array $params the additional name-value
pairs given in the rule
 */
public function validatePassword($attribute, $params)
{
```

```
    if (!$this->hasErrors())
    {
        if (!$this->getUser() || !$this->
        getUser()->validatePassword($this->password)) {
            $this->addError($attribute, 'Incorrect email
            or password.');
        }
    }
}
```

5. We'll finalize our `UserForm` class by adding a `login()` method that will validate the email and password submitted by our user and then log the user in.

```
/**
 * Logs in a user using the provided email and password.
 * @return boolean whether the user is logged
in successfully
 */
public function login()
{
    if ($this->validate())
{
    if (Yii::$app->user->login($this->getUser()))
        return true;
}

    return false;
}
```

6. With our form finalized, we can then implement the login action in our controller that will finish the workflow. In our case, let's have our login action redirect the user to a page that will display some information about the user after they're logged in. Since we've already defined the bulk of this action back in *Chapter 4, Active Record, Models, and Forms*, a small change is required for this action:

```
public function actionLogin()
{
    $model = new \app\models\UserForm(['scenario' => 'login']);

    if ($model->load(Yii::$app->request->post()))
    {
        if ($model->login())
            return $this->redirect('secure');
    }
```

```
    return $this->render('login', [
        'model' => $model,
    ]);
}
```

For illustration purposes, let's also dump the information from `\Yii::$app->user->identity` on this page so that we can see it. We can do this by creating the secure action we mentioned previously and then using the `VarDumper` helper to print this information.

```
public function actionSecure()
{
    echo "<pre>";
    \yii\helpers\VarDumper::dump(\Yii::
    $app->user->identity->attributes);
    echo "</pre>";
}
```

Since we already created our login view in *Chapter 4, Active Record, Models, and Forms*, we can authenticate ourselves into the application using the credentials listed in that chapter. For example, we can log in as an admin using the following credentials:

- Username: `admin@example.com`
- Password: `admin`

If authenticated successfully, we will be redirected to the secure page that dumps our user attributes on the page.

```
[
    'id' => 4
    'email' => 'admin@example.com'
    'password' => '$2y$13$f.1jE/cSFP42bHbqjtmJ5
    .6VkcOtKPp7Vu3UBC6clL7cHj84fltUC'
    'first_name' => 'Site'
    'last_name' => 'Administrator'
    'role_id' => 2
    'created_at' => 1439233885
    'updated_at' => 1439233885
]
```

Authorization

Though we're now able to authenticate ourselves against our database, we need to implement the necessary methods in order to ensure that the right people can access the right pages. To do this, we need to implement either an access control filter or a role-based access control filter.

Access control filters

One way to control access to certain pages is to create access control filters. Access control filters in Yii2 are behaviors we can bind to our controllers to ensure that the right people have access to the right content. The access control filter is implemented through `yii\filter\AccessControl` and is primarily used when simple access control is needed, such when needing to make sure users are logged in or not (although it can be configured for rules that are more complex). As a filter, `yii\filter\AccessControl` is implemented in the `behaviors()` method of our controller, as shown in the following example:

```php
<?php

namespace app\controllers;

use yii\web\Controller;
use yii\filters\AccessControl;

class SiteController extends Controller
{
    public function behaviors()
    {
        return [
            'access' => [
                'class' => AccessControl::className(),
                'only' => ['login', 'logout', 'register'],
                'rules' => [
                    [
                        'allow' => true,
                        'actions' => ['login', 'register'],
                        'roles' => ['?'],
                    ],
                    [
                        'allow' => true,
                        'actions' => ['logout'],
                        'roles' => ['@'],
                    ],
```

```
        ],
      ],
    ];
  }
}
```

The previously mentioned code does several things, so let's break it down:

1. As mentioned in previous chapters, behaviors return an array of options. In this case, the first behavior we're returning is the access behavior, which specifies the `yii\filter\AccessControl` filter as the class this behavior should use:

    ```
    return [
      'access' => [
        'class' => AccessControl::className(),
        // [...]
      ]
    ];
    ```

2. Next, we define the actions we want our filter to apply. In this case, we only want `yii\filter\AccessControl` to be applied to the login, logout, and register actions of our `SiteController` object.

    ```
    'only' => ['login', 'logout', 'register'],
    ```

3. Finally, we define the rules that our filter should obey. In the following snippet, we declare that we want unauthenticated users (designated by the special character ? within the roles section) to access the login and register action and allow any authenticated user (designated by the special character @ within the roles section) to access the logout action:

    ```
    'rules' => [
        [
            'allow' => true,
            'actions' => ['login', 'register'],
            'roles' => ['?'],
        ],
        [
            'allow' => true,
            'actions' => ['logout'],
            'roles' => ['@'],
        ],
    ]
    ```

By default, if a user is unauthenticated, our access control filter will redirect the user to our login page, and if they do not have access, `yii\web\ForbiddenHttpException` will be thrown. As this isn't always desirable, we can modify our filter by setting the `denyCallback` parameter of our filter. Also, we can, within the rules section of our filter, define the conditions upon which an error can occur by setting the `matchCallback` property. As an example, if we want to make our secure action accessible to only administrators, we can write the following code:

```php
<?php

namespace app\controllers;

use Yii;
use yii\filters\AccessControl;
use yii\web\Controller;
use yii\web\HttpException;
use yii\helpers\Url;

class SiteController extends Controller
{
    public function behaviors()
    {
        return [
            'access' => [
                'class' => AccessControl::className(),
                // Specifies the actions that the rules should
                be applied to
                'only' => ['secure'],
                // The rules surrounding who should and should
                not have access to the page
                'rules' => [
                    [
                        'allow' => true,
                        'matchCallback' => function($rule,
                        $action) {
                            return !\Yii::$app->user->isGuest &&
                            \Yii::$app->user->identity->role->id
                            === 2;
                        }
                    ],
                ],
                // The action that should happen if the user
                shouldn't have access to the page
                'denyCallback' => function ($rule, $action) {
                    if (\Yii::$app->user->isGuest)
```

```
                    return $this->redirect
                    (Url::to('/site/login'));
                else
                    throw new HttpException('403', 'You are
                    not allowed to access this page');
            },
        ],
    ];
  }
}
```

In this section, users are only allowed to use the secure action if they have a role of 2 (which is the role we designated as an administrator in *Chapter 3, Migrations, DAO, and Query Building*). If they aren't authenticated, we redirect them to the login page, and if they are authenticated but don't have sufficient permissions, we throw an HTTP 403 error.

 The example shown previously is to illustrate what we can do with the matchCallback and denyCallback properties of our access control filter.

With an access control filter, we can restrict access to certain actions by the IP address by setting the ips parameter within our rules section, as shown. IP addresses can be restricted either by a specific IP or by a subnet using the wildcard character, as shown in the following example:

```
return [
    'access' => [
        'class' => AccessControl::className(),
        // [..]
        'rules' => [
            [
                'allow' => true,
                'ips' => [
                    '10.0.0.5', // Allow 10.0.0.5
                    '192.168.*' // Allow 192.168.0.0/24 subnet
                ]
            ]
        ]
    ],
];
```

Additionally, we can restrict access to our action by specifying which HTTP verbs are permitted using the `yii\filter\VerbFilter` filter. For instance, if we want to ensure that only GET requests can be run against our secure action, we can define the following behavior:

```php
<?php

namespace app\controllers;

use Yii;
use yii\web\Controller;
use yii\filters\VerbFilter;

class SiteController extends Controller
{
    public function behaviors()
    {
        return [
            // [...]
            'verbs' => [
                'class' => VerbFilter::className(),
                'actions' => [
                    'secure' => ['get'],
                ],
            ],
        ];
    }
}
```

By default, our access control filter will attempt to apply itself to every action within our controller. To specify the actions that our filter should be restricted to, we can set the `only` property of our filter:

```php
'only' => ['secure'],
```

Additionally, we can specify actions that our access control rules should be applied to by setting the `actions` property of our `rules` array:

```php
'rules' => [
    [
        'allow' => true,
        'actions' => [ 'secure' ],
        'matchCallback' => function($rule, $action) {
            return !\Yii::$app->user->isGuest && \Yii::
            $app->user->identity->role->id === 2;
        }
```

```
        ],
        [
            'allow' => true,
            'actions' => [ 'authenticated' ],
            'roles' => ['@']
        ]
    ],
```

In a manner similar to the `only` parameter, we can exclude certain actions from the authentication filter by setting the `except` filter:

```
'except' => ['secure'],
```

Access control filters are broken down into rules, as shown in the previous example. Each rule applies only to a specific set of actions, which allows us to specify custom allow or deny callbacks for these rules. The parent options of `only` and `except`, however, specify when the parent access control filter should be applied.

Role-based access control

As an alternative to managing access with the user identity object, we can also manage access to actions by configuring **role-based access control** (**RBAC**) within our application. In Yii2, RBAC works by creating roles that represent a collection of permissions and then assigning roles to a specific user. Roles are represented by a check to determine if a given role or permission is applicable to the user in question. In this section, we'll cover the basics of configuring and working with RBAC in Yii2.

Yii2's implementation of RBAC follows the NIST RBAC model through the `authManager` component. The complete implementation details of the NIST RBAC model are located at http://csrc.nist.gov/rbac/sandhu-ferraiolo-kuhn-00.pdf.

Configuring RBAC

To start working with RBAC, we first need to configure our `authManager` component for RBAC and define the authorization manager we want to use. Yii2 provides two different authorization managers, the first being `yii\rbac\PhpManager`, which uses a PHP script to store authorization data, and `yii\rbac\DbManager`, which utilizes the application database to manage authorization data. For simple applications with nondynamic permissions and roles, `yii\rbac\PhpManager` may be preferred.

To configure `authManager`, we simply need to define the class that we want to use, as follows:

```
return [
    // [...],
    'components' => [
        'authManager' => [
            'class' => 'yii\rbac\PhpManager',
        ],
    ],
    // [...],
];
```

 By default, `yii\rbac\PhpManager` will store authorization data in the `@app/rbac` directory, which must be writable by your web server.

Alternatively, if we're using a database to manage our authorization data, we will configure `authManager` as follows:

```
return [
    // [...],
    'components' => [
        'authManager' => [
            'class' => 'yii\rbac\DbManager',
        ],
    ],
    // [...],
];
```

When using our database to manage our authorization data, we need to run RBAC migrations to configure our database appropriately, which can be done by running the following command from our command-line interface:

./ yii migrate --migrationPath=@yii/rbac/migrations

This will result in output similar to the following:

```
Yii Migration Tool (based on Yii v2.0.6)
Total 1 new migration to be applied:
    m140506_102106_rbac_init
*** applying m140506_102106_rbac_init
    > create table {{%auth_rule}} ... done (time: 0.006s)
    > create table {{%auth_item}} ... done (time: 0.005s)
```

```
> create index idx-auth_item-type on {{%auth_item}} (type) ... /
done (time: 0.006s)
> create table {{%auth_item_child}} ... done (time: 0.005s)
> create table {{%auth_assignment}} ... done (time: 0.005s)
*** applied m140506_102106_rbac_init (time: 0.050s)
Migrated up successfully.
```

After configuring RBAC, our `authManager` component can be accessed by \
`Yii::$app->authManager`.

Creating permissions and permission relationships

After configuring our `authManager` component, we need to define the permissions we want our users to have and the relationships between them. For most applications with fixed permission hierarchies, this can be achieved by writing an RBAC console command to initialize the data in our database. In the following example, we'll create three permissions for an imaginary issue management application, a permission for a user to create new issues, support for newly created issues, a supervisor to oversee supervisors, and an administrator permission:

```php
// Save to @app/commands
<?php
namespace app\commands;

use Yii;
use yii\console\Controller;

class RbacController extends Controller
{
    public function actionInit()
    {
        $auth = \Yii::$app->authManager;

        // Create the user permissions
        $user = $auth->createPermission('createIssue');
        $user->description = 'A permission to create a new issue
        within our incident management system';
        $auth->add($user);
```

```
            // Create the supporter permissions
            $supporter = $auth->createPermission('supportIssue');
            $supporter->description = 'A permission to apply supporter
            specific actions to an issue';
            $auth->add($supporter);

            // A supporter should have all the permissions of a user
            $auth->addChild($supporter, $user);

            // Create a permission to manage issues
            $supervisor = $auth->createPermission('manageIssue')
            $supervisor->description = 'A permission to apply
            management specific actions to an issue';
            $auth->add($supervisor);

            // A supervisor should have all the permissions of
            a supporter and a end user
            $auth->addChild($supervisor, $supporter);
            $auth->addChild($supervisor, $user);

            $admin = $auth->createRole('admin');
            $admin->description = 'A permission to perform
            admin actions on an issue';
            $auth->add($admin);

            // Allow an admin to perform all related tasks.
            $auth->addChild($admin, $supervisor);
            $auth->addChild($admin, $supporter);
            $auth->addChild($admin, $user);
        }
    }
```

Our newly created permission scheme can then be initialized by running the rbac/init command from our command line:

./yii rbac/init

After defining our roles, we can apply them to our users during our registration step or in the administrative dashboard, as shown. In this example, we're fetching the admin role and assigning it to our administrative user, which has a user ID of 4:

```
    $auth = \Yii::$app->authManager;
    $role = $auth->getRole('admin');
    $auth->assign($role, User::findOne([ 'email' =>
    'admin@example.com' ]));
```

Alternatively, we can define an implicit default role within our `authManager` component. This way, we do not need to explicitly assign new users to the lowest-level user role. This can be achieved as follows:

```
return [
    // [...],
    'components' => [
        'authManager' => [
            'class' => 'yii\rbac\PhpManager',
            'defaultRoles' => ['user'],
        ],
        // [...],
    ],
];
```

Custom authorization rules

In addition to basic authentication roles and permissions, we can also define custom rules by extending `yii\rbac\Rule` and implementing the `execute()` method, as shown in the following example:

```php
// Save to @app/rbac
<?php
namespace app\rbac;

use yii\rbac\Rule;

/**
 * Checks if a user can edit their own issue
 */
class SupervisorRule extends Rule
{
    public $name = 'isAuthor';

    /**
     * @param string|integer $user the user ID.
     * @param Item $item the role or permission that
     this rule is associated with
     * @param array $params parameters passed to
     ManagerInterface::checkAccess().
     * @return boolean a value indicating whether the rule
        permits the role or permission it is associated with.
     */
    public function execute($user, $item, $params)
    {
```

```
            return isset($params['issue']) ?
            $params['issue']->author == $user : false;
        }
    }
```

Custom rules can be added to our `authManager` component, as follows:

```
$auth = Yii::$app->authManager;

// Add a rule
$rule = new \app\rbac\SupervisorRule;
$auth->add($rule);

// Create a permission and associate the rule to it
$modifyOwnIssue = $auth->createPermission('modifyOwnIssue');
$modifyOwnIssue->description = 'Modify a issue that was self
submitted';
$modifyOwnIssue->ruleName = $rule->name;
$auth->add($modifyOwnIssue);
// Assign the supervisor role to the superviseIssue permissions
$superviseIssue = $auth->getRole('superviseIssue');
$auth->addChild($modifyOwnIssue, $superviseIssue);
```

Checking if a user has access to a role

After configuring RBAC, creating the required roles, and assigning users to these roles, we can check to see if a user has access to a particular role using the `yii\web\User::can()` method, as shown here:

```
if (\Yii::$app->user->can('createIssue'))
{
    // Create a new issue
}
```

We can also check accessibility against our newly created rule by checking against the parent role and passing in the required data, as shown here:

```
if (\Yii::$app->user->can('superviseIssue', ['issue'
=> Yii::$app->request->post('Issue')]))
{
    // Can modify an issue that they created
}
```

Though more explicit through the naming of roles and rules, using RBAC can quickly become confusing. When using RBAC, thoroughly document permissions, relationships, and rules for reference later.

Flash messages

Rather than blindly redirecting users without information, we can utilize flash messages in Yii2 to display one-time useful pieces of information to the user, such as what action they need to perform in order to complete another action (such as them having to log in to view the secure page).

In Yii1, user-specified flash messages can be tied directly to the user component. In Yii2, they're solely managed by the session object. In this section, we'll show how to use flash messages by example by enhancing our login view. We'll also take advantage of several of the other widgets and helpers we've covered in previous chapters.

As shown in the previous section, when a user is a guest and they try to access a secure page, we simply redirect them back to the login page without any information. To provide good user experience, we can set a flash message before redirecting the user and then display that flash message in our login view. As an example, the `behaviors()` method of our controller will change to the following. Note the use of the `setFlash()` method:

```
public function behaviors()
{
    return [
        'access' => [
            'class' => AccessControl::className(),
            'denyCallback' => function ($rule, $action) {
                if (\Yii::$app->user->isGuest)
                {
                    \Yii::$app->session->setFlash('warning', 'You
                    must be authenticated to access this page');
                    return
                    $this->redirect(Url::to('/site/login'));
                }
                else
                    throw new HttpException('403', 'You are not
                    allowed to access this page');
            },
```

```
                'only' => ['secure'],
                'rules' => [
                    [
                        'allow' => true,
                        'matchCallback' => function($rule, $action) {
                            return !\Yii::$app->user->isGuest && \Yii:
                            :$app->user->identity->role->id === 2;
                        }
                    ],
                ],
            ],
        ];
    }
```

Within our login view file, we can then check for the presence of a specific type of flash message using the hasFlash() method and then displaying a particular flash message using the getFlash() method, as shown here:

```
<?php use yii\bootstrap\Alert; ?>

<div class="site-login">
    <?php if (\Yii::$app->user->isGuest): ?>
        <div class="body-content">
            <?php if (\Yii::$app->session->hasFlash(
            'warning')): ?>
            <?php echo Alert::widget([
                    'options' => [
                    'class' => 'alert alert-warning'
                    ],
                    'body' => \Yii::$app->
                    session->getFlash('warning')
                ]); ?>
                <?php endif; ?>
            <?php echo $this->render('forms/LoginForm',
            [ 'model' => $model ]); ?>
        </div>
    <?php else: ?>
        <?php echo Alert::widget([
            'options' => [
                'class' => 'alert alert-info'
            ],
            'body' => 'You are already logged in. To login as a
            different user, logout first'
        ]); ?>
    <?php endif; ?>
</div>
```

Now if we navigate our browser to site/secure without being authenticated, we are shown the following. Moreover, if we refresh the page again, the flash message disappears, as flash messages are only intended to be displayed once.

Hashing and encryption

When dealing with user information, it's essential to be mindful of best security practices in order to ensure that user information such as passwords is stored in a way that if your database is compromised, the user's bare passwords are not exposed in plain text. As shown in *Chapter 3, Migrations, DAO, and Query Building*, we're using the native PHP `password_hash()` and `password_verify()` functions to encrypt and decrypt our users' passwords. While these standards are easy to use, in the development of your application, you may find it easier to take advantage of the Yii2 security component used to hash user passwords and for the encryption of sensitive data:

```
Yii::$app->getSecurity();
```

Hashing and verifying passwords

With Yii2, we can hash and verify user passwords using the `generatePasswordHash()` and `validatePassword()` methods of the security component. Like the `password_hash()` and `password_verify()` functions, the `generatePasswordHash()` and `validatePassword()` methods use bcrypt to hash the user passwords:

```
$hash = \Yii::$app->getSecurity()-
>generatePasswordHash($password);
```

Passwords can then be verified, as follows:

```
if (Yii::$app->getSecurity()->validatePassword(
$plainTextPassword, $hashedPassword))
{
    // Valid Password
}
else
{
    // Invalid Password
}
```

By default, Yii2 will use the PHP `crypt()` function to generate password hashes, but can, optionally, be configured to use the raw `password_hash()` methods using the `PASSWORD_DEFAULT` algorithm by setting the `passwordHashStrategy` property of the security component within the application configuration:

```
return [
    // [...],
    'security' => [
        'passwordHashStrategy' => 'password_hash'
    ],
    // [...],
];
```

It's highly recommended that you use the `password_hash` strategy over crypt as PHP will continue to strengthen the hashing algorithm of `PASSWORD_DEFAULT` to increase the security of PHP.

The password hashing methods implemented by Yii2, however, are simply wrappers around native PHP functions. Both the native functions and Yii2 implementations will remain backward-compatible with each other. For a more object-oriented approach, it's recommended that you use Yii2 methods.

Data encryption and decryption

For convenience, Yii2 provides a way to encrypt and decrypt data using a secret key or a user's passwords. To encrypt data with Yii2, we can use the `encryptByPassword()` method of the security component, as shown in the following example:

```
$encrypted = \Yii::$app->getSecurity()->encryptByPassword($data,
$secretPassword);
```

Data can then be decrypted using the `decryptByPassword()` method:

```
$data = \Yii::$app->getSecurity()->decryptByPassword($encrypted,
$secretPassword);
```

 The secret password used for the encrypt and decrypt methods should be unique to the user and be stored in a format that if our database is compromised, the secret password itself is not compromised. A good secret to use would be the separate password submitted by the user.

Data hashing

In addition to hashing passwords and encrypting data, we can also hash data for integrity verification using the `hashData()` and `validateData()` methods. These methods will be beneficial to present and validate checksums of files or raw data:

```
$hash = Yii::$app->getSecurity()->hashData($data, $secretKey);
$data = Yii::$app->getSecurity()->validateData($hash, $secretKey);
```

 Unlike encrypted data, hashed data cannot be recovered to its original state. Hashes are beneficial in order to verify that information hasn't been tampered with, and it ensures that the integrity of files or data is consistent after transmission.

Summary

In this chapter, we covered the basics of authenticating the identity of our users and granting them access to certain pages based upon attributes we set in the user identity interface, and how to implement Yii2's hierarchical role-based authentication. We also explored how to use flash messages to enhance our user experience. Additionally, we explored a few components of the security component, which enabled us to hash the user's passwords, hash and verify data, and encrypt and decrypt information utilizing the user's password.

In the next chapter, we'll cover more complex routing within our application, how to work with and modify our responses directly with Yii2, and the basics of listening and responding to events.

8

Routing, Responses, and Events

Like many modern web frameworks, Yii2 is built with a powerful router component, which we can utilize to handle a variety of URIs coming from both our end users and application. This functionality is further enhanced by Yii2's powerful request and response handlers, which we can use to manipulate request and response bodies. In this chapter, we'll cover the basics of how to manipulate Yii2's URL Manager to adjust routes, explore how to configure Yii2 to respond in different ways, and learn how to send and listen to events within our application.

Routing

As mentioned in previous chapters, routing within Yii2 is managed by the UrlManager component defined in our application configuration. The router in Yii2 is responsible for determining where Yii2 routes external URI requests to internal controllers and actions. In *Chapter 5, Modules, Widgets, and Helpers*, we covered the basics of how to create and manipulate URL routes with the `yii\helpers\Url` helper. In this section, we'll cover how Yii2 routes these requests inside our application by exploring Yii2's UrlManager in more detail.

Routing in Yii2 can be broken down into two basic steps. The first of these steps is to parse the incoming request and query parameters (which are stored in the GET parameters of our request with the r parameter by default but can be retrieved from the request URI if we have pretty URLs enabled). The second step is to create an instance of the corresponding controller action, which will ultimately handle the request.

By default, Yii2 will break the route down in the forward slashes of the URL to map it to the appropriate module, controller, and action pair. For instance, the site/login route will match the `site` controller and the action named `login` in the default module of the application instance. Internally, Yii2 will take the following steps to route the request:

1. By default, Yii2 will set the current module as the application.

2. Examine the controller map of the application to see whether it contains the current route. If so, a controller instance will be created according to the controller map defined within the module, at which point, the action will be created according to the action map defined in step 4. By default, Yii2 will create a controller map based upon the controllers found within the `@app/controllers` folder, but this may be customized within the module (or UrlManager):

    ```
    yii\base\Module::$controllerMap = [
        'account' => 'app\controllers\UserController',
        // Different syntax for the previous example
        //'account' => [
        //    'class' => 'app\controllers\AccountController'
        //],
    ]
    ```

3. If the controller map of the application module is found not within the application module, Yii2 will iterate through the module list in the `module` property of the application module to see if a route matches there. If a module is found, Yii2 will instantiate the module using the provided configuration and then create the controller using the details outlined in the previous step.

4. Yii2 will then look for the action within the action map defined in the module's configuration. If found, it will create an action according to that configuration; otherwise, it will attempt to create an inline action defined in the `action` method corresponding to the given action.

If an error occurs at any point during this process, Yii2 will throw `yii\web\NotFoundHttpException`.

Default and catch all routes

When Yii2 receives a request that is parsed into an empty route, the default route will be used instead. The default route is set to `site/index`, which references the `index` action of the `site` controller. This behavior can be changed by setting the `defaultRoute` property of the `application` component, as follows:

```
[
    // index action of main controller
    'defaultRoute' => 'main/index'
]
```

Additionally, Yii2 can be configured to forward all requests to a single route by setting the `catchAll` property of `yii\web\application`. This can be beneficial when you need to perform application maintenance.

```
[

    // Display a maintenance message
    'catchAll' => 'site/maintenance'
]
```

Custom routes and URL rules

Rather than relying upon the default controller/action routes Yii2 internally generates, custom URL rules can be written to define our own URL routes. URL routes in Yii2 are implemented by an instance of `yii\web\UrlRule`, and they consist of a pattern used to patch the path information and query parameters of a given route. When using custom URL rules, Yii2 will route a request to the first matching rule for the accompanying request. Moreover, the matching rule determines how the request parameters are split up. Additionally, using the `yii\helpers\Url` helper will also rely upon the list rules to internally route requests.

URL rules in Yii2 can be defined in our application configuration by setting the `yii\web\UrlManager:$rules` property as an array, with a key containing the URL pattern to be matched and the value being the corresponding route. For example, supposing we had a controller to manage published content, we could write custom rules, as follows, to route `posts` and `post` to our content:

```
[
    'posts' => 'content/index',
    'post/<id:\d+>' => 'content/view',
]
```

Now when navigating to the /posts endpoint of our application, the content/index controller action pair will be triggered. As shown in the previous example, URL rules can extend beyond simple strings and can contain complex regular expressions, which we can use to conditionally route rules. In the previous example, a route to the /post endpoint followed by an integer ID will route to the content/view controller action pair. Moreover, Yii2 will automatically pass the $id parameter to the action:

```
class ContentController extends yii\web\Controller
{
    // Responds to content/index and /posts
    public function actionIndex() {}

    // Responds to content/view/id/<id> or /post/<id>
    public function actionView($id) {}
}
```

 Regular expressions can only be specified for parameters. However, as we'll see later in this section, we can parameterize our routes to make the controller and action more dynamic.

These regular expressions can be further customized to include more complex routes. For instance, adding the following to our URL routes would enable us to pass additional information to our content/index action, such as the year, month, and the day we want to show published entries for.

```
// Creates a route that includes the year, month, and date of
a post
// eg: https://www.example.com/posts/2015/09/01
[
'posts/<year:\d{4}>/<month:\d{2}>/<day:\d{2}>' => 'content/index',
]
```

As you may expect from the expression, this route will only match four-digit years and two-digit months and days. Moreover, as mentioned previously, by adding this information to our URL rules, the yii\helper\Url helper will understand any URL created with this pattern:

```
// Routes to posts/2014/09/01
Url::to(['posts/index', 'year' => 2015, 'month' => 09,
'day' => 01]);
```

URL routes can also be defined to route domain names and schemes. For instance, the following routes can be written to ensure that different domain names route to different parts of the site:

```
[
    'https://dashboard.example.com/login' =>
    'dashboard/default/login',
    'https://www.example.com/login' => 'site/login'
]
```

This is beneficial when handling multiple frontend applications within the same codebase.

Parameterizing routes

In addition to named parameters, as described in the previous section, parameters can also be embedded within the URL rule itself. This approach enables Yii2 to match a single rule to multiple routes, which can greatly reduce the number of URL rules and, consequently, the performance of your router. Take, for instance, the following route:

```
[
    '<controller:(content|comment)>/<id:\d+>/<action:(
    create|list|delete)>' => '<controller>/<action>',
]
```

This route will match both the content and comment controller with a given ID for the create, list, and delete actions and pass it to the appropriate action. In order for a route to match, however, all named parameters must be defined. If a given route does not contain the given parameters, Yii2 will fail to match the route, which will most likely result in the route hitting a 404 error. One way to get around this limitation is to provide default parameters for the routes, as shown in the following example:

```
[
    // ...other rules...
    [
        // :\d+ is a regular expression for integers
        'pattern' => 'content/<page:\d+>/<name>',
        'route' => 'content/index',
        'defaults' => ['page' => 1, 'name' => NULL],
    ],
]
```

In this example, page will default to 1, and name will default to NULL. This URL rule can match multiple routes. In this specific instance, several routes will be matched:

- /content, page=1, name=NULL

- /content/215, page=215, name=NULL

- /content/215/foo, page=215, name=foo

- /content/foo, page=1, name=foo

URL suffixes

As an alternative to declaring a key-value pair for a URL route, routes can be defined as an array of key-value pairs containing the pattern, route, and even a custom URL suffix to specifically respond to.

```
[
    [
        'pattern' => 'posts',
        'route' => 'content/index',
        'suffix' => '.xml',
    ],
]
```

These routes can be used to configure your application to respond to certain types of requests in different formats.

 By default, rules created this way will be created as an instance of yii\web\UrlRule, but they can be changed by defining the class parameter.

HTTP method-specific URL rules

At times, you may find it beneficial to route different types of HTTP methods to the same route but handle them in different actions. In Yii2, this can be achieved by prefixing the method types before the route key, as shown in the following example:

```
[
    'PUT,POST users/<id:\d+>' => 'users/create',
    'DELETE users/<id:\d+>' => 'users/delete',
    'GET users/<id:\d+>' => 'users/view',
]
```

From an API perspective, all requests will ultimately route to users/<id>, but depending upon the HTTP method, a different action will be executed.

> URL rules with specified HTTP methods will only be used for routing purposes, and they won't be used to create URLs such as when using `yii\helper\Url`.

Custom URL rule classes

While `yii\web\Url` is extremely flexible, and it should cover the majority of use cases you need for a URL rule, often there are times when a custom URL may be required. For instance, a publisher may want to support a format to represent authors and books, such as `/Author/Book`, where both `Author` and `Book` are data retrieved from the database. Custom URL rules in Yii2 can be created to solve this problem by extending `yii\base\Object` and implementing `yii\web\UrlRuleInterface`, as shown in the following example:

```php
<?php

namespace app\components;

use yii\web\UrlRuleInterface;
use yii\base\Object;

class BookUrlRule extends Object implements UrlRuleInterface
{

    public function createUrl($manager, $route, $params)
    {
        if ($route === 'book/index')
        {
            if (isset($params['author'], $params['book']))
                return $params['author'] . '/' . $params['book'];
            else if (isset($params['author']))
                return $params['author'];
        }
        return false;
    }

    public function parseRequest($manager, $request)
    {
        $pathInfo = $request->getPathInfo();
        if (preg_match('%^(\w+)(/(\w+))?$%', $pathInfo, $matches))
        {
```

```
                // If the parameterized identified in
                $matches[] matches a database value
                // Set $params['author'] and $params['book'] to
                those attributes, then pass
                // those arguments to your route
                // return ['author/index', $params]
            }

            return false;
        }
    }
```

Our custom rule can then be implemented within our `yii\web\`
`UrlManager::$rules` section by declaring our desire to use that class:

```
[
    // [...],
    [
        // Reuslts in URL's like https://
        www.example.com/charlesportwodii/mastering-yii
        'class' => 'app\components\BookUrlRule'
    ],
    // [...],
]
```

Dynamic rule generation

Rules can be programmatically and dynamically added to your application in
several different ways. Dynamic rule generation can take the form of a custom
URL rule class, as outlined in the previous section, or a custom URL manager. The
simplest way to add new URL rules dynamically, however, is to use the `addRules()`
method of the URL Manager. For rules to take effect, they need to occur early in the
bootstrapping process of the application. For modules to dynamically add new rules,
they should implement `yii\base\BootstrapInterface` and add the custom URL
rules in the `bootstrap()` method, as shown in the following example:

```
public function bootstrap($app)
{
    $app->getUrlManager()->addRules([
        // Add new rules here
    ], false);
}
```

In complex web applications, it's important to monitor how many URL rules you have. Adding many different rules can seriously degrade the performance of your application as Yii2 needs to iterate over each rule until it finds the first matching rule. Parameterized routes and reducing the number of URL rules can significantly improve the performance of your application.

Requests

After handling where we want our request to go, we will often need to write specific logic to handle the details of our HTTP request. To help facilitate this, Yii2 represents the HTTP request within the `yii\web\Request` object, which can provide a variety of information about the HTTP request, such as the request body, GET and POST parameters, and headers. Each request in Yii2 can be accessed easily through the request application component, which is represented by `Yii::$app->request` in our code.

Retrieving request parameters and data

The most common task we'll perform when working with the request object is retrieving GET and POST parameters, which are implemented by `yii\web\Request::get()` and `yii\web\Request::post()` respectively. These methods enable us to consistently and safely access the `$_GET` and `$_POST` parameters of our application:

```
$request = \Yii::$app->request;

// Retrieve all of the $_GET parameters
// similar to $get = $_GET
$get = $request->get();

// Retrieve all of the $_POST parameters
$post = $request->post();
```

Unlike the native `$_GET` and `$_POST` PHP global variables, however, Yii2's request object allows us to safely access named parameters, as shown in the next example:

```
// Retrieves the name $_GET parameter, $_GET['id']
// https://www.example.com/controller/action/id/5
// https://www.example.com/controller/action?id=5
$id = $request->get('id');

// Retrieves the named $_POST parameter
$name = $request->post('name');
```

If the parameters are not defined, Yii2 will return NULL by default. This behavior can be modified by setting the second parameter of both `yii\web\Request::get()` and `yii\web\Request::post()`:

```
// Default to 1 if ID is not set
$id = $request->get('id', 1);

// Default to 'Guest' if name is not set
$name = $request->post('name', 'Guest');
```

> In addition to providing safe access to the $_GET and $_POST data, the request object can also be easily mocked when running tests. We'll cover how to work with tests and mocking data in *Chapter 10, Testing with Codeception*.

As an added convenience, Yii2 provides us with the ability to determine the type of request we're working with, such as a GET, POST, or PUT request. The easiest way to determine the request type is to query `\Yii::$app->request->method`, which will return the HTTP method type (such as GET, PUT, POST, DELETE, and so on). Alternatively, we can conditionally check the request by querying one of the request objects of many Boolean options, as shown in the following table:

Property	Explanation
`yii\web\Request::$isAjax`	If the request is an AJAX (XMLHTTPRequest) request
`yii\web\Request::$isConsoleRequest`	If the request is being made from the console
`yii\web\Request::$isDelete`	If the request is an HTTP DELETE request
`yii\web\Request::$isFlash`	If the request originated from Adobe Flex or Adobe Flash.
`yii\web\Request::$isGet`	If the request is an HTTP GET request
`yii\web\Request::$isHead`	If the request is an HTTP HEAD request
`yii\web\Request::$isOptions`	If the request is an HTTP OPTIONS request
`yii\web\Request::$isPatch`	If the request is an HTTP PATCH request
`yii\web\Request::$isPjax`	If the request is an HTTP PJAX request
`yii\web\Request::$isPost`	If the request is an HTTP POST request

Property	Explanation
`yii\web\Request::$isPut`	If the request is an HTTP PUT request
`yii\web\ Request::$isSecureConnection`	If the request was made over a secure (HTTPS) connection

Unlike GET and POST requests sent as forms, many of these requests submit data directly in the request body. To access this data, we can use `yii\web\ Request::getBodyParam()` and `yii\web\Request::getBodyParams()`, as shown:

```
$request = Yii::$app->request;

$allParamns = $request->bodyParams;

$name = $request->getBodyParam('name');

$manyParams = $request->getBodyParams(['name', 'age', 'gender']);
```

Request headers and cookies

In addition to the request body, Yii2's request object can also retrieve header and cookie information sent along with the request. The headers sent along with our request are ultimately represented by `yii\web\HeaderCollection`, which provides several methods used to work with headers, namely `yii\web\ HeaderCollection::get()` and `yii\web\HeaderCollection::has()`. In the following example, we're checking whether the X-Auth-Token header is set and then assigning it to the `$authToken` variable if it is set:

```
// $headers is an object of yii\web\HeaderCollection
$headers = Yii::$app->request->headers;

// If the header has 'X-Auth-Token', retrieve it.
if ($headers->has('X-Auth-Token'))
    $authToken = $headers->get('X-Auth-Token');
```

 If a parameter is not provided to the `yii\web\ HeaderCollection::get()` method, an array of all headers will be returned. More details on `yii\web\HeaderCollection` can be found at `http://www.yiiframework.com/doc-2.0/yii-web-headercollection.html`.

The request object has several built-in defaults to access some commonly queried headers, namely:

- `yii\web\Request::$userAgent` retrieves the user agent sent by the browser
- `yii\web\Request::$contentType` can be used to determine the appropriate response type
- `yii\web\Request::$acceptableContentTypes` returns all the acceptable content types that the client will accept
- `yii\web\Request::$acceptableLanguages` can be used if our application is configured to support multiple languages

 The request object can also tell us what the preferred language of the client is through `yii\web\Request::getPreferedLanguage()`. We'll work more with this variable and general translation and localization in *Chapter 11, Internationalization and Localization*.

Alongside our header information, we can also retrieve the cookie data sent with our request by querying `Yii::$app->request->cookies`, which will return an instance of `yii\web\CookieCollection`, which, as you may suspect, contains many of the same types of methods that `yii\web\HeaderCollection` provides, such as `get()` and `has()`.

 The Yii2 API documentation provides a complete set of methods for `yii\web\CookieCollection` at `http://www.yiiframework.com/doc-2.0/yii-web-cookiecollection.html`.

Retrieving client and URL information

In addition to information about the request, the Yii2 request object can also be used to retrieve information about the client and our application state. For instance, client information such as their hostname or IP address can be accessed using `yii\web\Request::$userHost` and `yii\web\Request::$userIP`.

 The user's IP address may not be accurate if your request is being forwarded through a proxy or load balancer. Ensure that your web server is properly configured to pass along the original data.

Data about the application state can be inspected by referencing a variety of methods, which are more convenient than querying the $_SERVER global variable. A few of the most common properties are shown in the following table:

Property	Explanation
yii\web\Request::$absoluteUrl	This is the absolute URL, including the hostname and all the GET parameters (for example, https://www.example.com/controller/action/?name=foo)
yii\web\Request::$baseUrl	This is the base URL used before the entry script.
yii\web\Request::$hostInfo	These are the host details (for example, https://www.example.com)
yii\web\Request::$pathInfo	This is the full path after the entry script (for example, /controller/action)
yii\web\Request::$queryString	This is the GET query string (for example, name=foo)
yii\web\Request::$scriptUrl	This is the URL without the path and query string (for example, /index.php)
yii\web\Request::$serverName	This is the server name (for example, example.com)
yii\web\Request::$serverPort	This is the port the server is running on (usually 80 or 443 for TLS connections)
yii\web\Request::$url	This is the complete URL sans the host and scheme information (for example, controller/action/?name=foo).

> The request object is capable of representing nearly every aspect of the HTTP request and the data that may be stored in the $_SERVER global variable. For more information on the request object refer to the Yii2 API documentation at http://www.yiiframework.com/doc-2.0/yii-web-request.html.

Responses

After finishing the processing of the request object, Yii2 then generates a response object, which is sent back to the client. The response contains a myriad of information, such as the HTTP status code, response body, and headers. In Yii2, the response object is implemented by yii\web\Response, which is represented by the response application component. In this section, we'll explore how to work with responses.

Setting status codes

In most cases, Yii2 is perfectly capable of setting the appropriate response code back to the end user; however, there may be situations that require us to explicitly define the HTTP response code for our application. To modify the HTTP status code within our application, we simply need to set `yii\web\Response::$statusCode` to a valid HTTP status code:

```
\Yii::$app->response->statusCode = 200;
```

Web exceptions

By default, Yii2 will return an HTTP 200 status code for any successful request. If we want to adjust the status code without interrupting our flow of logic, we can simply define a new status code for `yii\web\Response::$statusCode`. In other cases, it may be better to throw an exception to cause a short circuit in our application flow to prevent additional logic from being executed.

In general, web exceptions can be thrown by calling `yii\web\HttpException` with a valid HTTP status code:

```
throw new \yii\web\HttpException(409);
```

For convenience, Yii2 provides several specific methods for a few different types of requests, as shown in the following table:

Exception	Status Code	HTTP Error
yii\web\BadRequestHttpException	400	Bad request
yii\web\UnauthorizedHtpException	401	Unauthorized
yii\web\ForbiddenHttpException	403	Forbidden
yii\web\NotFoundHttpException	404	Not found
yii\web\MethodNotAllowedException	405	Method not allowed
yii\web\NotAcceptableHttpException	406	Not acceptable
yii\web\ConflictHttpException	409	Conflict
yii\web\GoneHttpException	410	Gone
yii\web\ UnsupportedMediaTypeHttpException	415	Unsupported media type
yii\web\TooManyRequestsHttpException	429	Too many requests
yii\web\ServerErrorHttpException	500	Sever error

As an alternative to throwing an empty `yii\web\HttpException` with a given status code, you can also extend `yii\web\HttpException` to implement your own `HttpException` exception.

Setting response headers

As with the `yii\web\Request object`, we can manipulate the HTTP headers of our response using the `add()` and `remove()` methods from `yii\web\HeaderCollection`, as shown in the following example:

```
yii\web\HeaderCollection
$headers = Yii::$app->response->headers;

// Add two headers
$headers->add('X-Auth-Token', 'SADFLJKBQ43O7AGB28948QT');
$headers->add('Pragma', 'No-Cache');

// Remove a header
$headers->remove('Pragma');
```

 Adding new headers will override any previously set headers with the same name. Moreover, all headers set through `yii\web\HeaderCollection` are case insensitive. Removing a header will remove any header with the name that is currently sent.

Headers can be manipulated at any time during the response up until `yii\web\Response::send()` is called, which, by default, is called right before the response body is sent out.

The response body

Typically, the response body will be represented by an instance of `yii\web\View`, which is usually displayed to the end user by returning a rendered view inside a controller action, as shown here. By default, Yii2 will return the response with a MIME type of text/HTML and will format the response using `yii\web\HtmlResponseFormatter`:

```
public function actionIndex()
{
    return $this->render('index');
}
```

There may be situations, however, where a different response type may be required, such as when displaying JSON or XML data. Within our controller action, we can change the output format from the default by setting the `yii\web\Response::$format` property and returning either an array or a string representing the data we want formatted, as shown in the following example:

```
public function actionIndex()
{
    \Yii::$app->response->format = \yii\web\Response::FORMAT_JSON;
    return [
        'message' => 'Index Action',
        'code' => 200,
    ];
}
```

The previous example will output the following JSON data to the client:

```
{
    "message": "Index Action",
    "code": 200
}
```

In addition to JSON formatting, `yii\web\Response::$format` can also be set to JSONP, HTML, RAW, and XML using the details outlined in the following table:

Type	Formatter class	Format value
HTML	`yii\web\HtmlResponseFormat`	FORMAT_HTML
RAW		FORMAT_RAW
XML	`yii\web\XmlResponseFormatter`	FORMAT_XML
JSON	`yii\web\JsonResponseFormatter`	FORMAT_JSON
JSONp	`yii\web\JsonResponseFormatter`	FORMAT_JSON

 RAW data will be submitted to the client as is without any additional formatting being applied to it.

In addition to working with the default response object, in Yii2, you can also create new response objects to be sent to the end user, as shown in the following example:

```
public function actionIndex()
{
    return \Yii::createObject([
        'class' => 'yii\web\Response',
```

```
        'format' => \yii\web\Response::FORMAT_JSON,
        'data' => [
            'message' => 'Index Action',
            'code' => 100,
        ],
    ]);
}
```

 Any custom configuration set for the response application component will not be applied to any custom response objects that you instantiate.

While controller actions are the primary place where you will find yourself editing the response body, the response body can be modified from anywhere in Yii by directly manipulating `\Yii::$app->response`. Any data that has been already formatted can be assigned directly to the response object by setting the `yii\web\Response::$content` property. Moreover, if you want to have the data being passed through a response formatted before being sent to the user, you can set `yii\web\Response::$content` and then set `yii\web\Response::$data` with the data you want formatted:

```
$response = \Yii::$app->response;
$response->format = yii\web\Response::FORMAT_JSON;
$response->data = [
    'message' => 'Index Action',
    'code' => 100
];
```

Redirection

In order to redirect a browser to a new page, the special header location must be set by the response. Yii2 provides special support for this through the `yii\web\Response::redirect()` method, which can be called from within a controller action, as follows:

```
public function actionIndex()
{
    return $this->redirect('https://www.example.com/index2');
}
```

By default, Yii2 will return a 302 status code, indicating that the redirect should be temporary. To notify the browser to permanently redirect the request, you can set the second parameter of `yii\web\Response::redirect()` to 301, which is the HTTP status code for a permanent redirection.

Outside a controller action, a redirect can be called by calling the `redirect()` method and then immediately sending the response, as shown in the following example:

```
\Yii::$app->response->redirect('https://www.example.com/index2', 301)->send();
```

The file output

Similar to browser redirection, outputting a file to the client requests several custom headers to be set. To facilitate the transfer of files to the browser, Yii2 provides three distinct methods to output files:

- `yii\web\Response::sendFile()` should be used when sending an existing file located on the disk

- `yii\web\Response::sendContentAsFile()` sends a string of data as a file (such as a CSV file)

- `yii\web\Response::sendStreamAsFile()` should be used for large files (typically, files larger than 100 MB), and it should be sent to the browser as it is more memory efficient. Within a controller, these methods can be called directly to send a file:

```
public function actionReport()
{
    return \Yii::$app->response->sendFile('path/to/report.csv');
}
```

Similar to redirecting a browser, these methods can be called outside a controller action by manipulating the response object directly:

```
\Yii::$app->response->sendFile('path/to/report.csv')->send();
```

More information on the response object can be found in the Yii2 documentation at http://www.yiiframework.com/doc-2.0/yii-web-response.html.

Events

Often when working with complex code bases, we may implement hooks and handlers so that our application can call custom code outside our main application flow. In Yii2, these handlers are called events, which can be automatically executed when a given event is triggered. For example, in a blogging platform, we may create an event to indicate that a post was published, which will trigger some custom code to send out an email to users in a specific mailing list. In this section, we'll cover how to create event handlers, trigger events, and write our own custom events.

Event handlers

Events in Yii2 are implemented within the `yii\base\Component` base class, which nearly every class in Yii2 extends from. By extending from this class, we can bind an event to nearly anywhere in our codebase. To begin working with events, we first need to create an event handler.

Event handlers in Yii2 can be bound by calling the `yii\base\Component::on()` method, and they specify a callback that should be executed when the event is triggered. These callbacks can take several different forms, ranging from a global PHP function specified as a string to an anonymous function written inline on the event. For instance, if we want to call a global PHP function (such as the one we defined or a built-in function such as `trim`), we can bind our event, as follows:

```
$thing = new app\Thing;
$thing->on(Thing::EVENT_NAME, 'php_function_name');
```

Events handlers can also be called on any PHP object: either the one that we already have an instance variable for or a namespaced class within our application:

```
$thing->on(Thing::EVENT_NAME, [$object, 'method']);
$thing->on(Thing::EVENT_NAME, ['app\components\Thing ',
'doThing']);
```

Moreover, event handlers can be written as an anonymous function:

```
$thing->on(Thing::EVENT_NAME, function($event) {
    // Handle the event
});
```

Additional data can be passed to event handlers by passing any data as the third parameter to the `yii\base\Component::on()` method:

```
$thing->on(Thing::EVENT_NAME, function($event) {
    echo $event->data['foo']; // bar
}, ['foo' => 'bar']);
```

Furthermore, multiple event handlers can be bound to a single event. When a given event is triggered, each event will execute in the order in which it was bound to the event. If an event handler needs to stop the execution of the other events that follow, it can set the `yii\base\Event::$handled` property of the `$event` object to `true`, which will prevent all the event handlers bound to the event from not executing:

```
$thing->on(Thing::EVENT_NAME, function($event) {
    // Handle the event
    $event->handled = true;
}, $data);
```

By default, the event handler in Yii2 is bound in the order in which it is called, which means that the last event handler bound to a given event will be called last. To prepend an event handler to the beginning of the event handler queue, you can set the `$append` parameter of `yii\base\Component::on()` to `false`, which will override the default behavior and cause the event handler to be triggered first when the event is raised:

```
$thing->on(Thing::EVENT_NAME, function($event) {
    // Handle the event
}, [], false);
```

Event handlers can also be unbound from the event they're listening to by calling `yii\base\Component::off()` using the same syntax used to attach the event listener to the event. Alternatively, all events handlers can be unbound from an event by calling `yii\base\Component::off()` without any additional parameters, as shown in the following example:

```
$thing->off(Thing::EVENT_NAME);
```

Triggering events

Events in Yii2 are triggered by calling the `yii\base\Component::trigger()` method, which takes the event name as the second parameter, and an optional instance of `yii\base\Event` as the second parameter. For example, we can call `Thing::EVENT_NAME` within our code, as follows:

```
$this->trigger(Thing::EVENT_NAME);
```

This event was previously bound with the following event:

```
$thing->on(Thing::EVENT_NAME, ['app\components\Thing', 'doThing']);
```

Now, the `app\components\Thing::doThing()` method will be triggered. This code may look as follows for our imaginary component:

```php
<?php
namespace app\components;

use yii\base\Component;
use yii\base\Event;

class Thing extends Component
{
    const EVENT_NAME = 'name';

    public function doThing()
    {
        // This is the event handler
    }
}
```

 Yii2 considers it a best practice to store event names as constants within classes.

Additional information can be sent to our event handlers by extending `yii\base\Event` and passing it as the second parameter of our trigger call, as shown in the following example:

```php
<?php

namespace app\components;

use yii\base\Component;
use yii\base\Event;

class LogEvent extends Event
{
    public $message;
}

class Logger extends Component
{
    const EVENT_LOG = 'log_event';
```

```
    /**
     * Log with $message
     * @param string $message
     */
    public function log($message)
    {
        $event = new LogEvent;
        $event->message = $message;
        $this->trigger(self::EVENT_LOG, $event);
    }
}
```

Due to the single-threaded nature of PHP, Yii2's events will occur synchronously rather than asynchronously, which will block all other application flows from occurring until all the events in the event handler queue are complete. Consequently, you should be careful when using many events as they may cause detrimental application performance.

> One way to use implemented asynchronous events (such as sending an email newsletter from a CMS) is to have your event handlers pass off the event to a third-party messaging queue, such as Gearman, Sidekiq, or Resque, and immediately return the event. The event can then be handled in a separate processing thread, which can be a Yii2 console command configured to read events from the messaging queue and process them separately from the main application.

Class-level events

The events described previously were bound at an instance level. In Yii2, events can be bound to every instance of a class rather than a specific instance, and they can also be bound to Yii2's global event handler.

Class-level events can be bound by attaching the event handler directly through yii\base\Event::on(). For instance, Active Record will trigger an EVENT_AFTER_ DELETE event whenever a record is deleted from the database. We can log this information for every Active Record instance, as shown in the following example:

```
<?php

use Yii;
use yii\base\Event;
use yii\db\ActiveRecord;
```

```php
Event::on(ActiveRecord::className(),
ActiveRecord::EVENT_AFTER_DELETE, function ($event) {
    Yii::trace(get_class($event->sender) . ' deleted a record.');
});
```

Whenever a trigger occurs, it will first call instance-level event handlers, then it will call class-level event handlers, and then it will call global event handlers. Class-level events can be explicitly called by calling `yii\base\Event::trigger()` directly. Additionally, class-level event handlers can be removed through `yii\base\Event::off()`.

Global events

Global events are supported in Yii2 by binding event handlers to the application singleton instance itself, as shown in the following example:

```php
<?php
use Yii;
use yii\base\Event;
use app\components\Foo;

Yii::$app->on('thing', function ($event) {
    echo get_class($event->sender);
});

Yii::$app->trigger('thing', new Event(['sender' => new Thing]));
```

 When using global events, be cautious as to not override Yii2's built-in global events. Any global event that you use should include some sort of prefix in order to avoid collision with Yii2's built-in events.

Summary

In this chapter, we covered the basics of how requests and responses are handled in Yii2. We first explored how Yii2 handles the routing of URL routes, and we learned how to manipulate and create our own custom URL rules. We then explored the `yii\web\Request` and `yii\web\Response` objects and gained a better understanding of how we can use these objects to manipulate the requests and responses coming to and from our application. Finally, we learned how events work in Yii2, and we also learned how to create our own events.

In the next chapter, we'll take the knowledge we've gained in this chapter to the next level by exploring how to implement RESTful APIs.

9
RESTful APIs

Representational State Transfer (REST) is a modern approach for client-server communications that decouple the client (such as Bowers and mobile applications) from the server components in applications. RESTful implementations enable backend implementations to speak a common language (usually, XML or JSON) while taking complete advantage of HTTP verbs, such as GET, POST, PUT, and DELETE. RESTful applications enable us to build stateless, scalable, and uniform applications that we can distribute to our clients. With Yii2, we can quickly implement RESTful APIs as either a part or the whole of our application.

ActiveController

The simplest way to create RESTful APIs in Yii2 is to take advantage of yii\rest\ActiveController. Like yii\web\Controller, yii\rest\ActiveController provides a controller interface that we can implement in our ./controllers directory. Unlike yii\web\Controller, implementing yii\rest\ActiveController with a yii\db\ActiveRecord model will immediately create a complete REST API for that model available, with very minimal coding. Models implemented with yii\rest\ActiveController also make the following additional features available out of the box:

- XML and JSON response formats
- Rate limiting
- Data and HTTP caching
- Authentication
- Full HTTP verb support (GET, POST, PATCH, HEAD, and OPTIONS)
- Data validation
- Pagination
- Support for HATEOAS

As an example, let's expose our User model that we created in *Chapter 4, Active Record, Models, and Forms*. To get started with `yii\rest\ActiveController`, we first need to create a controller in our `controllers/` directory called `UserController.php`, which references our User model that we created previously:

```php
<?php

namespace app\controllers;

use yii\rest\ActiveController;

class UserController extends ActiveController
{
    public $modelClass = 'app\models\User';
}
```

Next, we need to make some configuration changes to our `config/web.php` configuration file so that Yii2 can route the correct routes to our newly created controller and to ensure that our application can accept JSON input. As we've already enabled pretty URLs and disabled the script name being displayed in our `urlManager` component, we simply need to add a custom URL rule for our user class. This URL rule is an instance of `yii\rest\UrlRule`, and it will handle all the required routing for our controller:

```php
return [
    // [...],
    'components' => [
        // [...],
            'urlManager' => [
                'enablePrettyUrl' => true,
                'enableStrictParsing' => true,
                'showScriptName' => false,
                'rules' => [
                    ['class' => 'yii\rest\UrlRule',
                    'controller' => 'user'],
                ],
            ],
        ],
    ]
];
```

Next, we need to modify the base request object that our application uses so that it can parse the JSON input:

```
return [
    // [...],
    'components' => [
        // [...],
        'request' => [
            'parsers' => [
                'application/json' => 'yii\web\JsonParser',
            ]
        ]
    ]
];
```

 The change to the request parser is added for convenience as JSON is an easy input type to work with. Without this change, our application will only be able to parse the `application/x-www-form-urlencoded` and `multipart/form-data` request formats.

By simply adding a few lines of code, we've now implemented a complete REST API for our `Users` model. The following table exposes a complete list of methods that `yii\rest\ActiveController` exposes for us:

HTTP Method	Endpoint	Result
GET	/users	This is a list of all users
GET	/users/<id>	This has the information for the user with the given <id> tag
POST	/users	This creates a new user with the data supplied in the request body
PATCH	/users/<id>	This modifies a user with the given <id> tag with the data supplied in the request body
DELETE	/users/<id>	This deletes a user with a given <id> tag
HEAD	/users	This retrieves the header information
HEAD	/users/<idl>	This retrieves the header information for the given user <id> tag
OPTIONS	/users	This retrieves the HTTP options for Ajax-like requests
OPTIONS	/users/<id>	This retrieves the HTTP options for Ajax-like requests for a user with a given <id> tag

An easy way to query against our newly created REST API is to use the command-line tool called CURL. For example, to retrieve the headers for our /users endpoint, we can run the following command:

```
$ curl -i -X HEAD https://www.example.com/users
```

You'll get output similar to the following:

```
HTTP/1.1 200 OK
Content-Type: application/json; charset=UTF-8
Transfer-Encoding: chunked
Connection: keep-alive
Vary: Accept-Encoding
X-Pagination-Total-Count: 4
X-Pagination-Page-Count: 1
X-Pagination-Current-Page: 1
X-Pagination-Per-Page: 20
Link: <https://www.example.com/users?page=1>; rel=self
Access-Control-Allow-Origin: *
```

As mentioned previously, yii\rest\ActiveRecord immediately provides us with a bunch of useful information, such as CORS headers and pagination details.

With CURL, we can also query for the raw data itself. Our API can respond in either a JSON or an XML format depending upon the Accept headers we submit along with our request. The next example illustrates a request that will respond in the JSON format:

```
$ curl -I -H "Accept:application/json" https://www.example.com/users |
jq .
[
  {
    "updated_at": 1442602004,
    "created_at": 1442602004,
    "role_id": 1,
    "last_name": "Joe",
    "first_name": "Jane",
    "password": "$2y$13$pc0TEJged1BwmqpGL7
dywupNzG6bCBWRjBbDMzBXhv7FewvUR/qqm",
    "email": "jane.doe@example.com",
    "id": 1
  },
  {...}
]
```

By default, CURL will return data as a single line. As illustrated in the previous command, we're piping the JSON response from our cURL request to a tool called **jq** (`https://stedolan.github.io/jq/`), which is used to format the data in an easy-to-read format. Alternatively, you can install a graphic-based tool of your choice to submit and display responses in an easy-to-read format.

Additionally, we can filter specific fields by passing them as GET parameters within our request. For example, if we want to just retrieve the first and last name of the user with the ID of 1 in our database, we can execute the following command:

```
$ curl -H "Accept:application/json" /
https://www.example.com/users/1?fields=id,first_name,last_name | jq .
```

This will return the following response:

```
{
    "last_name": "Joe",
    "first_name": "Jane",
    "id": 1
}
```

Configuring ActiveController display fields

As you may have noticed, `yii\rest\ActiveController` only returns fields that are populated from the database and does not return extra fields that you may have created (such as a `full_name` field as the concatenation of the first and last name) or relations. Additionally, it exposes every field in the database, including sensitive data, such as encrypted password hashes. One way to get around this limitation is to modify the `fields()` method of our models.

For example, to prevent accidentally exposing our hashed passwords over our API, we can implement a custom `fields` method in our `User` model, as follows. We can also change the display name of certain fields:

```
class User extends \yii\db\ActiveRecord implements
\yii\web\IdentityInterface
{
    /**
     * API safe fields
     */
    public function fields()
    {
```

```
            return [
                'id',
                'email_address' => 'email',
                'first_name',
                'last_name',
                'full_name' => function($model) {
                    return $model->getFullName();
                },
                'updated_at',
                'created_at'
            ];
        }
    }
```

Now, let's query against our API, as follows:

```
$ curl -H "Accept:application/json" https://www.example.com/users/1 /
| jq .
```

We retrieve the following response:

```
    {
        "created_at": 1442602004,
        "updated_at": 1442602004,
        "full_name": "Jane Joe",
        "last_name": "Joe",
        "first_name": "Jane",
        "email_address": "jane.doe@example.com",
        "id": 1
    }
```

Additionally, we can expose relational data by implementing the extraFields()
method of our model, as shown in the next example:

```
    public function extraFields()
    {
        // Expose the 'role' relation
        return ['role'];
    }
```

 The extraFields() method will expose the entire model relationship
in our response, and it can consequently be a security risk if our relations
contain sensitive information. Ensure that you use the fields() method
in the related attribute to restrict what data will be returned.

We can expand this data by adding `expand=role` to our GET parameters, as shown in the following example:

```
$ curl -H "Accept:application/json" /
https://www.example.com/users/1?expand=role | jq .
    {
      "role": {
        "name": "User",
        "id": 1
      },
      "created_at": 1442602004,
      "updated_at": 1442602004,
      "full_name": "Jane Joe",
      "last_name": "Joe",
      "first_name": "Jane",
      "email_address": "jane.doe@example.com",
      "id": 1
    }
```

Data serialization within responses

In addition to modifying the fields that are displayed in our response, we can also modify our response to contain useful information, such as the information that is sent in our headers (such as pagination information and links), and wrap our response in a container that is easy to identify in our response. We can do this by adding and specifying a serializer in our `yi\rest\ActiveController`, as shown in the following example:

```php
<?php

namespace app\controllers;

use yii\rest\ActiveController;

class UserController extends ActiveController
{
    public $modelClass = 'app\models\User';

    public $serializer = [
        'class' => 'yii\rest\Serializer',
        'collectionEnvelope' => 'users',
    ];
}
```

Now, when we query our /users endpoint, we will have the following response:

```
$ curl -H "Accept:application/json" https://www.example.com /users /
| jq .
    {
      "_meta": {
        "perPage": 20,
        "currentPage": 1,
        "pageCount": 2,
        "totalCount": 21
      },
      "_links": {
        "self": {
          "href": "https://www.example.com/users?page=1"
        },
        "next": {
          "href": "https://www.example.com/users?page=2 "
        }

      },
      "users": [
        {
          "created_at": 1442602004,
          "updated_at": 1442602004,
          "full_name": "Jane Joe",
          "last_name": "Joe",
          "first_name": "Jane",
          "email_address": "jane.doe@example.com",
          "id": 1
        },
        {...},
        {...}
      ]
    }
```

Disabling ActiveController actions

While `yii\rest\ActiveController` provides many useful actions, there may be situations where you do not want to expose every method that is exposed by default. The following actions are automatically exposed by `yii\rest\ActiveController`:

Action name	Result
index	This lists all the resources provided by the model with pagination support
view	This returns the details of a specific model
create	This creates a new model instance
update	This updates an existing model instance
delete	This deletes a model
options	This returns the available methods

Apart from overriding the action method, there are several different ways to disable actions. Actions can be disabled by removing them from the actions list within the `actions()` method of your controller. For example, to disable `delete` and `create`, we can remove them, as follows:

```php
<?php

namespace app\controllers;

use yii\rest\ActiveController;

class UserController extends ActiveController
{
    public $modelClass = 'app\models\User';

    public function actions()
    {
        $actions = parent::actions();

        // disable the "delete" and "create" actions
        unset($actions['delete'], $actions['create']);
        return $actions;
    }
}
```

Alternatively, actions can be disabled by removing the route from `yii\rest\UrlRule` within our web configuration by setting the `only` or the `except` parameters of our rule. In the following example, the `delete`, `create`, and `update` actions have been disabled in our router:

```
[
    'class' => 'yii\rest\UrlRule',
    'controller' => 'user',
    // 'only' => [ 'index' ], // Only allow index
    'except' => ['delete', 'create', 'update'], // Disabled
]
```

Customizing ActiveController actions

There are several ways to modify the data that is returned by each action provided by `yii\rest\ActiveController`. Apart from directly overloading a specific method, the data providers for each action can be modified as well. For example, to change the data provider for our index action, we can write code that's similar to the following code block:

```php
<?php

namespace app\controllers;

use yii\rest\ActiveController;

class UserController extends ActiveController
{

    public function actions()
    {
        $actions = parent::actions();

        // Customize the data provider preparation with the
        "prepareDataProvider()" method
        $actions['index']['prepareDataProvider'] = [$this,
        'prepareDataProvider'];

        return $actions;
    }

    private function prepareDataProvider()
    {
        // Prepare a new data provider
    }
}
```

Authentication filters

In *Chapter 7, Authenticating and Authorizing Users*, we covered the basics of user access control filters to control which users can have access to our controllers. Unlike stateful applications that depend upon the presence of session data to persist user data across each request, RESTful APIs are stateless by nature, which means that each request must provide the required information to authenticate each user. To assist us in authenticating users over our API, Yii2 provides three built-in methods to control access to our API:

- HTTP basic authentication
- Query parameter authentication
- OAuth2 authentication

Additionally, we can define our own custom authentication methods.

To get started with authenticating users within our API, we need to make the following changes to our application:

- Configuring the user component of our configuration by doing the following:
    - Disabling sessions by setting `enableSession` to `false`
    - Setting the `loginUrl` property to null to prevent redirects to the login page

- Specifying the authentication method in the `behaviors()` method of our controller

- Implementing `yii\web\IdentityInterface::findIdentityByAccessToken()` in our user identity class

> You may encounter issues if you mix your REST API with your normal Yii2 application. For this reason, it is strongly encouraged that you run your API as a separate application from your Yii2 app.

HTTP basic authentication

The most basic way to handle authentication is to implement HTTP basic authentication. HTTP basic authentication is provided by the `yii\filters\auth\HttpBasicAuth` class, and it can be implemented as follows:

```php
<?php

namespace app\controllers;
use yii\filters\auth\HttpBasicAuth;
use yii\rest\ActiveController;

class UserController extends ActiveController
{
    public function behaviors()
    {
        $behaviors = parent::behaviors();
        $behaviors['authenticator'] = [
            'class' => HttpBasicAuth::className(),
        ];
        return $behaviors;
    }
}
```

Now, if we attempt to query our API without sufficient credentials, we will receive the following response:

```
{
    "name": "Unauthorized",
    "message": "You are requesting with an invalid credential.",
    "code": 0,
    "status": 401,
    "type": "yii\\web\\UnauthorizedHttpException"
}
```

If we attempt to navigate to any endpoint in our application, we will then receive the following popup asking us to authenticate:

By default, Yii2 will pass this information to yii\web\IdentityInterface::findId
entityByAccessToken() with just the username as the token. Generally, a username
isn't sufficient information to authenticate a user. This behavior can be overwritten
by specifying the auth property of yii\filters\auth\HttpBasicAuth, which will
allow us to pass both the username and password to a function of our choice:

```
public function behaviors()
{
    $behaviors = parent::behaviors();
    $behaviors['authenticator'] = [
        'auth'  => ['app\models\User', 'httpBasicAuth' ],
        'class' => HttpBasicAuth::className(),
    ];
    return $behaviors;
}
```

Within our User model, we can define the httpBasicAuth() method as follows:

```
/**
 * Handle HTTP basic auth
 * @param string $email
 * @param string $password
 * @return static self
 */
public function httpBasicAuth($email, $password)
{
    $model = static::findOne(['email' => $email]);
    if ($model == NULL)
```

```
        return NULL;

    if (password_verify($password, $model->password))
        return $model;

    return NULL;
}
```

In the example shown, we're validating the username and password
against the users we created in *Chapter 4, Active Record, Models, and Forms*.
In this situation, we're validating the password against the previously
created bcrypt hash. Ensure that you reference the credentials listed in
that chapter for an example.

Now, if we query against our API, we will receive a valid response if we have valid
credentials and an error if we provide the wrong credentials.

Query parameter authentication

As an alternative to query parameter authentication, we can grant access to our API
by specifying a query parameter. This can be a global query parameter that we treat
as a secret key, or it can be a per-user token that we issue on our login request. Query
parameter authentication can be implemented by implementing yii\filters\auth\
QueryParamAuth. In the following example, we're looking for a GET parameter called
token, which contains our token:

```php
<?php

namespace app\controllers;
use yii\filters\auth\QueryParamAuth;

use yii\rest\ActiveController;

class UserController extends ActiveController
{
    public function behaviors()
    {
        $behaviors = parent::behaviors();
        $behaviors['authenticator'] = [
            'tokenParam'  => 'token',
            'class' => QueryParamAuth::className(),
        ];
        return $behaviors;
    }
}
```

Authentication can be performed in our model by implementing `yii\web\Identit yInterface::findIdentityByAccessToken()`. The simplest example is to create a new migration that adds a new column to our user's table called `access_token` that is populated on our authentication request. We can then validate against it by adding the following code to our `User` model:

```
/**
 * @inheritdoc
 */
public static function findIdentityByAccessToken($token,
$type=null)
{
    return static::findOne(['access_token' => $token]);
}
```

OAuth2 authentication

The most complex authentication method in Yii2 is OAuth2 authentication, as implemented by `yii\auth\filters\HttpBearerAuth`. Like `yii\auth\filters\QueryParamAuth`, `yii\auth\filters\HttpBearerAuth` can be implemented by setting the appropriate behavior in the `behaviors()` method and then implementing `yii\web\IdentityInterface::findIdentityByAccessToken()`.

```php
<?php

namespace app\controllers;
use yii\filters\auth\HttpBearerAuth;

use yii\rest\ActiveController;

class UserController extends ActiveController
{
    public function behaviors()
    {
        $behaviors = parent::behaviors();
        $behaviors['authenticator'] = [
            'class' => HttpBearerAuth::className(),
        ];
        return $behaviors;
    }
}
```

If you're unfamiliar with the OAuth2 workflow, you can simulate a login request by setting the `Authorization` header with a specific Bearer token, as shown here:

```
Headers:
    Authorization: Bearer <token>
```

The `<token>` part of the header is what will ultimately be passed to `yii\web\Identi tyInterface::findIdentityByAccessToken()`.

Composite authentication

To increase the security of our API, we can bundle several different authentication filters together by implementing `yii\filters\auth\CompositeAuth`. To authenticate against our API, we need to satisfy all the authentication requirements, as listed in our `behaviors()` method. Composite authentication can be configured as follows within our controller:

```php
<?php

namespace app\controllers;
use yii\filters\auth\CompositeAuth;
use yii\filters\auth\HttpBasicAuth;
use yii\filters\auth\QueryParamAuth;

use yii\rest\ActiveController;

class UserController extends ActiveController
{
    public function behaviors()
    {
        $behaviors = parent::behaviors();
        $behaviors['authenticator'] = [
            'class' => CompositeAuth::className(),
            'authMethods' => [
                HttpBasicAuth::className(),
                QueryParamAuth::className(),
            ],
        ];
        return $behaviors;
    }
}
```

Custom authentication filters

As an alternative to built-in authentication providers, we can also define our own authentication filters. For example, as part of our login request, we may generate a unique token for the user to make all additional requests against. Rather than requiring clients of our API to store the users' raw password or pass the credentials as a GET parameter that may end up in our server log files, we can have our users submit their authentication token as a unique header. An example class of how to implement this is shown as follows:

```php
<?php

namespace app\filters\auth;

use yii\filters\auth\AuthMethod;
use yii\web\UnauthorizedHttpException;
/**
 * HeaderParamAuth is an action filter that supports the
authentication based on the access token passed through a query
parameter.
 */
class HeaderParamAuth extends AuthMethod
{
    /**
     * @var string the parameter name for passing the access token
     */
    public $tokenParam = 'x-auth-token';

    /**
     * @inheritdoc
     */
    public function authenticate($user, $request, $response)
    {
        $accessToken = $request->getHeaders()[$this->tokenParam];

        if (is_string($accessToken))
        {
            $identity = $user->loginByAccessToken($accessToken,
            get_class($this));

            if ($identity !== null)
                return $identity;
        }
```

```
        if ($accessToken !== null)
            $this->handleFailure($response);

        return null;
    }

    /**
     * @inheritdoc
     */
    public function handleFailure($response)
    {
        throw new UnauthorizedHttpException('The token you are
        using has is either invalid, or has expired. Please
        re-authenticate to continue your session.');
    }
}
```

Our custom authentication method can then be implemented in our controller, as follows:

```php
<?php

namespace app\controllers;
use app\filters\auth\HeaderParamAuth;

use yii\rest\ActiveController;

class UserController extends ActiveController
{
    public function behaviors()
    {
        $behaviors = parent::behaviors();
        $behaviors['authenticator'] = [
            'class' => HeaderParamAuth::className(),
        ];
        return $behaviors;
    }
}
```

As you would expect, the x-auth-token parameter will be the token that is passed to yii\web\IdentityInterface::findIdentityByAccessToken().

Action-specific authentication

Authentication can be restricted to certain actions using the `only` and `except` keywords as part of the authenticator behavior. For example, using our previously created `HeaderParamAuth` class, we can only require authentication to the `delete`, `create`, and `update` actions while allowing unauthenticated users to access the main index action:

```php
<?php

namespace app\controllers;
use app\filters\auth\HeaderParamAuth;

use yii\rest\ActiveController;

class UserController extends ActiveController
{
    public function behaviors()
    {
        $behaviors = parent::behaviors();
        $behaviors['authenticator'] = [
            'class' => HeaderParamAuth::className(),
            'only' => [ 'delete', 'update', 'create' ]
        ];
        return $behaviors;
    }
}
```

Checking access

When exposing API endpoints, you often need to bundle both authentication and authorization. With `yii\rest\Controller`, this can be handled by overriding the `yii\rest\Controller::checkAccess()` method:

```php
/**
 * Checks the privilege of the current user.
 *
 * This method should be overridden to check whether the current
 user has the privilege
 * to run the specified action against the specified data model.
 * If the user does not have access, a [[ForbiddenHttpException]]
 should be thrown.
 *
```

```
 * @param string $action the ID of the action to be executed
 * @param \yii\base\Model $model the model to be accessed. If
null, it means no specific model is being accessed.
 * @param array $params additional parameters
 * @throws ForbiddenHttpException if the user does not have access
 */
public function checkAccess($action, $model = null, $params = [])
{
    // check if the user can access $action or $model
    // throw ForbiddenHttpException if access should be denied
}
```

Alternatively, you can use the access control filter, as shown in *Chapter 7, Authenticating and Authorizing Users*.

> Authorization determines which actions require authenticated access. When working with APIs, you'll need to properly implement authentication to determine which users, or which set of users, have access to a specific command. Refer to the material in *Chapter 7, Authenticating and Authorizing Users* for more details on how to authenticate users in your app.

Verb filters

When creating custom API endpoints, you may want to only allow certain HTTP verbs to be issued against these actions. For instance, a PUT request to an endpoint that deletes a user doesn't make much sense. One way to control which HTTP verbs can be executed against our actions is to use yii\filters\VerbFilter. When using yii\filters\VerbFilter, we simply need to specify which HTTP verbs will be accepted by each of our public actions. The following example shows the default verb filter that is used by yii\rest\ActiveController:

```
public function behaviors()
{
    return [
        'verbs' => [
            'class' => \yii\filters\VerbFilter::className(),
            'actions' => [
                'index'  => ['get'],
                'view'   => ['get'],
                'create' => ['get', 'post'],
                'update' => ['get', 'put', 'post'],
```

```
                    'delete' => ['post', 'delete'],
            ],
        ],
    ];
}
```

Cross-origin resource headers

When working with JavaScript applications that issue AJAX requests against your API, you may want to use **cross-origin resource sharing (CORS)** headers to ensure that only domains that you specify can run against your domain. CORS headers can be implemented by adding yii\filters\Cors to your behaviors() method, as shown in the following example:

```
public function behaviors()
{
    return [
        'corsFilter' => [
            'class' => \yii\filters\Cors::className(),
        ],
    ];
}
```

This behavior can be extended by setting specific CORS headers that you want to specify for your controller:

```
public function behaviors()
{
    return [
        'corsFilter' => [
            'class' => \yii\filters\Cors::className(),
            'cors' => [
                // Only allow https://www.example.com to execute
                against your domain in AJAX
                'Origin' => ['https://www.example.com'],
                // Only allow POST and DELETE methods from the
                domain
                'Access-Control-Request-Method' => ['POST',
                'DELETE'],
                // Set cache control headers
                'Access-Control-Max-Age' => 3600,
                // Allow the X-Pagination-Current-Page header to
                be exposed to the browser.
```

```
                    'Access-Control-Expose-Headers' =>
                    ['X-Pagination-Current-Page'],
                ],


            ],
        ];
}
```

CORS headers have a very specific purpose when it comes to preventing AJAX requests from browsers and other domains from accessing content on your domain, and they are meant to be implemented as a security precaution for your end users rather than your API. CORS headers will not prevent tools such as CURL or noncompliant browsers from accessing your API. Before implementing CORS, ensure that you have a concrete understanding of what they are, what they protect against, and what headers to use. For more information on CORS, refer to the W3C reference guide at http://www.w3.org/TR/cors/.

Rate Limiting

When creating APIs, you may want to implement rate limiting within your API to prevent excessive requests being made to your API and exhausting server resources. This is extremely important if your API is dependent upon another API that has rate limits already in place. Rate limiting in Yii2 is implemented by yii\filters\ RateLimiter and yii\filters\RateLimitInterface.

To get started with rate limiting, we first need to add yii\filters\Ratelimiter to our controller behaviors. The yii\filters\RateLimiter class is coupled to our user identity class. Consequently, rate limiting will only be applied to actions that are protected by authentication. Any action that is not protected by an authenticate filter will not have rate limiting applied to it. The following example illustrates the code blocks required to implement yii\filters\RateLimiter within our controller:

```
<?php

namespace app\controllers;
use yii\filters\auth\HttpBasicAuth;
use yii\filters\RateLimiter;
use yii\rest\ActiveController;
```

```
class UserController extends ActiveController
{
    public function behaviors()
    {
        $behaviors = parent::behaviors();
        $behaviors['authenticator'] = [
            'class' => HttpBasicAuth::className(),
            'auth' => [ 'app\models\User', 'httpBasicAuth'],
            'only' => [ 'delete', 'update', 'create', 'index']
        ];
        $behaviors['rateLimiter'] = [
            'class' => RateLimiter::className(),
            'enableRateLimitHeaders' => true,
        ];

        return $behaviors;
    }
}
```

Next, we need to implement the required methods in our user identity class with the yii\filters\RateLimitInterface interface. The first method, yii\filters\Rate LimitInterface::getRateLimit(), defines the number of requests we can make in a unit of time. For global rate limiting, we can simply return [100, 600], which will allow 100 requests in 600 seconds. As the complete request and action are passed to the yii\filters\RateLimitInterface::getRateLimit() method, however, we can further refine our rate limits for each controller and action pairing:

```
/**
 * Returns the rate limit
 * @param yii\web\Request $request
 * @param yii\base\Action $action
 * @return array
 */
public function getRateLimit($request, $action)
{
    return [100, 600];
}
```

 yii\filters\RateLimiter is coupled with your user identity. If you want to implement rate limiting for unauthenticated users, you will need to implement a custom filter.

Next, we need to implement two methods to load the available rate limits and update the available rate limits after each request. These two methods are `yii\filters\RateLimitInterface::loadAllowance()` and `yii\filters\RateLimitInterface::saveAllowance()`. As rate limit data isn't considered sensitive and won't have a significant impact upon our application if the data is accidentally removed, this data can be stored either in our cache component or within a NoSQL solution, such as MongoDB or Redis. The method signatures are defined as follows:

```
/**
 * Returns the rate limit allowance
 * @param yii\web\Request $request
 * @param yii\base\Action $action
 * @return array
 */
public function loadAllowance($request, $action)
{
    $allowance = 100; // Fetch the allowance from a datasource
    return [$allowance, time()];
}

/**
 * Saves the rate limit allowance
 * @param yii\web\Request $request
 * @param yii\base\Action $action
 * @param integer $allowance
 * @param Integer $timestamp
 * @return array
 */
public function saveAllowance($request, $action, $allowance,
$timestamp)
{
    // Update a NoSQL solution or a cache
    return true;
}
```

Combined together, our extended class will look as follows:

```
<?php

namespace app\models;

use Yii;
```

```
class User extends \yii\db\ActiveRecord implements
\yii\web\IdentityInterface, \yii\filters\RateLimitInterface
{

    public function getRateLimit( $request, $action )
    {
        return [100, 600];
    }

    public function loadAllowance( $request, $action )
    {
        return [100, time();
    }

    public function saveAllowance( $request, $action,
    $allowance, $timestamp )
    {
        return true;
    }
}
```

Now, when your query against authenticated API endpoints, the following additional headers will be returned with the response:

```
x-rate-limit-remaining: <remaining_rate_limts>
x-rate-limit-limit: <rate_limit_upper_bound>
x-rate-limit-reset: <seconds_until_rate_limit_reset>
```

 Now that you have MinGW and MSYS, there's no need to be jealous of those with a Linux installation anymore, since they implement in your system the most important parts of a Linux development environment.

Error handling

By extending yii\rest\Controller (or yii\rest\ActiveController), we can easily implement error handling in our application by defining a proper error handler within our configuration, as illustrated in previous chapters:

```
<?php return [
    // [...],
    'components' => [
        // [...],
```

```
        'errorHandler' => [
            'errorAction' => 'user/error',
        ],
        // [...]
    ],
];
```

Unlike view-based responses, we do not need to include a definition within the `actions()` method of our controller for the error handler that we want to use. Instead, we can simply return the error as it occurs, or we can override the error to display a more generic response:

```php
<?php

namespace app\controllers;
use yii\rest\ActiveController;

class UserController extends ActiveController
{
    public function actionError()
    {
        $exception = Yii::$app->errorHandler->exception;

        if ($exception !== null)
            return ['exception' => $exception];

    }
}
```

Custom API controllers

While convenient, `yii\rest\ActiveController` doesn't solve every problem with creating APIs. When not using `yii\rest\ActiveController`, you'll want to extend your controller classes from `yii\rest\Controller` in order to take full advantage the built-in REST API defaults implemented by `yii\rest\Controller`. The following sections illustrate some additional information on creating custom API controllers.

Returning data

There are several way in which we can think about custom API controllers in Yii2. The easiest way to think about passing data to our clients is to bypass the view portion of our MVC model and directly return data from our controllers. For example, if we were to create a new controller called `SiteController` within our controller's namespace, we could directly return data from our newly created controller, as follows:

```php
<?php

namespace app\controllers;

use Yii;

class SiteController extends \yii\rest\Controller
{
    public function actionIndex()
    {
        return [ 'foo' => 'bar'];
    }
}
```

> Remember, once we start making changes to our default URL manager rules, we'll need to add the rules required to route data to other controllers. This rule will ensure that site/<action> maps back to our site controller: ['class' => 'yii\web\UrlRule', 'pattern' => 'site/<action>', 'route' => 'site/index'].

Curling against the site/index endpoint of our API will return the following:

```
$ curl -I -H "Accept:application/json" /
https://www.example.com/site/index | jq .

    {
        "foo": "bar"
    }
```

Response Formatting

Yii2 has a very specific response structure that it will return with the default `yii\rest\Controller`. When creating an API, you may already have a specific response structure you may want to use (for instance, if you're refactoring an existing but outdated API with a Yii2 API). You may also want to have a uniform structure in your API responses as the responses provided by `yii\rest\Controller` and `yii\rest\ActiveController` don't match up (as illustrated by the previous sections).

In these situations, you'll need to modify the response structure. To do this, we simply need to override the `response` component of our application and modify the `$response->data` variable within the `beforeSend` event with the actual response that we want. In this example, we will have the following response structure:

```
{
    "status": <http_status_code>,
    "message": <exceptions_or_messages>,
    "response": <response_data_from_controllers>
}
```

The code required to make this change is shown as follows:

```php
<?php return [
    // [...],
    'components' => [
        // [...],
        'response' => [
            'format'  => yii\web\Response::FORMAT_JSON,
            'charset' => 'UTF-8',
                'on beforeSend'  => function ($event) {
                $response = $event->sender;

                if ($response->data !== null)
                {
                    $return = ($response->statusCode == 200 ?
                    $response->data : $response->data['message']);

                    $response->data = [
                        'success'  => ($response->statusCode ===
                        200),
                        'status'   => $response->statusCode,
                        'response' => $return
                    ];
                }
```

```
        }
    ],
    // [...],
  ]
];
```

Now, if we were to query our API, we would receive a uniform response structure for both our SiteController and UserController. This is for SiteController:

```
$ curl -I -H "Accept:application/json" /
https://www.example.com/site/index | jq .

{
    "success": true,
    "status": 200,
    "response": {
        "foo": "bar"
    }
}
```

This query regards UserController:

```
$ curl -I -H "Accept:application/json" /
https://www.example.com/users | jq .

{
    "success": true,
    "status": 200,
    "response": {
        "users": [
            {
                "id": 1,
                "email_address": "jane.doe@example.com",
                "first_name": "Jane",
                "last_name": "Joe",
                "full_name": "Jane Joe",
                "updated_at": 1442602004,
                "created_at": 1442602004
            },
            {...},
        ],
        "_links": {
            "self": {
```

```
            "href": "https://www.example.com/users?page=1"
        }
    },
    "_meta": {
        "totalCount": 4,
        "pageCount": 1,
        "currentPage": 1,
        "perPage": 20
    }
}
}
```

Summary

In this chapter, we expanded upon our knowledge of everything we've learned thus far and also learned how to create RESTful JSON and XML APIs in Yii2. First, we covered the usage of yii\rest\ActiveController, which enabled us to quickly create CRUD APIs based upon our model classes. We then covered Yii2's built-in authentication filters and covered how we can protect our resources by requiring authentication. We also covered the creation of our own authentication filters to support different authentication schemes. We then covered several other useful API classes, including yii\filters\VerbFilter, yii\filters\Cors, and learned how to handle errors within our API. Additionally, we detailed some important information about creating our own API endpoints by extending yii\rest\Controller.

Having covered all the information required to build applications in Yii2, we'll spend the remaining chapters of this book exploring ways in which we can enhance our applications. In the next chapter, we'll specifically go over one of the most important aspect of building applications: testing. We'll cover how to set up testing within our application using a powerful called Codeception, and we will detail how to set up and create function, unit, and acceptance testing as well as how to create data fixtures to test with.

10
Testing with Codeception

An important but often overlooked aspect of software development is testing our application to ensure that it performs as expected. There are three basic ways in which we can test our applications:

- Unit testing
- Functional testing
- Acceptance testing

Unit testing enables us to test individual sections of code before coupling it with our application. **Functional testing** allows us to test the functional aspects of code within a simulated browser, and **acceptance testing** allows us to test our application within a real browser and verify that it does what we built it to do. With Yii2, we can use a tool called Codeception to create and execute unit, functional, and acceptance testing for our application. In this chapter, we'll cover how to create and run unit, functional, and acceptance testing in Yii2. In addition to these three types of testing, we can mock our data using fixtures, which we can use to bring our application to a fixed state before testing.

As we work through this chapter, we'll be using much of the code from previous chapters. For your convenience, the source code for this chapter is provided on GitHub at https://github.com/masteringyii/ chapter10 and is broken into three distinct branches. We'll use the unit branch in the unit testing section, the functional_and_acceptance branch in the functional and acceptance testing section, and the fixture branch in the fixtures section.

Reasons for testing

Most software developers will admit that testing is a good thing, but many developers don't write tests for their application for a variety of reasons, such as the following:

- The fear of testing
- Not knowing how to write tests
- Thinking that their application is too small for testing
- Not having enough time
- Budgetary reasons

While many of these reasons are valid, testing can have a profound effect on your application and can drastically improve the quality of your code. The following list provides several reasons why tests should be added to your codebase:

- Testing can reduce bugs as new features are added
- Testing verifies that your code does what you think it does
- Testing verifies that your code does what your client wants
- Features can be constrained by testing
- Testing forces us to slow down and break our applications into small, manageable components with constraining features
- Testing reduces the cost of change by ensuring that a change to a single feature doesn't break another feature
- Testing provides documentation of what our code is supposed to do
- Testing reduces the fear that a change will break something in our application

How to approach testing

There are many factors that go into modern development, costs and development time being the chief among them. There are several realistic approaches that we can take for testing in order to work around these constraints.

Testing manually

The most rudimentary approach to testing we can take is to test manually as we're writing code. Whether you realize it or not, every time you make a code change and reload your browser, you're testing your code. At a cursory glance, manual testing lets us verify new features and bug fixes that are working, but it requires us to manually verify the state of our applications after every change. Furthermore, manual testing requires us to remember every test case we've created. Automated testing with a tool such as Codeception can reduce this cognitive burden and free up our time to perform other tasks.

Testing a few core components

A better approach to testing is to automate the testing of just the core components of our applications. With this approach, we add tests for only the critical paths in our application, which enables us to verify the important bits of our application at the cost of reduced tests elsewhere. In situations where time and budget are constrained but you want to automate the verification of important flows and paths, this approach is a realistic alternative to no testing whatsoever.

Test-driven development

Test-driven development (TDD) is the philosophy that we should create tests for our application as we're building it. The primary idea behind TDD is that we can verify that our code is working by writing a test for it beforehand. With TDD, we generally write a test beforehand (which will fail), then we write code in order to make it pass the test, and then we continuously iterate between tests and code until our feature is completed and our test passes. TDD also forces us to ensure that we write usable code by passing tests before checking it into our versioning system, which then encourages us to write good tests.

With TDD, our goal is to have a test for every feature and component and have many tests that thoroughly cover our application. In an ideal world, TDD is the best approach to take when working with testing at the cost of requiring more time and budget to implement.

Configuring Codeception with Yii2

Before we can use Codeception to test our code, we first need to configure Codeception to work with Yii2:

1. The preferred way to set up Codeception with Yii2 is to install both the `yii2-codeception` package and the Codeception base package via Composer:

   ```
   $ composer require --dev codeception/codeception
   $ composer require --dev yiisoft/yii2-codeception
   $ composer require --dev yiisoft/yii2-faker
   ```

    The `--dev` flag on our composer command ensures that development packages are not installed in our production environment. Packages installed with `-dev` will be added to the `require-dev` section of our `composer.json` file. Storing Codeception and other testing code reduces the dependencies we need in production and makes our code more secure.

   The first package contains the Codeception binary that we'll use to generate and execute our tests, while the second package contains Yii2-specific helpers and bindings that Codeception will use to tightly integrate into Yii2.

    This process may take a long time as Codeception is dependent upon many different packages, including PHPUnit.

2. After installing Codeception, we can execute the command by running the following command:

   ```
   $ ./vendor/bin/codecept
   ```

By itself, `codecept` will output all the available commands that Codeception has to offer.

```
Codeception version 2.1.3

Usage:
  command [options] [arguments]

Options:
  -h, --help            Display this help message
  -q, --quiet           Do not output any message
  -V, --version         Display this application version
      --ansi            Force ANSI output
      --no-ansi         Disable ANSI output
  -n, --no-interaction  Do not ask any interactive question
  -v|vv|vvv, --verbose  Increase the verbosity of messages: 1 for normal output, 2 for
more verbose output and 3 for debug

Available commands:
  bootstrap             Creates default test suites and generates all requires files
  build                 Generates base classes for all suites
  clean                 Cleans or creates _output directory
  console               Launches interactive test console
  help                  Displays help for a command
  list                  Lists commands
  run                   Runs the test suites
 generate
  generate:cept         Generates empty Cept file in suite
  generate:cest         Generates empty Cest file in suite
  generate:environment  Generates empty environment config
  generate:groupobject  Generates Group subscriber
  generate:helper       Generates new helper
  generate:pageobject   Generates empty PageObject class
  generate:phpunit      Generates empty PHPUnit test without Codeception additions
  generate:scenarios    Generates text representation for all scenarios
  generate:stepobject   Generates empty StepObject class
  generate:suite        Generates new test suite
  generate:test         Generates empty unit test file in suite
```

3. After verifying that Codeception is installed, we need to bootstrap Codeception by running the following command:

```
$ ./vendor/bin/codecept bootstrap
```

```
Initializing Codeception in /var/www/chapter10

File codeception.yml created          <- global configuration
tests/unit created                    <- unit tests
tests/unit.suite.yml written          <- unit tests suite configuration
tests/functional created              <- functional tests
tests/functional.suite.yml written    <- functional tests suite configuration
tests/acceptance created              <- acceptance tests
tests/acceptance.suite.yml written    <- acceptance tests suite configuration
tests/_output was added to .gitignore
---
tests/_bootstrap.php written <- global bootstrap file
Building initial Tester classes
Building Actor classes for suites: acceptance, unit, functional
 -> AcceptanceTesterActions.php generated successfully. 0 methods added
\AcceptanceTester includes modules: PhpBrowser, \Helper\Acceptance
 -> UnitTesterActions.php generated successfully. 0 methods added
\UnitTester includes modules: Asserts, \Helper\Unit
 -> FunctionalTesterActions.php generated successfully. 0 methods added
\FunctionalTester includes modules: \Helper\Functional

Bootstrap is done. Check out /var/www/chapter10/tests directory
```

4. The bootstrap process will create several files. The first file is called codeception.yml and lives within the root of our application. The remaining files exist within the tests folder and will be the directory to which we add our tests.

5. Next, we need to configure Codeception to work with the Yii2 Codeception module in our codeception.yml file. The required additions are highlighted in the following code block:

```
actor: Tester
paths:
    tests: tests
    log: tests/_output
    data: tests/_data
    support: tests/_support
    envs: tests/_envs
settings:
    bootstrap: _bootstrap.php
    colors: true
```

```
    memory_limit: 1024M
extensions:
    enabled:
        - Codeception\Extension\RunFailed
```

6. Additionally, we need to tell Codeception to autoload our composer dependencies and Yii2. We can do this by updating the `tests/_bootstrap.php` file. To ensure that we test our application in a manner similar to our `web/index.php` loads data, we should add the following:

```php
<?php

// Define our application_env variable as provided by nginx/apache
if (!defined('APPLICATION_ENV'))
{
    if (getenv('APPLICATION_ENV') != false)
        define('APPLICATION_ENV', getenv('APPLICATION_ENV'));
    else
        define('APPLICATION_ENV', 'prod');
}

$env = require(__DIR__ . '/../config/env.php');

// comment out the following two lines when deployed to production
defined('YII_DEBUG') or define('YII_DEBUG', $env['debug']);
defined('YII_ENV') or define('YII_ENV', APPLICATION_ENV);

require(__DIR__ . '/../vendor/autoload.php');
require(__DIR__ . '/../vendor/yiisoft/yii2/Yii.php');
$config = require(__DIR__ . '/../config/web.php');

(new yii\web\Application($config));
```

7. With Codeception now configured, we can run all of our tests by running the following command:

```
$ ./vendor/bin/codecept run
```

The run command will output the following:

```
Codeception PHP Testing Framework v2.1.3
Powered by PHPUnit 4.8.10 by Sebastian Bergmann and contributors.

Acceptance Tests (0) ----------------------
------------------------------------------

Unit Tests (0) ----------------------------
------------------------------------------

Functional Tests (0) ----------------------
------------------------------------------


Time: 183 ms, Memory: 13.00Mb

No tests executed!
```

Unit testing

The most basic type of tests we can create are called unit tests. As the name suggests, **unit tests** are designed to test a unit of work (whether that be a single method, function, or a larger work unit), and then check a single assumption about that unit of work. A good unit test will be composed of the following components:

- **Fully automated**: A good unit test is a test that can be fully automated without human intervention.

- **Thorough**: Thorough unit tests provide good coverage of the code block they are testing.

- **Independent**: Good unit tests can be run in any order, and their output should have no effect or side effect on other tests that occur. Furthermore, each unit test should only test a single logical unit of code. Tests that fail should pinpoint the exact section of code that failed.

- **Consistent and repeatable**: Unit tests should always produce the same result and should be dependent upon static data as opposed to generated or random data.

- **Fast**: Unit tests need to execute quickly. Long tests mean that fewer tests will be run in a given amount of time, and tests that take too long to execute will encourage developers to either write fewer tests or skip writing tests altogether. As unit tests are intended to test small individual units of code, long-running tests can also be an indicator of a bad or incomplete test.

- **Readable**: Good unit tests should be readable and should be either self-explanatory or thoroughly documented if they require additional explanation.

- **Maintainable**: Finally, good unit tests should be maintainable. A test we don't maintain is a test that we don't use or work with.

 In this section, we'll be using the source code in the `unit` branch located at `https://github.com/masteringyii/chapter10`.

Generating unit tests

If you're familiar with PHPUnit, writing tests in Codeception should feel very familiar. For unit testing, Codeception can generate a PHPUnit-like test, but it can also generate a Codeception-specific unit test that doesn't require PHPUnit to execute.

To generate PHPUnit-specific tests, we can run the following command, which will generate a PHPUnit unit test called `Example`:

```
$ ./vendor/bin/codecept generate:phpunit unit Example
```

Alternatively, we can generate a Codeception-specific test called `Example` by running the following command:

```
$ ./vendor/bin/codecept generate:test unit Example
```

 Unless you have a specific need for PHPUnit-like tests, Codeception unit tests should be preferred.

After generating our Codeception test, a file called `tests/unit/ExampleTest.php` will be generated, and it will contain the following code. Before we start writing unit tests for our application, let's explore the basic structure of a Codeception unit test class:

```php
<?php


class ExampleTest extends \Codeception\TestCase\Test
{
    /**
```

```
     * @var \UnitTester
     */
    protected $tester;

    protected function _before()
    {
    }

    protected function _after()
    {
    }

    // tests
    public function testMe()
    {

    }
}
```

By default, our Codeception unit tests will extend \Codeception\TestCase\Test, and will implement two protected methods (_before() and _after()) and a protected property called $tester for Codeception to use internally. The _before() and _after() methods are intended to set up and tear down tasks that execute immediately before and after each of our predefined tests within our class.

After the _before() and _after() methods, we have all of the tests that we want to run. In general, any test that we want to run should be in a public method with a method name prefix of test. Any public method with this signature will be executed as a test. As a brief example, let's modify our testMe() method to make a simple assertion (a statement of whether a given predicate (a function, method, or variable) evaluates to a boolean value which we can verify is true):

```
public function testMe()
{
    // Assert that the boolean value "true" is indeed true
    $this->assertTrue(true);
}
```

Using this simple assertion as an example, we can verify our tests run by running this:

```
$ ./vendor/bin/codecept run
```

Alternatively, we can just run our unit tests by running the following command:

```
$ ./vendor/bin/codecept run unit
```

```
Codeception PHP Testing Framework v2.1.3
Powered by PHPUnit 4.8.10 by Sebastian Bergmann and contributors.

Acceptance Tests (0) ----------------------
-------------------------------------------


Unit Tests (1) -----------------------------------------------------------
Test me (ExampleTest::testMe)                                          Ok
-------------------------------------------------------------------------


Functional Tests (0) ----------------------
-------------------------------------------



Time: 193 ms, Memory: 13.50Mb

OK (1 test, 1 assertion)
```

As you can see from the previous screenshot, our unit test case executed successfully. We can add extra unit tests by defining additional test methods, as shown in the following example:

```
public function testMeToo()
{
    $this->assertFalse(false);
}
```

Running a second test will then show up in our Codeception output.

```
Powered by PHPUnit 4.8.10 by Sebastian Bergmann and contributors.


Unit Tests (2) -----------------------------------------------------------
Test me (ExampleTest::testMe)                                         Ok
Test me too (ExampleTest::testMeToo)                                  Ok
-------------------------------------------------------------------------


Time: 279 ms, Memory: 11.75Mb

OK (2 tests, 2 assertions)
```

Unit test examples

Now that we know the basics of unit testing with Codeception, let's explore a couple of examples we can test within applications we've built previously. Starting with the source code we developed in *Chapter 9, RESTful APIs*, let's write a few unit tests for our models.

Testing User model methods

1. Our User model is a significant part of our application. Since we've added both custom code and custom validators, we can write unit tests to verify that our validators are accurate and that our custom code works as expected. To get started, let's create a new unit test for our User model:

    ```
    $ ./vendor/bin/codecept generate:test unit User
    ```

2. Since we're testing our User model, we need to explicitly specify that we want to use that model within our test:

    ```php
    <?php

    namespace app\tests\unit\UserTest;

    use Codeception\TestCase\Test;
    use app\models\User;
    use Yii;

    class UserTest extends Test {}
    ```

3. Next, let's define a method to test that our app\models\ User::setFullName() method works:

    ```php
    public function testSetFullName()
    {
        $user = new User;
        $user->setFullName('John Doe');

        // Asser the setFullName method works
        $this->assertTrue($user->first_name == "John");
        $this->assertTrue($user->last_name == "Doe");
        $this->assertFalse($user->first_name == "Jane");
        unset($user);

        $user = new User;
        $user->fullName = 'John Doe';
    ```

```
    // Asser the full_name setter method works
    $this->assertTrue($user->first_name == "John");
    $this->assertTrue($user->last_name == "Doe");
    $this->assertFalse($user->first_name == "Jane");

    unset($user);
}
```

4. After executing our tests, we can verify our newly passed test case by viewing the output.

```
Codeception PHP Testing Framework v2.1.3
Powered by PHPUnit 4.8.10 by Sebastian Bergmann and contributors.

Acceptance Tests (0) -----------------------
--------------------------------------------

Unit Tests (3) ------------------------------------------------------------------------
Test me (ExampleTest::testMe)                                                          Ok
Test me too (ExampleTest::testMeToo)                                                   Ok
Test set full name (app\tests\unit\UserTest\UserTest::testSetFullName)                 Ok..
--------------------------------------------------------------------------------------

Functional Tests (0) -----------------------
--------------------------------------------


Time: 224 ms, Memory: 15.00Mb
```

> The test cases illustrated here are very rudimentary. Try expanding upon this test case to ensure complete code coverage of this method.

Let's write another test to the `app\models\User::validatePassword()` method that correctly validates the password of an existing user:

1. For this test case, we'll be relying upon the data supplied by our migrations. Before creating the test, ensure that you migrate the database:

    ```
    $ ./yii migrate/up --interactive=0
    ```

2. Next, we'll add a test case that will load our four default users and verify that their passwords match, as we expect:

    ```
    public function testValidatePassword()
    {
        $user = User::find()->where(['id' => 1])->one();
        $this->assertTrue(
        $user->validatePassword('password1'));
    ```

```
$this->assertFalse(
$user->validatePassword('password2'));

$user = User::find()->where(['id' => 2])->one();
$this->assertTrue(
$user->validatePassword('password2'));
$this->assertFalse(
$user->validatePassword('password1'));

$user = User::find()->where(['id' => 3])->one();
$this->assertTrue(
$user->validatePassword('password3'));
$this->assertFalse(
$user->validatePassword('password4'));

$user = User::find()->where(['id' => 4])->one();
$this->assertTrue($user->validatePassword('admin'));
$this->assertFalse(
$user->validatePassword('notadmin'));
}
```

In this case, information about our users is being loaded from our migrations, which in some cases makes sense if we want to provide our end users with sensible defaults. Later on in this chapter, we'll explore how we can use fixtures to create and populate defaults for testing, which will eliminate the need to have these defaults as part of our migration file.

3. After running our unit tests, we should see the following output:

```
Powered by PHPUnit 4.8.10 by Sebastian Bergmann and contributors.

Acceptance Tests (0) -----------------------
-------------------------------------------


Unit Tests (4) ---------------------------------------------------------------
--
Test me (ExampleTest::testMe)                                               Ok
Test me too (ExampleTest::testMeToo)                                        Ok
Test set full name (app\tests\unit\UserTest\UserTest::testSetFullName)      Ok
Trying to test validate pas (app\tests\unit\UserTest\UserTest::testValidatePassword)...
Test validate password (app\tests\unit\UserTest\UserTest::testValidatePassword)   Ok
------------------------------------------------------------------------------
--

Functional Tests (0) -----------------------
-------------------------------------------


Time: 5.92 seconds, Memory: 16.25Mb
```

Note how in the previous test case, we tested both the expected result and the several results that we were expecting to fail. An important part of unit testing is verifying that both the expected passing cases pass and invalid or wrong input is not accepted. This ensures that our application does what we want, while not allowing rogue or bad inputs to be accepted.

Have you gotten the hang of unit testing yet? Before moving on to functional testing, let's write a test case to verify that our validators are working:

1. Since the validator for our `User` model validates several different attributes, we're going check whether our `app\models\User::validate()` method returns the expected `true` or `false` result and whether the appropriate validator is called.

2. To make our test output more readable, we can include the `codeception/specify` composer module in our project, which will allow us to specify what the expected result for each test section in the output of our tests is in the event that a test fails. This package can be installed by running the following command:

    ```
    $ composer require codeception/specify
    ```

    To use `specify`, we need to use it inside our `UserTest` class, as shown in the following example:

    ```php
    <?php

    namespace app\tests\unit\UserTest;

    use Codeception\TestCase\Test;

    use app\models\User;
    use yii\codeception\TestCase;
    use Yii;

    class UserTest extends Test
    {
        use \Codeception\Specify;
    }
    ```

3. `specify` can then be used as follows:

    ```php
    public function testValidate()
    {
    ```

```
        $this->specify('false is false', function() {
            $this->assertFalse(false);
        });
    }
```

Now if we run our test case, we should see the following output indicate specifically that our "false is false" test case has failed:

Test validate (app\tests\unit\UserTest\UserTest::/

testValidate)   Ok

4. Now that we know how to use the specify module, let's write several test cases for our validator:

```
public function testValidate()
{
    $this->specify('email and password are required',
    function() {
        $user = new User;
        // Verify our validation fails as we didn't
        provide any attributes
        $this->assertFalse($user->validate());

        // Verify that the email and password properties
        are required
        $this->assertTrue($user->hasErrors('email'));
        $this->assertTrue($user->hasErrors('password'));
        $user->email = 'user@example.com';
        $user->password =  password_hash('example',
        PASSWORD_BCRYPT, ['cost' => 13]);
        $this->assertTrue($user->validate());
    });

    $this->specify('email is unique', function() {
        $user = new User;
        // Verify email is unique
        $user->email = 'jane.doe@example.com';
        $user->password =  password_hash('example',
        PASSWORD_BCRYPT, ['cost' => 13]);
        $this->assertFalse($user->validate());
        $this->assertTrue($user->hasErrors('email'));
    });

    $this->specify('first and last name are strings',
    function() {
        $user = new User;
```

```
$user->email = 'user@example.com';
$user->password =  password_hash('example',
PASSWORD_BCRYPT, ['cost' => 13]);
// Verify first and last name has to be strings
$user->first_name = (int)7;
$user->last_name = (int)5;

$this->assertFalse($user->validate());
$this->assertTrue($user->hasErrors('first_name'));
$this->assertTrue($user->hasErrors('last_name'));

// Verify that strings work
$user->setFullName('Example User');
$this->assertTrue($user->validate());
    });
}
```

5. After running our unit tests, we should see the following output, indicating that our tests have passed. If our tests fail at any point, the specify module will output the first parameter, indicating what specific part of the test failed. As our test passes, we will see the following output:

```
Powered by PHPUnit 4.8.10 by Sebastian Bergmann and contributors.

Acceptance Tests (0) ------------------------
-----------------------------------------


Unit Tests (5) ---------------------------------------------------------------------
--
Test me (ExampleTest::testMe)                                                    Ok
Test me too (ExampleTest::testMeToo)                                             Ok
Test set full name (app\tests\unit\UserTest\UserTest::testSetFullName)           Ok
Trying to test validate pas (app\tests\unit\UserTest\UserTest::testValidatePassword)..
Test validate password (app\tests\unit\UserTest\UserTest::testValidatePassword)  Ok
Test validate (app\tests\unit\UserTest\UserTest::testValidate)                   Ok
---------------------------------------------------------------------------------
--

Functional Tests (0) -----------------------
-----------------------------------------


Time: 8.33 seconds, Memory: 21.25Mb
OK (5 tests, 20 assertions)
```

Yii2 already has a test case for `yii\db\`
`ActiveRecord::validate()`. Adding our own test case isn't to
verify that this method works but rather to verify that we have the
correct validators in place.

For more information on the specify module, refer to `https://`
`github.com/Codeception/Specify`.

Functional testing

The next type of tests that we can generate are called functional tests. **Functional tests** allow us to emulate our application without running it through a web server. This provides us with a way to quickly test the output of our application without introducing the overhead of a web server.

This emulation process is achieved by directly manipulating the `$_REQUEST`, `$_POST`, and `$_GET` parameters before executing our application. As a side effect of this behavior, however, certain variables, such as `$_SESSION` and `$_COOKIE`, as well as headers, can result in `junk` errors being thrown, which wouldn't necessarily be thrown in a real environment. Moreover, with Codeception, our functional tests will be executing within a single memory container, which may result in a test failing when run as part of a group as opposed to running a single test. Additionally, unlike acceptance testing, functional testing can't emulate JavaScript and Ajax requests.

Overall, functional testing provides us with a fast and easy way to prove that the output of our code does both what we programmed it to do and what our end users and customers expect it to do. Despite the minor issues functional testing brings up, at a high level, the report it provides can give us confidence that our code works as expected and that future changes in our codebase won't change our application significantly. In this section, we'll go over how to generate and run functional tests within our application.

In this section, we'll be using the source code in the `functional_`
`and_acceptance` branch located at `https://github.com/`
`masteringyii/chapter10`.

Setting up functional tests

Since functional testing and API don't really make sense, we'll be writing our functional tests using the code we wrote earlier in *Chapter 6, Asset Management*, as the code outlined in that chapter has several good components we can test. Functional tests behave quite differently from unit tests, so before we can start writing test code, we need to make a few changes to our test configuration:

1. To get started with functional tests, we first need to make sure that Codeception is initially installed and configured. This process is identical to what we performed in the previous section:

    ° Install the required composer dependencies:

    ```
    $ composer require --dev codeception/codeception
    $ composer require --dev yiisoft/yii2-codeception
    $ composer require --dev yiisoft/yii2-faker
    $ composer require --dev codeception/specify
    ```

    ° Install Bootstrap Codeception:

    ```
    $ ./vendor/bin/codecept bootstrap
    ```

    ° Add the required configuration to `tests/_bootstrap.php`. Note that because we're emulating a complete request flow, we need to prepopulate several variables, such as `$_SERVER['SCRIPT_FILENAME']` and `$_SERVER['SCRIPT_NAME']`. The relevant sections are highlighted as follows:

    ```php
    <?php
    define('DS', DIRECTORY_SEPARATOR);

    defined('YII_TEST_ENTRY_URL') or define('YII_TEST_ENTRY_
    URL',
    parse_url(\Codeception\Configuration::config()['config']
    ['test_entry_url'], PHP_URL_PATH));
    defined('YII_TEST_ENTRY_FILE') or define('YII_TEST_ENTRY_
    FILE',
    dirname(__DIR__) . '/web/index-test.php');

    // Define our application_env variable as provided by
    nginx/apache
    if (!defined('APPLICATION_ENV'))
    {
        if (getenv('APPLICATION_ENV') != false)
            define('APPLICATION_ENV',
            getenv('APPLICATION_ENV'));
        else
    ```

```
            define('APPLICATION_ENV', 'prod');
    }
    $env = require(__DIR__ . '/../config/env.php');
    // comment out the following two lines when deployed to
    production
    defined('YII_DEBUG') or define('YII_DEBUG', $env['debug']);
    defined('YII_ENV') or define('YII_ENV', APPLICATION_ENV);
    require(__DIR__ . '/../vendor/autoload.php');
    require(__DIR__ . '/../vendor/yiisoft/yii2/Yii.php');
    $config = require(__DIR__ . '/../config/web.php');


    $_SERVER['SCRIPT_FILENAME'] = YII_TEST_ENTRY_FILE;
    $_SERVER['SCRIPT_NAME'] = YII_TEST_ENTRY_URL;
    $_SERVER['SERVER_NAME'] = parse_url(\Codeception\
    Configuration::config()['config']
    ['test_entry_url'], PHP_URL_HOST);
    $_SERVER['SERVER_PORT'] = parse_url(\Codeception\
    Configuration::config()['config']
    ['test_entry_url'], PHP_URL_PORT) ?: '80';


    Yii::setAlias('@tests', dirname(__DIR__));

    (new yii\web\Application($config));
```

  ○ Verify that Codeception is running:

```
$ ./vendor/bin/codecept bootstrap
```

2. The first change we need to make is the inclusion of the Yii2 Codeception module. This module will enable us to take advantage of Yii2-specific bindings within our test that will help us test our Yii2 application better. Rather than enabling our module for all of our test types, we can just enable it for our functional tests by adding the following to tests/functional. suite.yml:

```
# Codeception Test Suite Configuration
#
# Suite for functional (integration) tests
# Emulate web requests and make application process them
# Include one of framework modules (Symfony2, Yii2,
Laravel5) to use it

class_name: FunctionalTester
modules:
    enabled:
```

```
        - Filesystem
        - Yii2
    config:
        Yii2:
            configFile: 'tests/config/functional.php'
```

3. Next, we need to disable cross-site request forgery (CSRF) validation on our forms. Rather than making a global configuration change to our `config/web.php` file, we can create a custom configuration in `tests/config/functional.php` that includes our `config/web.php` file and disables CSRF validation in that file:

```php
<?php
$_SERVER['SCRIPT_FILENAME'] = YII_TEST_ENTRY_FILE;
$_SERVER['SCRIPT_NAME'] = YII_TEST_ENTRY_URL;
/**
 * Application configuration for functional tests
 */
return yii\helpers\ArrayHelper::merge(
    require(__DIR__ . '/../../config/web.php'),
    [
        'components' => [
            'request' => [
                'enableCsrfValidation' => false,
            ],
        ],
    ]
);
```

4. Next, we need to enable our Yii2 module. To enable a new module in Codeception, we simply need to run the following command:

```
$ ./vendor/bin/codecept build
```

```
Building Actor classes for suites: acceptance, unit, functional
 -> AcceptanceTesterActions.php generated successfully. 0 methods added
\AcceptanceTester includes modules: PhpBrowser, \Helper\Acceptance
 -> UnitTesterActions.php generated successfully. 0 methods added
\UnitTester includes modules: Asserts, \Helper\Unit
 -> FunctionalTesterActions.php generated successfully. 0 methods added
\FunctionalTester includes modules: Filesystem, Yii2
```

5. Finally, we can execute the run command of Codeception to verify that our changes took place:

```
$ ./vendor/bin/codecept run
```

6. If successful, we should see output similar to what is shown in the following figure:

```
Acceptance Tests (0) ------------------------
--------------------------------------------

Unit Tests (0) ------------------------------
--------------------------------------------

Functional Tests (0) ------------------------
--------------------------------------------


Time: 341 ms, Memory: 12.25Mb
No tests executed!
```

Generating functional tests

Unlike unit tests, functional tests are not executed within a generated class. Instead, they run within a plain PHP file within the tests/functional folder. To get started with generating functional tests, we need to use the generate:cept command once again:

```
$ ./vendor/bin/codecept generate:cept functional Page
```

Our functional test will then be generated in tests/functional/PageCept.php and will contain the following:

```php
<?php
$I = new FunctionalTester($scenario);
$I->wantTo('perform actions and see result');
```

Now if we execute our tests again, we should see the following:

```
Codeception PHP Testing Framework v2.1.3
Powered by PHPUnit 4.8.10 by Sebastian Bergmann and contributors.


Functional Tests (1) ----------------------------------------------------------

Trying to perform actions and see result (PageCept)...
Perform actions and see result (PageCept)                                    Ok
--------------------------------------------------------------------------------


Time: 180 ms, Memory: 12.50Mb
```

Examples of functional tests

Now that we know how to generate functional tests, let's explore a few examples of functional testing. If you remember from *Chapter 6, Asset Management*, our home page looks as follows:

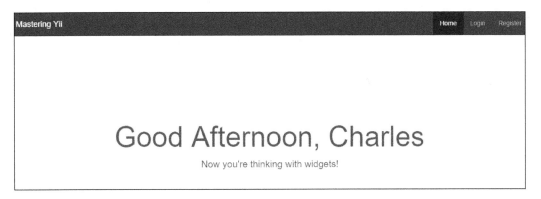

Let's write a quick functional test to verify that our home page loads and contains the elements we see on screen:

1. With Yii2's Codeception binding, we have several ways to navigate to and load the data from a page. Within our `tests/functional/PageCept.php` test, we can write the following to verify that the home page loads. We can do this using the `FunctionalTester::amOnPage()` method, which verifies that `FunctionalTester` was able to access the given page:

```php
<?php
$I = new FunctionalTester($scenario);
$I->wantTo('Verify that homepage loads');
$I->amOnPage('/');
$I->amOnPage('site/index');
$I->amOnPage(['/site/index']);
```

2. As you can see, we can load the home page either by querying the root URI or the `site/index` action either as a string or an array. If we use the array syntax, we can pass additional parameters to our page as GET parameters.

3. Now that we've verified that we're on the home page, let's verify that the `'Now you're thinking with widgets!'` string is displayed. With Codeception, this is exceptionally easy with the following line of code:

    ```
    $I->see('Now you\'re thinking with widgets!');
    ```

4. We can additionally verify that the `'Home'`, `'Register'`, and `'Login'` link text is displayed using the `FunctionalTester::see()` method, which scans the requested document for the presence of the provided text:

    ```
    $I->see('Home');
    $I->see('Register');
    $I->see('Login');
    ```

5. Now let's run our functional tests. As an alternative to running both our unit and acceptance tests with every run, we can just run our functional tests by specifying the test type we want to run, as shown in the following example:

    ```
    $ ./vendor/bin/codecept run functional
    ```

```
Codeception PHP Testing Framework v2.1.3
Powered by PHPUnit 4.8.10 by Sebastian Bergmann and contributors.

Functional Tests (1) ------------------------------------------------------------

Trying to Verify that homepage loads (PageCept)...
Verify that homepage loads (PageCept)                                        Ok
--------------------------------------------------------------------------------



Time: 211 ms, Memory: 17.00Mb
```

Even though we're running several different tests, Codeception will only report a pass or fail result for the entire test file we created. To gain more insight into what Codeception is doing, we can tell Codeception to be more verbose by passing the "-v" flag to our command. Additional verbosity can be added by adding more "v" flags to our verbose flag (for example, "-vv" or even "-vvv"):

```
$ ./vendor/bin/codecept run functional -vv
```

```
Functional Tests (1) -----------------------------------------

Modules: Filesystem, Yii2
---------------------------------------------------------------

Verify that homepage loads (PageCept)
Scenario:

* I am on page "/"

  [Page] https://localhost/
  [Response] 200
  [Cookies] []
  [Headers] {"content-type":["text/html; charset=UTF-8"]}
* I am on page "site/index"
  [Page] https://localhost/site/index
  [Response] 200
  [Cookies] []
  [Headers] {"content-type":["text/html; charset=UTF-8"]}
* I am on page "/site/index"
  [Page] https://localhost/site/index
  [Response] 200
  [Cookies] []
  [Headers] {"content-type":["text/html; charset=UTF-8"]}
* I see "Now you're thinking with widgets!"
* I see "Home"
* I see "Login"
* I see "Register"
PASSED

^^^^^^^^^^^^^^^^^^^^^^^^^^^^^^^^^^^^^^^^^^^^^^^^^^^^^^^^^^^^^^^^^^^^^^^^^^

---------------------------------------------------------------

Time: 220 ms, Memory: 17.00Mb
```

6. Since we're creating a new test, we should first create a new functional test file for us to work with. Running the following command will generate a test file at tests/functional/LoginCept.php:

```
$ ./vendor/bin/codecept generate:cept functional Login
```

7. First, let's write a test to verify that we can click on the "Login" link on our home page and navigate to our login page:

```php
<?php
$I = new FunctionalTester($scenario);
$I->wantTo('Verify login page');

// Verify homepage link works
$I->amOnPage('/');
$I->click('Login');
$I->amOnPage(['site/login']);
```

8. After verifying that our tests pass, we can verify that the form is present and that there aren't any errors using the seeElement() and dontSeeElement() methods:

```php
// Verify form is present
$I->seeElement('input', ['id' => 'userform-email']);
$I->seeElement('input', ['id' => 'userform-password']);
```

9. Then, after verifying that we can see the form elements on the page, let's test whether our form works by first submitting an invalid username and password and then submitting a valid username and password combination:

```php
// Verify bad user/pass fails
$I->fillField(['id' => 'userform-email'], 'foo');
$I->fillField(['id' => 'userform-password'], 'bar');
$I->click("Submit");

$I->SeeCurrentUrlEquals('/site/login');

// Verify bad user/pass fails
$I->fillField(['id' => 'userform-email'], 'admin@example.com');
$I->fillField(['id' => 'userform-password'], 'admin');
$I->click("Submit");

$I->SeeCurrentUrlEquals('/site/index');
```

10. Now let's run our Login test. We can run this test independently of all other tests by calling it directly, as shown in the following example:

```
$ ./vendor/bin/codecept functional LoginCept -vv
```

11. As shown in the following screenshot, our functional test iterates through all of our test and verifies that the login form flow works as expected:

```
Verify login page (LoginCept)
Scenario:

* I am on page "/"

  [Page] https://localhost/
  [Response] 200
  [Cookies] []
  [Headers] {"content-type":["text/html; charset=UTF-8"]}
* I click "Login"
  [Page] https://localhost/site/login
  [Response] 200
  [Cookies] []
  [Headers] {"content-type":["text/html; charset=UTF-8"]}
* I am on page "site/login"
  [Page] https://localhost/site/login
  [Response] 200
  [Cookies] []
  [Headers] {"content-type":["text/html; charset=UTF-8"]}
* I see element "input",{"id":"userform-email"}
* I see element "input",{"id":"userform-password"}
* I fill field {"id":"userform-email"},"foo"
* I fill field {"id":"userform-password"},"bar"
* I click "Submit"
  [Uri] https://localhost/site/login
  [Method] POST
  [Parameters] {"UserForm[email]":"foo","UserForm[password]":"bar"}
  [Page] https://localhost/site/login
  [Response] 200
  [Cookies] []
  [Headers] {"content-type":["text/html; charset=UTF-8"]}
* I see current url equals "/site/login"
* I fill field {"id":"userform-email"},"admin@example.com"
* I fill field {"id":"userform-password"},"admin"
* I click "Submit"
  [Uri] https://localhost/site/login
  [Method] POST
  [Parameters] {"UserForm[email]":"admin@example.com","UserForm[password]":"admin"}
  [Headers] {"location":["https://localhost/site/index"],"content-type":["text/html; ch
arset=UTF-8"]}
  [Page] https://localhost/site/login
  [Response] 302
  [Cookies] []
  [Headers] {"location":["https://localhost/site/index"],"content-type":["text/html; ch
arset=UTF-8"]}
  [Redirecting to] https://localhost/site/index
  [Page] https://localhost/site/index
  [Response] 200
  [Cookies] []
  [Headers] {"content-type":["text/html; charset=UTF-8"]}
* I see current url equals "/site/index"
 PASSED

^^^^^^^^^^^^^^^^^^^^^^^^^^^^^^^^^^^^^^^^^^^^^^^^^^^^^^^^^^^^^^^^^^^^^^^^^^^^^^^^^^^^^^^^^^^^^^^^
-------------------------------------------------------------------------------------------


Time: 1.06 seconds, Memory: 22.75Mb
```

The Yii2 module provides several methods that can be used when running both functional and unit tests. For a complete list of the methods provided by the Yii2 Codeception module, ensure that you refer to the Yii2 Codeception module page at `http://codeception.com/docs/modules/Yii2`.

Acceptance testing

The last type of testing we can automate with Codeception is called acceptance testing. It is very similar to functional testing, with the exception that your application is tested using a real browser rather than a simulated one. This gives the advantage of being able to completely simulate end user behavior. Acceptance testing doesn't have many of the limitations of functional testing, such as memory limitations, `$_COOKIE`, `$_SESSION`, and header limitations. Moreover, acceptance testing can be done by anyone on your team, as what is tested using acceptance testing replicates the work you would do to test manually. In fact, one of the only downsides of running acceptance tests is that due to the entire browser flow, acceptance tests can be extremely slow for specific tests. In this section, we'll cover how to set up and run acceptance testing with Codeception.

In this section, we'll be using the source code on the `functional_and_acceptance` branch located at `https://github.com/masteringyii/chapter10`.

Setting up acceptance testing

Like functional testing, acceptance testing requires some setup in order to get working with Yii2:

1. To get started, we first need to specify the browser we want to use. In our case, we'll be using a combination of PHP and browser. To do this, we first need to add the following to our `tests/acceptance.suite.yml` file. Additionally, since we want to take advantage of Yii2-specific plugins, we'll enable the Yii2 module as well:

```
---
class_name: AcceptanceTester
modules:
  enabled:

    -

      PhpBrowser:
        url: "http://localhost:8082"
```

```
    - \Helper\Acceptance
    - Yii2
config:
    Yii2:
        configFile: 'tests/config/acceptance.php'
```

> If we want to use a real browser, we can do that by enabling the
> WebDriver module by adding the following to our `modules:enabled`
> section:
>
> ```
>     - WebDriver:
>         url: http://localhost
>         browser: firefox
>         restart: true
> ```

2. Next, we need to rebuild our tests to include the added modules:

   ```
   $ ./vendor/bin/codecept build
   ```

3. Then, we need to configure our `tests/acceptance/_bootstrap.php` file so
   that we can load our Yii2 app in our tests. Fortunately, this is more or less the
   same as our functional test bootstrap file:

```php
<?php
    define('DS', DIRECTORY_SEPARATOR);

    defined('YII_TEST_ENTRY_URL') or
    define('YII_TEST_ENTRY_URL', parse_url(\Codeception\
    Configuration::config()['config']['test_entry_url'],
    PHP_URL_PATH));
        defined('YII_TEST_ENTRY_FILE') or
    define('YII_TEST_ENTRY_FILE', dirname(dirname(__DIR__)
    ) . '/web/index-test.php');

    // Define our application_env variable as
    provided by nginx/apache
    if (!defined('APPLICATION_ENV'))
    {
        if (getenv('APPLICATION_ENV') != false)
            define('APPLICATION_ENV',
            getenv('APPLICATION_ENV'));
        else
        define('APPLICATION_ENV', 'prod');
    }
    $env = require(__DIR__ . '/../../config/env.php');
```

```
// comment out the following two lines when
deployed to production
defined('YII_DEBUG') or define('YII_DEBUG',
$env['debug']);
defined('YII_ENV') or define('YII_ENV',
APPLICATION_ENV);
require(__DIR__ . '/../../vendor/autoload.php');
require(__DIR__ . '/../../vendor/yiisoft/yii2/Yii.php');
$config = require(__DIR__ . '/../../config/web.php');

Yii::setAlias('@tests', dirname(__DIR__));

(new yii\web\Application($config));
```

4. Next, we need to define our `tests/config/acceptance.php` file as follows:

```php
<?php
$_SERVER['SCRIPT_FILENAME'] = YII_TEST_ENTRY_FILE;
$_SERVER['SCRIPT_NAME'] = YII_TEST_ENTRY_URL;

/**
 * Application configuration for functional tests
 */
return require(__DIR__ . '/../../config/web.php');
```

5. Then, we need to generate our first acceptance test using the `generate:cept` command:

```
$ ./vendor/bin/codecept generate:cept acceptance Page
```

6. Finally, we can run our newly created test by running the run command:

```
$ ./vendor/bin/codecept run acceptance
```

```
Codeception PHP Testing Framework v2.1.3
Powered by PHPUnit 4.8.10 by Sebastian Bergmann and contributors.


Acceptance Tests (2) --------------------------------------------------------

Perform actions and see result (PageCept)                              Ok
Perform actions and see result (PageclearCept)                         Ok
-----------------------------------------------------------------------------



Time: 176 ms, Memory: 12.50Mb
```

Note that we're passing the required `APPLICATION_ENV` variable to our built-in server. Additionally, we're using a `8082` high port, as defined previously in our `tests/acceptance.suite.yml` file. The high port number is to avoid the need to run PHP's built-in server with root access, which is required for ports under `1024`.

Examples of acceptance tests

Since acceptance tests are extremely similar to functional tests, we can reuse a lot of the same tools and methods we used in the previous section. For instance, we can write an acceptance test to check the home page for the links and text we looked for earlier in our functional tests, as follows:

```php
<?php
$I = new AcceptanceTester($scenario);
$I->wantTo('Verify that homepage loads');
$I->amOnPage('/');
$I->amOnPage('site/index');
$I->see('Now you\'re thinking with widgets!');
$I->see('Home');
$I->see('Login');
$I->see('Register');
```

Note that the only substantial difference here is the usage of `AcceptanceTester` instead of `FunctionalTester`. Running our tests in the verbose mode now will reveal the following:

```
$ ./vendor/bin/codecept run acceptance -vv
```

```
Acceptance Tests (1) ----------------------------------------------------------

Modules: PhpBrowser, \Helper\Acceptance, Yii2
-------------------------------------------------------------------------------

Verify that homepage loads (PageCept)
Scenario:

* I am on page "/"

  [Page] https://localhost/
  [Response] 200
  [Cookies] []
  [Headers] {"content-type":["text/html; charset=UTF-8"]}
* I am on page "site/index"
  [Page] https://localhost/site/index
  [Response] 200
  [Cookies] {"_csrf":"905c7478999c93c59f7a4d05f66c549922067adf7fcc35ed43890c30a4520b81a
:2:{i:0;s:5:"_csrf";i:1;s:32:"7ahDi7DQoNnzPJq3kUCCtggrklkVbM-L";}"}
  [Headers] {"content-type":["text/html; charset=UTF-8"]}
* I see "Now you're thinking with widgets!"
* I see "Home"
* I see "Login"
* I see "Register"
  PASSED

^^^^^^^^^^^^^^^^^^^^^^^^^^^^^^^^^^^^^^^^^^^^^^^^^^^^^^^^^^^^^^^^^^^^^^^^^^^^^^^^^^


-------------------------------------------------------------------------------



Time: 221 ms, Memory: 17.50Mb
```

Fixtures

The last testing component we'll talk about in this chapter is fixtures. **Fixtures** are an important part of testing as they enable us to set up our application state to a known and precise state before running our unit tests. Unlike these other test types, however, fixtures are provided directly by Yii2 and integrate into Codeception via the Yii2 Codeception module.

In this section, we'll be using the source code on the `fixtures` branch located at https://github.com/masteringyii/chapter10.

Creating fixtures

To get started with using fixtures, we first need to install the required composer dependencies and then add some configuration to our `config/console.php` file:

1. First, we need to make sure that the `yii2-faker` composer package is installed:

   ```
   $ composer require --dev yii2-faker
   ```

2. Alternatively, the `yii2-faker` extension can be installed by adding the following to your `composer.json`'s `require-dev` section and then by executing `composer update`:

   ```
   "yiisoft/yii2-faker": "*",
   ```

3. Then, we need to add the relevant section to our console configuration file:

   ```php
   <?php

   Yii::setAlias('@tests', dirname(__DIR__) . '/tests');

   return [
       // [...],
       'controllerMap' => [
           'fixture' => [
               'class' => 'yii\faker\FixtureController',
           ],
       ],
       'controllerNamespace' => 'app\commands',
       // [...]
   ];
   ```

4. Finally, we need to define a configuration file for our unit tests to load from `tests/config/unit.php`. To keep things simple, we'll just load our web configuration file:

   ```php
   <?php
   /**
    * Application configuration for functional tests
    */
   return require(__DIR__ . '/../../config/web.php');
   ```

With the required extension installed, we can create and load fixtures into our app via the `./yii` command-line tool:

```
./yii help fixture
```

```
SUB-COMMANDS

- fixture/generate          Generates fixtures and fill them with Faker data.
- fixture/generate-all      Generates all fixtures template path that can be found.
- fixture/load (default)    Loads the specified fixture data.
- fixture/templates         Lists all available fixtures template files.
- fixture/unload            Unloads the specified fixtures.

To see the detailed information about individual sub-commands, enter:

  yii help <sub-command>
```

Defining fixtures

To define new fixtures, we can either extend `yii\test\Fixture` (for general fixtures) or `yii\test\ActiveFixture` (for ActiveRecord entries) and place our newly created classes in the `tests/fixtures` folder of our application. After defining a new fixture, we'll then want to declare the model class we'll want to use for fixtures. As an example, let's create a fixture of our `app\models\User` class, as shown in the following example:

```php
<?php
namespace app\tests\fixtures;

use yii\test\ActiveFixture;

class UserFixture extends ActiveFixture
{
    public $modelClass = 'app\models\User';
}
```

Now that we've defined our fixture class, we need to create the data that our fixture will populate. When using `yii\test\ActiveFixture`, we'll want to place our data files in `@tests/fixtures/data/<database_table_name>.php` or `@tests/fixtures/data/user.php`, in our case. In this fixture file, we'll provide all the required mock data that we want to test against:

```php
<?php return [
    'user1' => [
        'id'        => 1,
        'email'     => 'jane.doe@example.com',
```

```
        'password' => '$2y$13$iqINH3RvfW29zPupoz2Zeu9cTXUPosjn1V
.yhihP0iZEWFkEPSl6.',
        'first_name'  => 'Jane',
        'last_name'   => 'Doe',
        'role_id'     => 1,
        'created_at'  => 1448926013,
        'updated_at'  => 1448926013
    ],
    'admin' => [
        'id'          => 4,
        'email'       => 'admin@example.com',
        'password'    => '$2y$13$uHCvsJWJr.M0vRcDlhWhVO9tTPLh8qD9
.ngnhwThzzwGNC62.Ugl6',
        'first_name'  => 'Site',
        'last_name'   => 'Administrator',
        'role_id'        => 2,
        'created_at'  => 1448926013,
        'updated_at'  => 1448926013
    ]
];
```

Our fixtures can be loaded by calling the `fixture` command with the appropriate namespace:

```
$ ./yii fixture/load User --namespace=app/tests/fixtures
```

Fixtures can then be unloaded using the `fixture/unload` command:

```
$ ./yii fixture/unload User --namespace=app/tests/fixtures
```

By default, Yii2 will try to load our fixtures from the `@app/tests/unit/fixtures` folder. In the previous examples, we overwrote this behavior by supplying the `--namespace` parameter. To avoid having to write this each time, we can modify our console configuration file as follows:

```php
<?php

Yii::setAlias('@tests', dirname(__DIR__) . '/tests');

return [
    // [...],
    'controllerMap' => [
        'fixture' => [
            'class' => 'yii\faker\FixtureController',
            'namespace' => 'tests\fixtures',
        ],
    ],
    // [...]
];
```

With this change, we can load and unload our fixtures without the need to specify a namespace.

Using fixtures in unit tests

Now that we know how to create and load fixtures, let's explore how to load them as part of our tests. To get started with testing with fixtures, we first need to create a new unit test for our fixtures to run in. As a reminder, new unit tests in Codeception can be generated as follows:

```
$ ./vendor/bin/codecept generate:test un it UserFixture
```

After creating our unit test, we need to modify our newly created `UserFixtureTest` in `tests/unit/UnitFixtureTest.php` with several changes:

1. First, we need to properly namespace our test and include our `UserFixture` class:

    ```php
    <?php

    namespace app\tests\unit\UserFixtureTest;

    use app\tests\fixtures\UserFixture;
    use app\models\User;
    use Yii;
    ```

2. Next, we need to have our `UserFixtureTest` extend `\yii\codeception\DbTestCase` and include the unit test configuration file that we created previously:

    ```php
    class UserFixtureTest extends \yii\codeception\DbTestCase
    {
        /**
         * @var \UnitTester
         */
        protected $tester;

        public $appConfig = "@app/tests/config/unit.php";
    }
    ```

3. Finally, we need to tell our test case to load our `UserFixture` class:

    ```php
    public function fixtures()
    {
        return [
            'users' => UserFixture::className(),
        ];
    }
    ```

Now, after every test we create within our newly created `UserFixtureTest` class, our previously created fixtures will be loaded into our database before each test and then removed after the test is complete. For instance, we can create the following test to verify that password verification works:

```
public function testValidatePassword()
{
    $user = User::find()->where(['id' => 1])->one();
    $this->assertTrue($user->validatePassword('password1'));
    $this->assertFalse($user->validatePassword('password2'));
    unset($user);

    $user = User::find()->where(['id' => 4])->one();
    $this->assertTrue($user->validatePassword('admin'));
    $this->assertFalse($user->validatePassword('notadmin'));
    unset($user);
}
```

Our newly created tests and fixtures can then be run with the following command:

$ ./vendor/bin/codecept run unit

```
Powered by PHPUnit 4.8.10 by Sebastian Bergmann and contributors.

Unit Tests (1) --------------------------------------------------------------
Test vali (app\tests\unit\UserFixtureTest\UserFixtureTest::testValidatePassword) Ok..
----------------------------------------------------------------------------



Time: 8.79 seconds, Memory: 15.25Mb
```

At the beginning of this test, our fixtures will be loaded, and then our tests will run. After our test runs, our fixtures will be unloaded, and then we can run another test. The use of fixtures in this case prevents the results of one test from affecting the results of another.

Automatic change testing

An important aspect of testing is ensuring that your tests are run regularly and often. If you're following the test-driven development philosophy, you should be writing your tests before writing code and adapting your tests as new code is added. While this will give you a good idea of what is working and what isn't, it can be extremely time-consuming, and it doesn't cover cases where team members make changes but either don't write tests or don't run them before committing and pushing them to your DCVS repository.

The best way to ensure that your tests are run after every change is to use a third-party service, such as Travis CI. A tool such as Travis CI will add a webbook to your repository, and after every commit, it can be configured to run all your tests and notify you if and when your tests ever start failing.

> In general, you should always verify that your code runs and that your tests pass before committing it to your repository.

Using Travis CI as an example, let's add our repository to Travis CI and enable automated builds:

1. To get started with Travis CI, we first need to log in to `https://travis-ci.org` with our GitHub account and then navigate to our profile at `https://travis-ci.org/profile`.

> Travis CI has tight coupling with GitHub and does not work with other services, such as GitLab or Bitbucket. The service is free only for public repositories. There are many other services, however, that can perform the same service as Travis CI, such as Atlassian Bamboo, drone.io, circleci.com, GitLab CI, and others. Before using a continuous integration tool, ensure that you do your research to determine what is best for your team. For projects that you don't mind being public, Travis CI provides a good free option.

2. After navigating to your profile, you need to enable Travis CI for your repository. Thanks to the tight coupling Travis CI has with GitHub, this is as simple as toggling a single switch.

3. After establishing your connection to Travis CI, you need to create a `.travis.yml` file in your repository. This file contains instructions on how to build and test your project. While there are many different possible configurations and matrices that Travis CI can work with, we'll be using a relatively simple one, as shown in the next section:

```
sudo: false

env:
  - "APPLICATION_ENV=dev"

language: php

cache:
  directories:
    - vendor

php:
  - 5.6
  - 7

install:
  - composer selfupdate
  - composer global require "fxp/composer-asset-plugin:~1.0"
  - composer install -o -n
```

```
before_script:
  - ./yii migrate/up --interactive=0

script:
  - ./vendor/bin/codecept run
```

4. Our `.travis.yml` file contains several sections:

    ° The `language` section defines what language we want to use when Travis CI runs our build.

    ° The `cache` option exists simply to speed up our build and test process. At the end of each successful build, Travis CI will cache the contents of our `vendor/folder`, which will reduce the time it takes for Composer to install all the required dependencies.

    ° The `php` section lists all the PHP versions we want to test against. Generally, we want to test against the current and next versions of PHP so that when that version comes out, we're ready to start using it. Testing against future versions of PHP allows us to quickly adapt our code to take advantage of new performance enhancements of new PHP versions.

    ° The `install` section allows us to define software that needs to be installed before our build runs. In this section, we define things such as the composer-asset-plugin and our composer dependencies.

    ° The `before_script` section defines things that should occur before our `build/test` script executes.

    ° Finally, the `script` section defines what we want to build or test.

5. After defining our `.travis.yml` file, we need to simply commit the file to our repository. Since we've already linked Travis CI to our GitHub project, pushing our project will automatically trigger a build that we can view on Travis CI. On Travis CI, we can view a history of all the builds that have occurred for our project. In the event that someone pushes code to our repository that breaks our build, we will receive a notification and can notify the person who broke our tests to fix their code before trying again. Additionally, we can view a complete build output for each commit, which gives us insight into what is happening in each build.

 As an example, the repository for this chapter was linked to Travis CI. You can see builds in action by navigating to `https://travis-ci.org/masteringyii`.

Summary

We learned quite a bit about testing in this chapter! We first covered how to set up and configure Codeception to run within our project. We then covered how to set up unit, functional, and acceptance testing in order to ensure that we had adequate test coverage of our code base. Next, we covered how to create and use fixtures to mock data so that our tests run with a consistent test base. Finally, we covered how to automate the testing of our code with Travis CI, a third-party continuous integration service.

In the next chapter, we'll cover how to use Yii2's internationalization and localization features to make our applications capable of running in multiple languages.

11
Internationalization and Localization

When developing modern web applications, we often find the need to ensure that our language is readable to users who speak and read languages different from our own. To help facilitate this, Yii2 provides built-in support for both internationalization (i18n) and localization (l10n). **Internationalization** is the process of planning and implementing messages and views such that they can be easily adapted into other languages. On the other hand, **localization** is the process of adapting our applications to a particular language or culture, and including things such as the look and feel of our application to match the accepted presentation of information to speakers of a given language or users in a given region or market. In this chapter, we'll discover how we can use Yii2's built-in features to translate and localize our applications into multiple languages.

i18n and l10n are numeronyms, not acronyms. Internationalization is abbreviated to i18n because it begins with the letter "I", is followed by 18 more characters, and ends with the letter "N". Similarly, localization shortens to l10n because it starts with the letter "L", has 10 more letters, and then ends with the letter "N". These abbreviations simply exist to shorten the word and have no other meaning. In this chapter, we'll use both the full and abbreviated versions to refer to both words.

Configuring Yii2 and PHP

Before we can start using Yii2's localization features, we first need to make sure the `intl` PHP extension is installed. This extension is used to provide Yii2 with the majority of the i18n features, including Yii2's message and date formatters. While Yii2 has some built-in fallbacks in case this extension is not installed, it is highly recommended that you install it beforehand.

The intl extension

Many default PHP installations come with the `intl` extension built into the PHP package, but many do not. Fortunately, there are several ways to check whether the `intl` extension is installed. For those who prefer viewing this information in a web browser, simply create a blank PHP file in your webroot containing the following and scan the output to check whether the `intl` extension exists and is enabled:

```
<?php phpinfo();
```

If you prefer using the command line, you can run the following command to check whether intl is installed with your PHP instance:

php -m | grep intl

If the `intl` extension does not appear in any output, you can either install it through your systems package manager (`apt` or `yum` depending upon your OS), or you can install it manually. Generally speaking, the extension can be compiled and installed manually through the `pecl` command:

sudo pecl install intl

> If you're installing the `intl` extension from the source, you'll need to make sure that you have the `intl` library installed, preferably version 49 or higher. If your system has an outdated version of the `intl` library, you can download and compile a newer version from http://site.icu-project.org/download. Additionally, the time zone data shipped with your `intl` library may be outdated. Ensure that you refer to the `intl` documentation for information on how to update your `intl` time zone data at http://userguide.icu-project.org/datetime/timezone#TOC-Updating-the-Time-Zone-Data.

After the compilation finishes, you can then add the following to your `php.ini` configuration file:

```
extension=intl.so
```

After restarting your web server and PHP process, you should see the `intl` extension appear using one of the previously listed commands.

 More information on how to install the `intl` extension can be found on the PHP manual page at `https://secure.php.net/manual/en/intl.installation.php`.

The application language

Before we can start using Yii2's translation features, we need to define the application our language is written in. Application languages in Yii2 are defined by a unique ID consisting of a language ID as defined by the ISO-639 format and a region ID defined by the ISO-3166 format. As an example, `en-US` represents English as the spoken language in the United States of America.

 Details on ISO-639 can be found at `http://www.loc.gov/standards/iso639-2/`, and details on IISO-3166 can be found at `https://www.iso.org/obp/ui/#search`.

Yii2 defines two language properties within our configuration file that we can define. The first `sourceLanguage` property represents the language or locale our application is written in and generally does not change during the request life cycle of our application. The second, `language`, represents the language or locale that our user is using, and it can be changed by the end user at any point in time (typically through the use of a `language` selector widget placed somewhere on the page). Combined, these two configuration options allow us to inform Yii2 about how it should treat messages we wish to be translated. Within our `config/web.php` or `config/console.php` configuration files, these two options can be set as follows:

```
return [
    'language' => 'ru-RU',
    'sourceLanguage' => 'en-US',
];
```

 By default, Yii2 will set the `sourceLanguage` property to `en-US`.

Programmatically setting the application language

If you're developing a multilingual site, rather than specifying a single default language, you may want to allow the user to select their language from a drop-down list and change your language programmatically. To do this, simply define the `Yii::$app->language` property within your code with the language code of your choice.

When setting the language property programmatically, you'll typically want to store the user's language setting either with their user information or as a session variable. Additionally, you'll want to ensure that you apply the language setting before Yii2 begins processing your messages. A good place to set this would be early in your controller flow, such as in the `init()` method of our controller.

Dynamically setting the application language

In addition to manually setting the application language within our controller, we can also use the content negotiator filter (`yii\filters\ContentNegotiator`) to determine the user's language from their `Accept-Language` headers sent by their browser. To use the content negotiator filter, we simply need to add `yii\filters\ContentNegotiator` to the `bootstrap` section of your `config/web.php` configuration file and specify the languages that we want to support automatically:

```
return [
    // [...],
    'bootstrap' => [
        [
            'class' => 'yii\filters\ContentNegotiator',
            'languages' => [
                'en',
                'de',
            ],
        ],
    ],
];
```

The languages property specifies which languages Yii2 will automatically set `Yii::$app->language` to if they are present in the `Accept-Language` headers. In the previous example, we only set the language to en or de. If a language other than the ones listed in our application configuration is present in our `Accept-Language` headers, we'll default to the language specified in our `sourceLanguage` property.

Rather than being set globally, we can also set a content negotiator within our controller's `behaviors()` methods and specify the languages we want to support within that controller. This is beneficial when you have a module that may support more or different languages than your base application. Within our controllers, we can configure `yii\filters\ContentNegotiator` as follows:

```
public function behaviors()
{
    return [
        [
            'class' => 'yii\filters\ContentNegotiator',
            'languages' => [
                'en',
                'de',
            ],
        ],
    ];
}
```

> This `yii\filters\ContentNegotiator` path can provide more features than just setting the application language. For more information on the content negotiation filter, ensure that you check out the Yii2 documentation at `http://www.yiiframework.com/doc-2.0/yii-filters-contentnegotiator.html`.

Message translations

Yii2's message translation service translates a given text message from the source language to another by looking up the message to be translated in a message source file. If a message is found in a source for the target language, that string is returned instead of the original message. If the translated text is not found, Yii2 will return the original message.

The use of Yii2's message translation service is extremely straightforward. The first step toward translating messages in Yii2 is to wrap any and all messages you want translated in the `Yii::t()` static method, which can be called as follows:

```
Yii::t('app', 'My message to be translated');
```

The first parameter indicates the category we want to store our messages in, and the second parameter indicates the message we wanted to be translated.

Message sources

Before Yii2 can translate our messages, however, we first need to define a message source that will store our base messages and our translated message files. Yii2 provides three distinct message source options:

- `yii\i18n\PhpMessageSource` stores message files in a key value array format

- `yii\i18n/DbMessageSource` stores messages in a database table

- `yii\i18n\GettextMessageSource` uses GNU Gettext MO or PO files to store translated messages

The message source we wish to use can be declared in your application configuration file within the components section, as follows:

```php
<?php return [
    // [...],
    'components' => [
        // [...],
        'i18n' => [
            'translations' => [
                'app*' => [
                    'class' => 'yii\i18n\PhpMessageSource',
                ],
            ],
        ],
    ]
];
```

In the previous code block, the message source is provided by `yii\i18n\PhpMessageSource`. The `app*` pattern indicates that all messages that begin with `app` should be handled by the specified message source. By default, Yii2 will store messages within the `@app/messages` folder and will default the source language to `en-US`; however, this behavior can be changed by specifying the `basePath` and `sourceLanguage` properties within the category block, respectively, as shown here:

```php
<?php return [
    // [...],
    'components' => [
        // [...],
        'i18n' => [
            'translations' => [
                'app*' => [
                    'class' => 'yii\i18n\PhpMessageSource',
                    //'basePath' => '@app/messages',
                    //'sourceLanguage' => 'en-US',
                ],
```

```
            ],
        ],
    ]
];
```

Furthermore, Yii2 will create message files with the same name as the category. This behavior can be altered by specifying the `fileMap` property within the category configuration. Unless otherwise specified with the `fileMap` property, all messages will be stored in `@app/messages/<language>/<category>.php`.

Default translations

Yii2 also allows us to create fallback messages for categories that don't match other translations. This can be set by declaring a `*` category within our configuration file, as shown in the following example:

```php
<?php return [
    // [...],
    'components' => [
        // [...],
        'i18n' => [
            'translations' => [
                '*' => [
                'class' => 'yii\i18n\PhpMessageSource'
            ],
            ],
        ],
    ]
];
```

Framework messages

In addition to specifying default messages, we can also modify the built-in messages that Yii2 provides natively. By default, Yii2 comes with several translations for things such as validation errors and other basic strings, all of which are stored within the `yii` category. As there may be times where the default Yii messages may not be appropriate or accurate, you can redefine the default message by setting the `yii` category within your configuration file:

```php
<?php return [
    // [...],
    'components' => [
        // [...],
        'i18n' => [
            'translations' => [
```

```
            'yii' => [
                'class' => 'yii\i18n\PhpMessageSource',
                'sourceLanguage' => 'en-US',
                'basePath' => '@app/messages'
            ],
            ],
        ],
    ]
];
```

Handling missing translations

If a message translation is missing from the source file, Yii2 will display the original message content by default. While it's convenient to ensure that our site displays at least something, this behavior can be troublesome to debug and identify. Moreover, we may want to perform additional processing in the event of missing translations. Fortunately, we can accomplish this by creating an event handler for the missingTranslation event triggered by yii\i18n\MessageSource, as shown in the following example:

```php
<?php return [
    // [...],
    'components' => [
        // [...],
        'i18n' => [
            'translations' => [
                'app*' => [
                    'class' => 'yii\i18n\PhpMessageSource',
                    'on missingTranslation' =>
                    ['app\components\TranslationEventHandler',
                    'handleMissingTranslation']
                ],
            ],
        ],
    ]
];
```

As an example, we can write an event handler to output something notable:

```php
<?php

namespace app\components;

use yii\i18n\MissingTranslationEvent;
```

```
class TranslationEventHandler
{
    public static function
    handleMissingTranslation(MissingTranslationEvent $event)
    {
        $event->translatedMessage = "@{$event->category}.
        {$event->message}-{$event->language}@";
    }
}
```

The event handler is only processed for messages in that category. If
you wish to handle the same event for multiple categories, you must
assign the event handler to each category or, alternatively, assign it to
the * category.

Generating message files

After configuring our message sources, we need to generate our message files. To do
this, we will use the `message` command:

1. The first step toward generating our messages files is to create a
   configuration file that will define what languages we want to support as well
   as specific paths for where the messages should be stored. This can be done
   by running the following command:

   `./yii message/config path/to/messagesconfig.php`

2. Depending upon the languages we previously specified in our web or
   console configuration file, this will generate something similar to the
   following:

```
<?php return [
    // string, required, root directory of all source files
    'sourcePath' => __DIR__ . DIRECTORY_SEPARATOR . '..',

    // array, required, list of language codes that the
    extracted messages
    // should be translated to. For example, ['zh-CN',
    'de'].

    'languages' => ['de'],
    // string, the name of the function for translating
    messages.
    // Defaults to 'Yii::t'. This is used as a mark to find
    the messages to be
```

```
// translated. You may use a string for single function
name or an array for
// multiple function names.
'translator' => 'Yii::t',

// boolean, whether to sort messages by keys when
merging new messages
// with the existing ones. Defaults to false, which
means the new (untranslated)
// messages will be separated from the old
(translated) ones.
'sort' => false,

// boolean, whether to remove messages that no
longer appear in the source code.
// Defaults to false, which means each of these
messages will be enclosed with a pair of '@@' marks.
'removeUnused' => false,

// array, list of patterns that specify which
files/directories should NOT be processed.
// If empty or not set, all files/directories will
be processed.
// A path matches a pattern if it contains the
pattern string at its end. For example,
// '/a/b' will match all files and directories
ending with '/a/b';
// the '*.svn' will match all files and directories
whose name ends with '.svn'.
// and the '.svn' will match all files and directories
named exactly '.svn'.
// Note, the '/' characters in a pattern matches
both '/' and '\'.
// See helpers/FileHelper::findFiles() description
for more details on pattern matching rules.
'only' => ['*.php'],

// array, list of patterns that specify which files (not
directories) should be processed.
// If empty or not set, all files will be processed.
// Please refer to "except" for details about the patterns.
// If a file/directory matches both a pattern in "only" and
"except", it will NOT be processed.
'except' => [
    '.svn',
    '.git',
```

```
            '.gitignore',
            '.gitkeep',
            '.hgignore',
            '.hgkeep',
            '/messages',
             '/vendor,
    ],

    // 'php' output format is for saving messages to php files.
    'format' => 'php',

    // Root directory containing message translations.
    'messagePath' => __DIR__,

    // boolean, whether the message file should be overwritten
with the merged messages
    'overwrite' => true
];
```

3. For the most part, the default values provided by Yii2 in this file should be sufficient. The only values you should consider changing are the `languages` option and the `format` option. Ensure that you set these values appropriately before proceeding.

4. After making the required changes to our `messagesconfig.php` file, we can generate our message files by running the message command directly, as shown in the following example:

   `./yii message path/to/messagesconfig.php`

5. The `message` command is an extremely powerful tool that allows us to quickly generate messages files that can be handed off to translators. Several options exist within the configuration file to make message translation easier. For example, the `removedUnused` parameter can be set to `true` to automatically remove strings from our message file if they are no longer listed in our source code. Additionally, by setting the `overwrite` parameter to `true`, we can run the `message` command over and over again to regenerate our translation files.

> Note that the `message` command doesn't support all path aliases. When working with a messages file, it's recommended that you use absolute paths. Additionally, it's recommended that you store your `messagesconfig.php` file within the `messages/` directory of your application.

Message formatting

When translating messages, you may want to inject variables or data from your models into the message. To do this, we simply need to embed a `placeholder` within our message and then define what the `placeholder` is as a parameter within the third property of our `Yii::t()` method. For example, if we want to greet our user using their name, we can do that as follows:

```php
<?php
// $model = User::find(1)->one();
echo Yii::t('app', 'Good Morning {name}', [
    'name' => $model->first_name
]);
```

As an alternative to named parameters, we can also use positional parameters, as shown in the following example:

```php
$price = 500;
$count = 2;
$subtotal = 1000;
echo \Yii::t('app', 'Price: ${0}, Count: {1}, Subtotal: ${2}', [
    $price,
    $count,
    $subtotal
]);
```

Yii2 also supports parameter formatting for numbers, currency, dates, times, original, and plural data. More information can be found on the Yii2 API at `http://www.yiiframework.com/doc-2.0/yii-i18n-formatter.html` and under the parameter formatting section of the Yii2 guide at `http://www.yiiframework.com/doc-2.0/guide-tutorial-i18n.html#parameter-formatting`.

Viewing file translations

As an alternative to translating individual messages, we can also translate entire view files by saving a translated view file within the subdirectory of our `views` folder. As an example, supposing that we had a view script located at `views/site/login.php`, we could create a Spanish view file for `es-MX` by placing a translated message file in `views/site/es-MX/login.php`. Assuming that our target and source language is appropriately set, Yii2 will automatically render the translated file instead of the base file when our target language is set to `es-MX`.

Note that if the source and target language are the same, the original view will be rendered regardless of the existence of a translated view file.

Additionally, the use of view file translations doesn't follow the DRY pattern we've emphasized throughout this book. Also, handing off complete HTML files with PHP code to your translators may make the translation of these files difficult, as the translation industry is based upon string translations rather than strings within code translations. To keep your application DRY and avoid any issues that may arise during the translation process, it is highly recommended that you use the previously mentioned message translation method rather than view file translations.

Module translations

As separate entities, modules should contain their own message files separate from your application message files. The recommended way to use messages within modules is as follows:

1. Within the `init()` method of your module, define a new translation section for your module:

```
parent::init();
Yii::$app->i18n->translations['modules/mymodule*'] = [
    'class' => 'yii\i18n\PhpMessageSource',
    'sourceLanguage' => 'en-US',
    'basePath' => '@app/modules/mymodule/messages'
];
```

2. Create a static method wrapper for `Yii::t()`:

```
public static function t($category, $message, $params = [],
$language = null)
{
    return Yii::t('modules/mymodule/' . $category, $message,
$params, $language);
}
```

3. Finally, create a separate message configuration file within the `messages/` directory of your module that specifies the translator to be `<ModuleName>::t`:

```
<?php return [
    'sourcePath' => __DIR__ . DIRECTORY_SEPARATOR . '..',
    'languages' => ['de'],
    'translator' => 'MyModule::t',
```

```
            'sort' => false,
            'removeUnused' => false,
            'only' => ['*.php'],
            'except' => [
                '.svn',
                '.git',
                '.gitignore',
                '.gitkeep',
                '.hgignore',
                '.hgkeep',
                '/messages',
                '/vendor'
            ],
            'format' => 'php',
            'messagePath' => __DIR__,
            'overwrite' => true
    ];
```

Messages within our module can then be translated by calling `MyModule::t()`.
Additionally, translated message files can be generated by running the following
command:

```
./yii message modules/mymodule/messages/messages.php
```

Widget translations

In a similar vein, widgets can also have their own message translation files by
following the same process outlined for modules. Using our `GreetingWidget` class
we created in *Chapter 5, Modules, Widgets, and Helpers* would look as follows:

```php
<?php
namespace app\components;

use yii\base\Widget;
use yii\helpers\Html;

use Yii;
class GreetingWidget extends Widget
{
    public $name = null;

    public $greeting;
```

```
public function init()
{
    parent::init();

    Yii::$app->i18n->translations['widgets/GreetingWidget*'] = [
        'class' => 'yii\i18n\PhpMessageSource',
        'sourceLanguage' => 'en-US',
        'basePath' => '@app/components/widgets/GreetingWidget'
    ];

    $hour = date('G');

    if ( $hour >= 5 && $hour <= 11 )
        $this->greeting = GreetingWidget::t("Good Morning");
    else if ( $hour >= 12 && $hour <= 18 )
        $this->greeting = GreetingWidget::t("Good Afternoon");
    else if ( $hour >= 19 || $hours <= 4 )
        $this->greeting = GreetingWidget::t("Good Evening");
}

public function run()
{
    if ($this->name === null)
        return HTML::encode($this->greeting);
    else
        return HTML::encode($this->greeting . ', ' . $this->name);
}

    public static function t($category, $message, $params = [],
$language = null)
    {
        return Yii::t('widgets/GreetingWidget/' . $category, $message,
$params, $language);
    }
}
```

Consequently, a call to `GreetingWidget::t()` will render a translated message that's specific to our widget. Additionally, because widgets support view rendering, they can also support completely translated view files by following the same process outlined previously.

Summary

Yii2 provides powerful tools to support internationalization and localization within our application. In this chapter, we covered how to generate and store message source files, how to generate message and view translations, and how to support translations within modules and widgets. In the next chapter, we'll cover Yii2's performance feature, as well as explore several built-in security features that Yii2 offers.

12

Performance and Security

Out of the box, Yii2 is an both a performant and efficient PHP framework. It was designed to be as fast as possible while still providing a feature-rich toolbox to work with. There are many factors that determine the performance of our application that can negatively affect the performance of our application, such as long running queries and data generation. In this chapter, we'll cover several ways in which we can optimize and fine-tune Yii2 so that our applications remain performant. We'll also cover several important aspects of securing our code.

Caching

One of the easiest ways to improve the performance of our applications is to implement caching. By implementing caching within our application, we can reduce the amount of time it takes to generate and deliver data to our end users. With Yii2, we can cache everything from generated data, database queries, and even entire pages and page fragments. We can also instruct our browsers to cache pages for us. In this section, we'll cover several different caching techniques that we can implement within Yii2 in order to improve the performance of our application.

Caching data

Data caching is all about storing commonly generated data so that we can generate it once for a given period of time rather than on every request, and in Yii2, it is implemented through the cache component of our application. Yii2 provides a variety of different classes that we can use to cache data, all of which follow and use a consistent API by implementing the `yii\caching\Cache` abstract class.

This consistent API enables us to swap out our caching component with any of the caches listed in the following table without having to make any change to the code within our application:

Cache Name	Description	Class reference
yii\caching\ ApcCache	A cache that uses APC PHP extensions. On a single server configuration, an APC cache is very performant but suffers from compatibility issues if PHP Opcache is enabled.	http://www. yiiframework. com/doc-2.0/ yii-caching- apccache.html
yii\caching\ DbCache	A cache that uses a database table to store information.	http://www. yiiframework. com/doc-2.0/yii- caching-dbcache. html
yii\caching\ DummyCache	A placeholder cache that doesn't do any caching but serves as a standing for a real cache that can be used during development in order to ensure that our applications will work with a real cache.	http://www. yiiframework. com/doc-2.0/ yii-caching- dummycache.html
yii\caching\ FileCache	A cache that stores data in a file store and is recommended for the storing of pages or page fragments.	http://www. yiiframework. com/doc-2.0/ yii-caching- filecache.html
yii\caching\ MemCache	An in-memory cache that uses the PHP memcache or memcached extensions to store data.	http://www. yiiframework. com/doc-2.0/ yii-caching- memcache.html
yii\caching\ WinCache	A cache that uses the WinCache PHP extension.	http://www. yiiframework. com/doc-2.0/ yii-caching- wincache.html
yii\redis\Cache	A cache that implements the Redis key value store.	http://www. yiiframework. com/doc-2.0/yii- redis-cache.html
yii\caching\ XCache	A cache that uses the XCache PHP extension.	http://www. yiiframework. com/doc-2.0/yii- caching-xcache. html

> While each cache that's listed implements the `yii\caching\Cache` API, some caches, such as `yii\redis\Cache` and `yii\caching\MemCache`, require some additional configuration. Ensure that you refer to the class reference for the cache you decide to use in your application.

Using `yii\caching\FileCache` as an example, we can implement caching within our application by adding the following to our application configuration file:

```php
<?php return [
    // [...],
    'components' => [
        // [...]
        'cache' => [
            'class' => 'yii\caching\FileCache',
        ]
    ]
];
```

After implementing a specific caching system, we can then use our cache by referencing `Yii::$app->cache` within our application code.

As mentioned previously, each cache implements a consistent API, as defined by the `yii\caching\Cache` abstract class. Consequently, each cache provides the following methods that we can use to manipulate the data in our cache.

Method	Explanation
`yii\caching\Cache::add()`	Stores the value with a given key in the cache if it does not exist. If the cached item exists, no operation will occur.
`yii\caching\Cache::get()`	Retrieves an item with a given key from the cache.
`yii\caching\Cache::set()`	Sets an item with a given key into the cache with the option to specify an expiration date. The cached items set with an expiration date will automatically be expunged by either the underlying cache mechanism or by Yii2 itself.
`yii\caching\Cache::madd()`	Stores multiple items in the cache as a key value array. If a given cache key already exists, nothing will occur. In Yii 2.1, this method will be marked as deprecated and will be superseded by `yii\caching\Cache::multiAdd()`.

Method	Explanation
`yii\caching\Cache::mget()`	Retrieves multiple data keys from the cache simultaneously. In Yii 2.1, this method will be marked as deprecated and will be superseded by `yii\caching\Cache::multiGet()`.
`yii\caching\Cache::mset()`	Sets multiple cached items represented as a key value simultaneously into the cache. The cached items set with an expiration date will automatically be expunged by either the underlying cache mechanism or by Yii2 itself. In Yii 2.1, this method will be marked as deprecated and will be superseded by `yii\caching\Cache::multiSet()`.
`yii\caching\Cache::exists()`	Returns `true` or `false` if a given cache key exists within the cache.
`yii\caching\Cache::delete()`	Deletes a given cache key from the cache.
`yii\caching\Cache::flush()`	Flushes all the data from the cache.

For more information on each method and its use, refer to the noninherited public methods described by the `yii\caching\Cache` abstract class at `http://www.yiiframework.com/doc-2.0/yii-caching-cache.html`.

In general, our cache can be used by calling any of these methods against our `Yii::$app->cache` component, as shown in the following example:

```
$cache = Yii::$app->cache;
if ($cache->exists('example'))
    $data = $cache->get('example');
else
{
    // Generate data here...
    $data = [];
    // Cache the $data for 100 seconds
    $cache->set('example', $data, 100);
}
return $data;
```

Caching dependencies

In addition to setting a cache with a given expiration time, we can also cache data with certain dependencies, such as the last modification time of a file of an expression of some kind, and automatically expire our data should that dependency change. Yii2 provides several dependencies that we can use.

Method	Explanation	Class Reference
yii\caching\ChainedDependency	A dependency that allows us to chain multiple dependencies together and expire a cache item if any of the dependencies fail.	http://www.yiiframework.com/doc-2.0/yii-caching-chaineddependency.html
yii\caching\DbDependency	A dependency upon a given SQL query. Should the result of the query change, the cache will be invalidated.	http://www.yiiframework.com/doc-2.0/yii-caching-dbdependency.html
yii\caching\FileDependency	A dependency upon a file based upon the last modification time of the file.	http://www.yiiframework.com/doc-2.0/yii-caching-filedependency.html
yii\caching\ExpressionDependency	A dependency represented by a Boolean expression.	http://www.yiiframework.com/doc-2.0/yii-caching-expressiondependency.html
yii\caching\TagDependency	A dependency upon an array of tags that can be managed.	http://www.yiiframework.com/doc-2.0/yii-caching-tagdependency.html

 Check out the class reference for each dependency for more information on its available properties and methods.

Expanding upon our previous example, we can add a cache dependency, as shown in the following example. In the following code, we create a dependency upon a file called `data.csv`, which can contain a report or some other data that we wish to generate or import into our application:

```
$cache = Yii::$app->cache;
if ($cache->exists('example'))
    $data = $cache->get('example');
else
```

```
{
    // Generate data here...
    $data = [];

    $dependency = new \yii\caching\FileDependency(['fileName' =>
    'data.csv']);
    // Cache $data for 100 seconds using the key "example" with a
    FileDependency
    $cache->set('example', $data, 100, $dependency);
}
return $data;
```

Database query caching

With Yii2, we can also cache the result of a database query. To enable
query caching, we need to set three properties within our database
component: $enableQueryCache, which toggles the query cache on and off;
$queryCacheDuration, which sets the duration queries should be cached for;
and $queryCache, which specifies the cache component that should be used.

The following connection example illustrates how to enable the query cache:

```
<?php return [
    // [...],
    'components' => [
        // [...]
        'db' => [
            'class'        => 'yii\db\Connection',
            'dsn'          =>
        'mysql:host='127.0.0.1;dbname=masteringyii',
            'username'     => '<username>,
            'password'  => '<password>',
            'charset'   => 'utf8',

            'queryCacheEnabled'  => true,
            // 0 = Never expires
            'queryCacheDuration' => 0,
            'queryCache'       => 'cache'
        ],

    'cache' => [
            'class' => 'yii\caching\FileCache',
        ]
    ]
];
```

After configuring database query caching, we can then cache the results of a single DAO query by adding or chaining the cache method to our query, as shown in the following example:

```
$duration = 100; // 100 seconds
$results = $db->createCommand('SELECT * FROM users WHERE id=1;')-
>cache($duration)->queryOne();
```

Alternatively, if we have multiple queries we'd like to cache, we can call the yii\db\ Connection::cache() function directly:

```
$result = $db->cache(function ($db) {
    $result = $db->createCommand('SELECT * FROM users WHERE
    id=1;')->queryOne();
    return $result;
}, $duration, $dependency);
```

ActiveRecord can also take advantage of query caching by fetching the database component from the ActiveRecord model, as shown in the next example:

```
$result = User::getDb()->cache(function ($db) {
    return User::find()->where(['id' => 5])->one();
}, $duration, $dependency);
```

Moreover, within a query cache, we can exclude certain queries from being cached by chaining the noCache() method to our query, as illustrated by the following examples:

```
$result = $db->cache(function ($db) {
    // Cache queries in this block

    $db->noCache(function ($db) {
        // Do not cache queries in this block
    });

    // Don't cache this query either
    $customer = $db->createCommand('SELECT * FROM
    users WHERE id=1')->noCache()->queryOne();
    return $result;
});
```

> Some databases such as MySQL have their own built-in caching implemented in the software layer. Implementing both MySQL's native query cache and Yii2's query cache can cause problems in ensuring that the right data is presented. Additionally, any data that is returned as a resource handler cannot be cached by Yii2. Furthermore, some caches, such as Memcache, limit how much data can be associated with a specific key. Be cognizant of these limitations when using query caching.

Fragment caching

Fragment caching is built on top of data caching. Fragment caching in Yii2 allows us to cache a fragment of a page and present that cached fragment rather than regenerating the entire contents of the page on every request. In general, we can use fragment caching by wrapping our code in the following block:

```
// $id = ...a unique key...
// $this = ...instance of yii\web\View...;
// Begin our cache and check to see if the data is already cached.
// If content is found, beginCache will output data, otherwise
// the conditional will execute.
if ($this->beginCache($id))
{
    // Our cached content goes here
    $this->endCache();
}
```

Like data caching, fragment caching has support for several conditions, such as duration, dependencies, variation, and toggling the fragment cache on and off. These conditions can be added as key value arrays to the second parameter of the beginCache() method, as shown in the following example:

```
if ($this->beginCache($id, [
    // Time we want the fragment cache valid for
    'duration' => 100,

    // Any dependencies we want to add
    'dependency' => [
        'class' => 'yii\caching\DbDependency',
        'sql' => 'SELECT MAX(updated_at) FROM user',
    ],

    // Conditionally enable the cache for any boolean value
    'enabled' => Yii::$app->request->isGet,

    // Have a variation of this page for every language
    'variations' => Yii::$app->language
```

```
]))
{
    // Our cached content goes here
    $this->endCache();
}
```

Page caching

As an alternative to caching just a fragment of a web page, with Yii2, we can also cache an entire page and serve the cached copy instead of generating the page on every page load. This is exceptionally useful when we have a read-heavy application, such as a blog. Page caching in Yii2 is implemented by adding the `yii\filters\PageCache` filter to the `behaviors()` method of our controller, as shown in the following example. Like fragment caching, we can specify variations for our page, dependencies upon which our content should be invalidated, and the duration it should be cached for. Like other filters, we can also specify the actions we want our cache to apply to using the `only` and `except` parameters. The following example illustrates the use of page caching:

```
public function behaviors()
{
    return [
        [
            'class' => 'yii\filters\PageCache',
            'only' => ['article'],
            'duration' => 60,
            'variations' => [
                Yii::$app->language,
                Yii::$app->user->isGuest
            ],
            'dependency' => [
                'class' => 'yii\caching\DbDependency',
                'sql' => 'SELECT MAX(updated_at) FROM articles',
            ],
        ],
    ];
}
```

HTTP caching

Data, fragment, and page caching are all strategies that we can use to optimize the server-side performance of our application. To further improve the performance of our application, we can also send across headers with our application in order to indicate that we want the client's browser to cache the output of our page. These three headers are `Last-Modified`, `ETag`, and `Cache-Control`. By sending these headers along with our application, we can significantly reduce the number of HTTP requests sent to our application from our clients for pages that don't change often. HTTP caching in Yii2 is implemented by the `yii\filtersHttpCache` filter:

- The first header, `Last-Modified`, informs the client about the last time the page was changed. If a client makes a HEAD request to the server and sees that the `Last-Modified` header differs from what it currently has, it will re-request the page and cache it instead. Otherwise, it will load the page from the client's cache.

- The `ETag` header is used to represent a hash of the tag. Like the `Last-Modified` header, if the `ETag` hash changes, the browser knows that it had to re-download the page.

- Finally, the `Cache-Control` header indicates what type of cache the page should be stored in and for how long. By default, Yii2 will send `public; max-age: 3600` for this header, which will indicate that the client should cache the content for 3600 seconds or 1 hour.

 More information on the Cache-Control header can be found on the w3c specification reference guide at `http://www.w3.org/Protocols/rfc2616/rfc2616-sec14.html#sec14.9`.

An example illustrating the use of all three of these headers combined is illustrated as follows:

```
public function behaviors()
{
    return [
        [
            'class' => 'yii\filters\HttpCache',
            'only' => ['index'],
            'lastModified' => function ($action, $params) {
                $q = new \yii\db\Query();
                return $q->from('articles')->max('updated_at');
            },
```

```
        'etag' => function($action, $params) {
            $article = Article::find()->where(['id' =>
            \Yii::$app->request->get('id')])->one();
            return serialize([$article->title,
            $article->content]);
        },
        'cacheControlHeader' => 'public; max-age:3600'
    ],
  ];
}
```

Note that for HTTP caching, you only need to specify the headers you want to send. Specifying multiple headers can give you more fine grain control over when caches should be expired.

Caching database schema

In order to make `ActiveRecord` models work automagically, Yii2 will automatically query the database to determine the schema of our application at the beginning of each query. While useful in a development environment, this operation is unnecessary in production environments where our schema rarely changes. We can tell Yii2 to cache our database schema to improve the performance of our database operations by enabling three properties of database component: $schemeCache, which represents the cache component we want to use; $schemaCacheDuration, which defines how long we want Yii2 to cache our schema; and $enableSchemaCache, which enables or disables the schema cache.

The following MySQL database component illustrates the use of the schema cache properties:

```
<?php return [
    // [...],
    'components' => [
        // [...]
        'db' => [
            'class'       => 'yii\db\Connection',
            'dsn'         =>
            'mysql:host='127.0.0.1;dbname=masteringyii',
            'username'    => '<username>,
            'password' => '<password>',
            'charset'  => 'utf8',
```

```
                'enableSchemaCache'      => true,
                'schemaCacheDuration' => 0,
                'schemaCache'               => 'cache'
        ],

        'cache' => [
            'class' => 'yii\caching\FileCache',
        ]
    ]
];
```

> When schema cache is enabled, run the cache/flush command after applying new migrations so that Yii2 can pick up your new database structure.

General performance enhancements

For considerable performance gains, there are several changes that you can make to your application as well as your web server environment that can significantly increase the performance of your application.

Enabling OPCache

Unlike compiled languages such as C and C++, PHP is an interpreted scripting language. Consequently, every time our web server requests a new page or every time we run a command from our command line, PHP needs to interpret our code into machine code that our servers can actually run. Even if our source code doesn't change, PHP will automatically perform this step on every request. In our development environments, this allows us to simply make a change to our source code, save the file, and then reload it in the page to see our changes. In a production environment, however, this step is unnecessary since our code will only change if we perform a deployment.

Starting in PHP 5.5, a new tool called OPCache was released by Zend Framework Technologies Ltd and built into the PHP core. Once enabled, OPCache will cache the compiled and optimized opcode that our PHP code is generated from and store it in a shared memory store. If our code is ever run again, OPCache will look inside that shared memory store for our code and execute it rather than re-interpreting our raw source code file. Depending upon the size of our application, enabling OPCache can have significant performance implications for our app. Moreover, since OPCache is now built into PHP, enabling it is fairly simple.

Note that Zend OPCache and APCCache both can be configured to cache PHP's opcode. It's highly recommended that you do not run both Zend OPCache and APCCache at the same time as it can cause instability within PHP. As Zend OPCache is maintained by PHP maintainers, it's recommended that you use it instead of APC.

Depending upon your package managed, OPCache may either be built into your PHP instance or provided as an external extension. A simply way to check whether OPCache is installed or not is to run the following command from your command line:

```
$ php -m
```

If OPCache is installed, you should see **Zend OPcache** appear in the output. If you don't see this output, you'll need to install OPCache from your package manager. Once OPCache is installed, you can enable it by adding the following to your php. ini file or to a file in your PHP INI includes folder and restarting your web server:

```
zend_extension=opcache.so
opcache.enable = true
opcache.enable_cli = true
opcache.save_comments = false
opcache.enable_file_override = true
```

When you perform a deployment, you'll need to clear OPCache for your new code to take effect. Typically, this is done by restarting your web server or your PHP process. Alternatively, you can use a tool such as cachetool (available at https://github.com/gordalina/cachetool) to clear the cache tool. Using a tool like cachetool is beneficial because it allows you to clear your OPCache without restarting your web server and facing potential downtime.

Optimizing Composer dependencies

Another performance change you can make as part of your deployment is to exclude your development dependencies from your production deployments:

```
$ composer install --no-dev
```

Since our development dependencies are used in development, loading and registering that code with our application only adds extra overhead to our application.

Additionally, we can instruct Composer to optimize the autoloader that it generates by running the following command when we install our composer dependencies:

```
$ composer install -o
```

Alternatively, we can generate an optimized autoloader file after installing our dependencies by running the following command:

```
$ composer dumpautoload -o
```

By optimizing Composer's autoloader file, we can reduce the number of file and disk lookups with which we need to load our classes in our source code, which in turn will make our application faster.

Upgrading to PHP 7

At the time of publication, PHP 7 has been released, and it contains a refactored PHP engine that is able to interpret, compile, and execute the same PHP code with significantly less instructions. By reducing the number of CPU instructions and memory usage, PHP 7 is significantly faster than PHP 5.6. For significant performance gains, consider upgrading your PHP instance from 5.6 to 7.

Switch to Facebook's HHVM

As an alternative to upgrading to PHP 7, you can consider leaving the PHP engine and switching to HHVM, a reengineered engine for PHP created by Facebook. Like PHP 7, HHVM is significantly faster than PHP 5.6, and for high traffic applications, it can significantly reduce the costs associated with hosting a high traffic application. Unlike PHP 7, however, HHVM doesn't have support for all the PHP modules you may be accustomed to. Moreover, while Yii2 is fully compatible with HHVM, third-party Composer packages may not be, which may cause problems if thorough testing is not performed. For more information on HHVM, check out the HHVM documentation at http://docs.hhvm.com/manual/en/index.php.

Security considerations

When using Yii2, it's important to remember to follow security best practices in order to ensure the security of your application, the servers they run on, the data we collect, and our end users who entrust us with this information. In previous chapters, we explored how we can use the `yii\base\Security` class to safely encrypt and hash data and how to use hazing algorithms such as Bcrypt to secure passwords. In this section, we'll cover some additional security best practices that we can apply when building our applications.

Certificates

In almost every application that Yii2 will be providing the backend for, our clients (browsers or native clients) will communicate with our application over HTTP (Hypertext Transfer Protocol). An easy way to ensure that the information our client submits from their clients reaches our servers in the same state it left in is to encrypt the traffic between our clients and the server with a certificate signed by a trusted certificate authority transmitted over the TLS (Transport Layer Security) protocol.

TLS is the successor to SSL (Secure Sockets Layer), and both are often referred to as SSL certificates. As of 2014, all versions of SSL (1.0, 2.0, and 3.0) have been deprecated due to known security issues with the SSL protocol itself. Its successor, TLS versions 1.1 and 1.2, are not vulnerable and are the recommended protocol to use when encrypting data between clients and servers over HTTP.

Adding a signed and trusted certificate to our server has several major advantages:

- Encrypting data in transit prevents data from being viewed and manipulated by third parties. Health information, credit card information, usernames, and passwords can all be protected by encrypting data while in transit

- Clients can pin certificates that we publish so that they know to communicate with us only if our certificate matches the one they have pinned. This prevents Man-in-the-Middle attacks (MITM) and prevents others from learning about our data. Additionally, when using pinned certificates, our clients will know not to communicate with servers masquerading as ours. Again, this protects us and our users

- Search engines such as Google and Bing give higher rankings to sites that use TLS

- Implementing TLS in our web server is a simple task, and on modern computers, it incurs almost no overhead

When implementing TLS, there are several resources you can use to determine the most secure cipher suites and to verify that your configuration is secure. For instance, the `https://cipherli.st` site provides a list of modern cipher suites for a variety of web servers and configurations. Qualys' SSL Labs site (`https://www.ssllabs.com/ssltest/`) can also give you a complete report of your TLS configuration and can validate your web server configuration. Combined, these tools can help better secure your application and infrastructure.

Cookies

When retrieving data from cookies using `yii\web\Request` and `yii\web\Response`, Yii2 will automatically encrypt your cookie information using your cookie validation key:

```
return [
    // [...],
    'components' => [
        // [...]
        'request' => [
            'cookieValidationKey' => '<your secret key here>',
        ],
    ],
];
```

When working with cookies and session cookies, we can take additional protections by adding additional attributes to our cookies, such as `yii\web\Cookie::$secure` and `yii\web\Cookie::$httpOnly`. By marking our cookies as `secure`, we can ensure that our cookies will only be sent over a secure connection, as described in the previous section. Moreover, by setting our cookies to be `httpOnly`, we can ensure that JavaScript and other web scripting languages cannot read our cookies. By configuring our cookies with these two flags, we can significantly improve the security of our application.

Protecting against cross-site scripting

As a general rule of web development, any time we display information submitted by an end user, we should encode it so that we can protect our site and users against XSS or cross-site scripting. XSS occurs when a user submits data that, when displayed on our page, can be interpreted by our browser. This could be something innocuous, such as adding `<em>` or `<b>` tags to our markup, or it could be something more sinister, such as injecting a `<script>` tag that tracks information about the user or redirects them to another site all together. Fortunately, Yii2 provides two ways of working with data submitted by end users that we can display.

The first method we can use to protect our site from XSS is to encode end user data using the `yii\helpers\Html::encode()` method, as illustrated in the following example:

```php
<?php echo \yii\helpers\Html::encode($data); ?>
```

When encoding our data using this method, Yii2 will convert tags such as `<` and `>` into HTML-encoded entities that modern browsers know how to display and interpret.

In the instance where we do want end user data to be displayed as HTML, we can use `yii\web\HtmlPurifier::purify()` to correctly parse our data with the rich HTML we want without allowing JavaScript code to be injected:

```php
<?php \yii\helpers\HtmlPurifier::process($longData);
```

> HtmlPurifier can be extremely slow even when configured properly. Be sure you understand and configure HtmlPurifier properly before deploying your code as it can significantly hurt the performance of your application. More information on how to configure HtmlPurifier within Yii2 can be found at `http://www.yiiframework.com/doc-2.0/yii-helpers-htmlpurifier.html`, and HtmlPurifier's complete documentation can be found at `http://htmlpurifier.org/`.

Enabling cross-site request forgery protection

CSRF (cross-site request forgery) is another common vulnerability that many sites deal with, which Yii2 can help protect us against. When dealing with client requests, we generally assume that the request came from the user himself. With JavaScript, however, we can send false requests in the background without the user's knowledge. These requests can be as simple as logging a user out of a given service without their knowledge or scraping a specific page for information about the user then transmitting it to a malicious server. Yii2 automatically protects us from CSRF attacks. The only additional protection you can perform is to follow the HTTP specification (such as not allowing state changes on GET requests).

> Note that there may be many times when CSRF needs to be disabled for one reason or another. Within our controller, we can disable CSRF for specific actions by adding this code within our action by setting `Yii::$app->controller->enableCsrfValidation` to false.

Summary

In this chapter, we covered several different ways in which we can improve and explore the performance of our application and learned how to improve the security of our application. We explored how we can use data, page, fragment, HTTP, database, and schema caching to improve the performance of our application. We also discovered general improvements we can make to Yii2 and PHP in order to make our application run faster. Finally, we discovered several ways in which we can improve the security of our application through the use of certificates, enabling certain cookie attributes, and protecting our site against XSS and CSRF attacks.

In our final chapter, we'll cover how we can speed up our already fast development time with Yii2, learn how to explore our application through logging, and discover fast and secure ways to deploy our application with almost no downtime or interruption of service.

13
Debugging and Deploying

One of the most important tasks when working with modern web applications is determining what went wrong during the development and runtime of our application. Without knowing what went wrong, it's impossible to determine the correct steps to correct the problem. Yii2 provides several tools and components that make the debugging of our applications painless and simple. In this chapter, we'll explore several different ways in which we can debug our applications. We'll also outline some of the best practices for the deployment of our Yii2 application once we've completed the development.

Debugging

Debugging is an important process in which we can discover what went wrong with our application. Whether we're solving a problem locally or trying to identify an issue in our production, our applications need to be configured to supply us with the required information to quickly and effectively identify and resolve issues as they arise. In this section, we'll cover how to enable logging within our application, how to benchmark certain sections of code and handler errors, and general debugging tools and guidelines.

Logging

To help us debug our applications, Yii2 comes built with several different logging components and log methods that we can implement within our application. To get started with logging in Yii2, we first need to implement a log component within our application. Yii2 comes with several different components that we can implement in concert with one another or disjointedly.

Logger Class	Description	Class Reference
yii\log\DbTarget	Logs information to a database table	http://www.yiiframework.com/doc-2.0/yii-log-dbtarget.html
yii\log\EmailTarget	On logging events, sends an email to a specified email address	http://www.yiiframework.com/doc-2.0/yii-log-emailtarget.html
yii\log\FileTarget	Logs events to a file	http://www.yiiframework.com/doc-2.0/yii-log-filetarget.html
yii\log\SyslogTarget	Logs events using PHP's syslog() function	http://www.yiiframework.com/doc-2.0/yii-log-syslogtarget.html

> Each of the previously listed loggers have slight variations in their configuration. For more information on how to specifically configure each log target, refer to the class reference for that logger class.

To enable a log target within our application, we first need to bootstrap the log component and then specify the logger target that we want to use within the components section of our application configuration, as shown in the following example:

```
return [
    // [...],
    'bootstrap' => ['log'],

    // [...],
    'components' => [
        // [...],
```

```
'log' => [
    'targets' => [
        [
            'class' => 'yii\log\FileTarget',
            'levels' => ['error', 'warning'],
        ]
    ],
    ],
],
];
```

 In the previous example, we enabled yii\log\FileTarget by itself for any error and warning log events. Note that multiple loggers can be enabled concurrently by specifying additional loggers within the targets array.

Each logging target can be configured to listen to certain events. Yii2 provides five distinct events that we can log to and several logging methods that we can add to our code:

- **Error**: This is triggered by Yii:error() when a regular error or a fatal error occurs. These types of events should be acted upon immediately as they indicate failure within the application.
- **Warning**: This is triggered by Yii::warning(). These events indicate that something went wrong within the application.
- **Info**: This is triggered by Yii::info(). Typically, these events are used to log something useful or interesting that has occurred.
- **Trace**: This is triggered by Yii::trace(), which is usually used during development to trace a particular piece of code.
- **Profile**: This is triggered by Yii::beginProfile() and Yii::endProfile().

 Most of these methods are simply wrappers around Yii::log().

Each log target can be configured to listen to a specific set of events by specifying the level property of that logger target, and by default, if the level property is not specified, Yii2 will process messages of any severity.

Each log method shares a similar method signature:

```
function($message, $category='application')
```

Yii2's log method will allow strings and complex data objects or arrays through the `yii\helpers\VarDumper::export()` method. When logging information, it's important that you specify a category, as that category can be searched and filtered within our log. As shown in the method signature, Yii2 will log information to the `application` category by default. When specifying a category, it's generally good to specify it in a hierarchical way, such as in a slash-like format:

```
app\components\MyEvent
```

Another effective format is to use the PHP magic method, __METHOD__, which will return the namespace and method the logger was called in:

```
app\components\MyEvent::myMethod
```

Within our logger components, we can specify which categories we want our logger to handle by specifying the `categories` parameter. The categories parameter can be configured to listen to specific categories such as `yii\db\Connection`, but it can also be configured with wildcards. For instance, if we want to send an email anytime a category within `yii\db` is called, we can configure the following logger target:

```
return [
    // [...],
    'bootstrap' => ['log'],

    // [...],
    'components' => [
        // [...],
        'log' => [
            'targets' => [
                [
                    'class' => 'yii\log\EmailTarget',
                    'categories' => ['yii\db\*'],
                    'message' => [
                        'from' => ['systems@example.com'],
                        'to' => ['administrator@example.com'],
                        'subject' => 'Database errors for
                        example.com',
                    ],
                ]
            ],
        ],
    ],
];
```

If you decide to use email logging, you can quickly flood your inbox with multiple messages or even be rate-limited by your email provider. It's highly recommended that you specify only the most critical categories for email logging.

In situations where we're logging multiple categories, such as `yii\web\HttpException`, we can also exclude certain categories from being logged by specifying the `except` property. For instance, if we want to log all non-HTTP 404 exceptions, we can configure our logger as follows to accomplish this:

```
return [
    // [...],
    'bootstrap' => ['log'],

    // [...],
    'components' => [
        // [...],
        'log' => [
            'targets' => [
                [
                    'class' => 'yii\log\FileTarget',
                    'levels' => ['error', 'warning', 'info'],
                    'categories' => ['yii\web\HttpException:*'],
                    'except' => [
                        'yii\web\HttpException:404',
                    ],
                ]
            ],
        ],
    ],
];
```

Finally, within our application, loggers can be toggled on and off by setting the `enabled` property of the logger target. To programmatically disable a logging target, we first need to specify a key for our logger target:

```
return [
    // [...],
    'bootstrap' => ['log'],

    // [...],
    'components' => [
        // [...],
        'log' => [
```

```
              'targets' => [
                  'file' => [
                  'class' => 'yii\log\FileTarget',
                  'levels' => ['error', 'warning', 'info'],
                  'categories' => ['yii\web\HttpException:*'],
                  'except' => [
                      'yii\web\HttpException:404',
                  ],
              ]
              ],
          ],
      ],
  ];
```

Then, within our code, we can temporarily disable our `file` target, as specified in the previous example, using the following code:

```
Yii::$app->log->targets['file']->enabled = false;
```

Benchmarking

Another tool that we can use to debug our applications is the profiler tool. The profile tool allows us to gain an insight into how long a certain piece of code takes to execute. To use the profiler, we simply need to wrap the code we want to examine in the following code block:

```
Yii::beginProfile('myProfile');
    // Code inside this will be profiled
Yii::endProfile('myProfile');
```

> The `beginProfile()` and `endProfile()` methods can be nested within another profiler section. The code within these methods will be outputted to your log targets for profiling. In production, you should disable profiling.

Error handling

By default, Yii2 has a fairly comprehensive error handler that will automatically catch and display all nonfatal PHP errors. The error handler can be an extremely powerful tool during development as it can provide complete stack traces in the event that something fails.

PHP Fatal Error – yii\base\ErrorException

Class 'yii\base\HttpException' not found

1. in /var/www/chapter5/controllers/SiteController.php   at line   27

```
                'captcha' => [
                    'class' => 'yii\captcha\CaptchaAction',
                    'fixedVerifyCode' => YII_ENV_TEST ? 'testme' : null,
                ],
            ];

    public function actionIndex()
    {
        throw new \yii\base\HttpException(500, 'Invalid something');
        return $this->render('index');
    }

    public function actionLogin()
    {
        $model = new \app\models\UserForm(['scenario' => 'login']);

        if ($model->load(Yii::$app->request->post())) {
            if ($model->validate()) {
```

2. yii\base\ErrorHandler::handleFatalError()

By default, the error handler is automatically enabled as part of our application, but it can be disabled by setting the YII_ENABLE_ERROR_HANDLER constant within our bootstrap file to false.

The error handler is configured within our main application configuration file, and it supports several different configuration options, as shown in the following example:

```
return [
    // [...],
    'components' => [
        // [...],
        'errorHandler' => [
            'maxSourceLines' => 20,
            'errorAction' => 'site/error',
            'maxTraceSourceLines' => 13,
            // [...]
        ],
    ],
];
```

More information on the error handler and its properties can be found on the Yii2 class reference page at http://www.yiiframework.com/doc-2.0/yii-web-errorhandler.html.

By default, the error handler will use two views to display errors:

- @yii/views/errorHandler/error.php: This will be used to display errors without a call stack and is the default view that is used when YII_DEBUG is set to false
- @yii/views/errorHandler/exception.php: This will be used when errors display a complete call stack

We can define our own error view files by specifying the errorView and exceptionView properties of our error handler.

As an alternative to the default error page, as presented in the previous screenshot, errors can be redirected to a different action by specifying the errorAction property of the error handler. We can then handle errors separately from our application by adding an errors action to our actions() method and defining an actionError() action within the specified controller:

```php
<?php
namespace app\controllers;

use Yii;
use yii\web\Controller;

class SiteController extends Controller
{
    public function actions()
    {
        return [
            'error' => [
                'class' => 'yii\web\ErrorAction',
            ],
        ];
    }

    public function actionError()
    {
        $exception = Yii::$app->errorHandler->exception;
        if ($exception !== null) {
```

```
        return $this->render('error', ['exception'
        => $exception]);
    }
}
}
```

Our custom error handler page can then be created within our `views/site/error.php` file.

Handling errors within non HTML responses

When working with non-HTML responses such as JSON or XML, Yii2 will be presented as a simplified error response, as shown in the following example:

```
{
    "name": "Not Found Exception",
    "message": "The requested resource was not found.",
    "code": 0,
    "status": 404
}
```

In the event that you wish to display more debugging information in nonproduction environments, you can create a custom response handler by overwriting the on `beforeSend` event of the response component. Our response handler can be rewritten as follows to achieve this:

```
<?php
return [
    // [...],
    'components' => [
        // [...],
        'response' => [
            'format' => yii\web\Response::FORMAT_JSON,
            'charset'        => 'UTF-8',
            'on beforeSend'  =>
            ['app\components\ResponseEvent', 'beforeSend']
        ],
        // [...]
    ]
];
```

Our response handler class located at @app/components/ResponseEvent.php can be written as follows to change the error behavior when YII_DEBUG is set to true:

```php
<?php

namespace app\components;

use Yii;

/**
 * Event handler for response object
 */
class ResponseEvent extends yii\base\Event
{
    /**
     * Before Send event handler
     * @param yii\base\Event $event
     */
    public function beforeSend($event)
    {
        $response = $event->sender;

        if (\Yii::$app->request->getIsOptions())
        {
            $response->statusCode = 200;
            $response->data = null;
        }

        if ($response->data !== null)
        {
            $return = ($response->statusCode == 200 ? $response->data : $response->data['message']);

            $response->data = [
                'data'  => $return
            ];

            // Handle and display errors in the API for easy
            debugging
            $exception = \Yii::$app->errorHandler->exception;
            if ($exception && get_class($exception) !==
            "yii\web\HttpException" &&
            !is_subclass_of($exception,
            'yii\web\HttpException') && YII_DEBUG)
```

```
        {
            $response->data['success'] = false;
            $response->data['exception'] = [
                'message'    => $exception->getMessage(),
                'file'       => $exception->getFile(),
                'line'       => $exception->getLine(),
                'trace'      => $exception->getTraceAsString()
            ];
        }
    }
}
}
```

Now when an error occurs, output similar to the following will be displayed, saving us the time taken to flip between our browser and our application log:

```
{
    "data": "<message>",
    "success": false,
    "exception": {
        "message": "Invalid",
        "file": "/path/to/SiteController.php",
        "line": 48,
        "trace": "#0 [internal function]:
        app\\controllers\\SiteController->actionIndex()\n# ...
        {main}"
    }
}
```

Debugging with the Yii2 debug extension

Another powerful tool that we can use to debug our applications is the `yii2-debug` extension. When enabled, the debug extension provides deep insights into every aspect of our request, ranging from logs, configurations, profiling, requests, asset bundles, and even emails sent by our application. With this tool, we can find out exactly what happened during a specific request.

To get started with using the `yii2-debug` extension, we first need to install it as part of our composer dependencies:

```
composer require --dev --prefer-dist yiisoft/yii2-debug
```

After installing the package and running the composer update, we can configure the debug extension by adding the following to our config/web.php configuration file:

```
if (YII_DEBUG)
{
    $config['bootstrap'][] = 'debug';
    $config['modules']['debug'] = [
        'class' => 'yii\debug\Module',
        'allowedIPs' => ['*']
    ];
}
```

After enabling the extension, we will be able to view it at the bottom of every view of our application.

By default, the extension will show some basic things about our application; however, if we click on it, we can gain deep insights into every aspect of our application for a particular request.

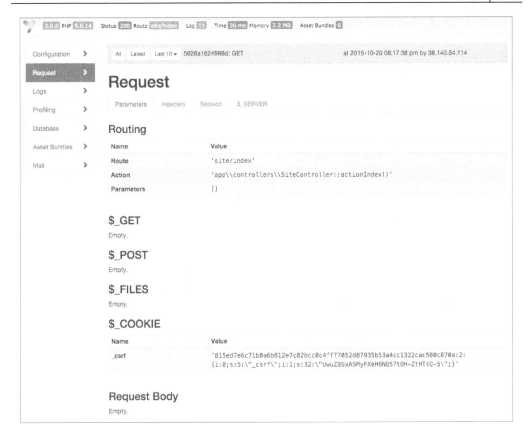

Alternatively, we can navigate to the /debug endpoint of our application to view all the debug requests captured by the extension.

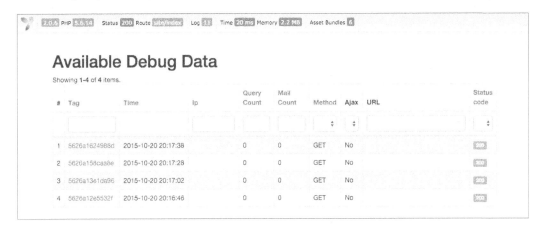

Deploying

The final step in working with any Yii2 application is to move it to production and create a deployment strategy. There are many different tools that we can use to deploy our code, ranging from Bamboo, TravisCI, Jenkins, Capistrano, and even manual SSH deployments—just to name a few.

In general, however, there are several key concepts we should keep in mind when deploying our code:

- Deployments should be automated and hands off. In order to be consistent, your deployments should be run by a tool or service that can run the same tasks every time. This eliminates any human error during the deployment and ensures consistency.

- Deployments should be fast, providing you with the ability to quickly push out new features and bug fixes.

- The actual building of your application (such as combined and compressed JavaScript, CSS, and other configurations) should occur on a build server and then be pushed to your production server in a pre-build manner. This ensures that your production servers don't have extra tools on them that may contain security vulnerabilities while also ensuring that your project is built with the same tools each time.

- Deployments should be reversible. If we deploy code and our application breaks, we should be able to easily roll back to a previous version.

- When deploying, we should remove any development tools, scripts, and our DCVS repository information. This ensures that in case there is a bug or security vulnerability in our code or our web server, this information is not exposed.

- Directories that contain logs of our other information (such as `runtime`) should be stored in a persistent directory and then symlinked back into our project. This ensures that our logs and other data can persist across multiple deployments.

- Our deployments should be structured in such a way that there is no interruption of service. Typically, this is achieved by storing our deployment in a specific folder and then renaming or symlinking it into the directory our web server is pointed to. This ensures that our site does not experience an outage when we are making a change.

- When deploying new code, we should clear any application-specific caches, such as our schema cache, configuration cache, and PHP OPCache, to ensure that our new code changes take effect.

- Configuration files should never be committed to our DCVS as they contain database usernames, passwords, and other secret information. Consider storing this data as environment variables on the servers themselves, or encrypting them in a way such that only your production servers can decrypt and use the data.

By following these general guidelines, we can ensure that our Yii2 applications are deployed seamlessly and easily.

Summary

In this chapter, we covered the basics of debugging and deploying our application. We covered how to set up logging and benchmarking and how to debug our application with the `yii2-debug` extension while also detailing general guidelines and a few tools we can use to deploy our applications to production.

As you may expect, there's more to Yii2 than what is covered in this book. When developing Yii2 applications, remember that the Yii2 API documentation located at `http://www.yiiframework.com/doc-2.0/` provides excellent class reference documentation along with superb documentation on how to use many of the classes. Having reached the end of the book, you should feel confident in your knowledge and mastery of Yii2, and you should feel ready to take on any project with Yii2.

Index

automatic change testing
    defining 292-294

B

base drivers, PHP manual
    URL 43
behaviors
    URL 104
Boolean options
    defining 210
bootstrap-specific widgets
    defining 138
    URL 138
Bower
    about 167
    URL 167
built-in console commands
    about 25
    asset command 26
    cache command 26-28
    fixture command 28, 29
    Gii command 29
    help command 25, 26
    message command 30
    migration command 30, 31
built-in validators
    URL 97
built-in widgets
    Bootstrap widgets 137, 138
    jQuery UI widgets 138
    using 137
    Yii-specific widgets 139, 140

C

Cache-Control header
    URL 322
cachetool
    URL 325
caching
    about 313
    database schema, caching 323, 324
    data caching 313-316
    fragment caching 320
    HTTP caching 322, 323
    page caching 321

Cascading Style Sheets (CSS) 151
certificates
    advantages 327
cipher suites
    URL 328
Codeception
    configuring, with Yii2 258-261
    URL 272
components 14, 15
components, unit test
    Consistent and repeatable 262
    Fast 262
    fully automated 262
    independent 262
    Maintainable 263
    Readable 263
    references 263
    thorough 262
Composer
    about 1
    defining 1-7
    modules, managing with 133-135
    URL 1
Composer Asset Plugin
    about 3
    URL 3
Composer CLI
    URL 29
configuration
    about 7
    application environment, setting up 13
    configuration files 10
    entry scripts 8
    requirements checker 7, 8
    web environment, setting for Apache 14
    web environment, setting for NGINX 13
configuration and usage, Yii2
    configuration file 21, 22
    console commands, running 22-24
    console environment, setting 22
    defining 19
    entry script 19, 20
configuration files
    about 10
    database configuration file 10
    environment configuration 11-13
    parameter configuration 11

migrations
URL 55
models
about 110
attributes 111
scenarios 111, 112
URL 111
module components
controllers 125, 126
defining 124
module class structure 124, 125
views and layouts 126, 127
modules
about 123
accessing 132
bootstrapping 131
components 124
managing, with Composer 133-135
registering 128
registering dynamically 128-131
summary 135
module translations 309, 310

N

new records
creating 109
NodeJS
about 166, 167
URL 166

O

object-relational mapping (ORM) 88
objects 14-16
OCI8 driver
URL 43
Open Database Connectivity (ODBC) 43

P

passwords
hashing 197, 198
verifying 197, 198
path aliases
about 16, 17
URL 17

performance enhancements
Composer dependencies, optimizing 325
defining 324
OPCache, enabling 324, 325
switching, to HHVM 326
upgrading, to PHP 7 326
PHP
configuring 298

Q

Query Builder
about 65
Query construction methods 65
select method 66

R

rate limiting 246-249
Representational State Transfer (REST) 225
request object
URL 213
requests
about 209
client and URL information,
retrieving 212, 213
headers and cookies 211, 212
properties 213
request parameters and data,
retrieving 209-211
response object
URL 218
responses
about 213
file output 218
redirection 217
response body 215-217
response headers, setting 215
status codes, setting 214
role-based access control (RBAC)
about 189
URL 189
routes
parameterizing 205
routing
about 201, 202
catch all route 203

Y

Thank you for buying
Mastering Yii

About Packt Publishing

Packt, pronounced 'packed', published its first book, *Mastering phpMyAdmin for Effective MySQL Management*, in April 2004, and subsequently continued to specialize in publishing highly focused books on specific technologies and solutions.

Our books and publications share the experiences of your fellow IT professionals in adapting and customizing today's systems, applications, and frameworks. Our solution-based books give you the knowledge and power to customize the software and technologies you're using to get the job done. Packt books are more specific and less general than the IT books you have seen in the past. Our unique business model allows us to bring you more focused information, giving you more of what you need to know, and less of what you don't.

Packt is a modern yet unique publishing company that focuses on producing quality, cutting-edge books for communities of developers, administrators, and newbies alike. For more information, please visit our website at www.packtpub.com.

About Packt Open Source

In 2010, Packt launched two new brands, Packt Open Source and Packt Enterprise, in order to continue its focus on specialization. This book is part of the Packt Open Source brand, home to books published on software built around open source licenses, and offering information to anybody from advanced developers to budding web designers. The Open Source brand also runs Packt's Open Source Royalty Scheme, by which Packt gives a royalty to each open source project about whose software a book is sold.

Writing for Packt

We welcome all inquiries from people who are interested in authoring. Book proposals should be sent to author@packtpub.com. If your book idea is still at an early stage and you would like to discuss it first before writing a formal book proposal, then please contact us; one of our commissioning editors will get in touch with you.

We're not just looking for published authors; if you have strong technical skills but no writing experience, our experienced editors can help you develop a writing career, or simply get some additional reward for your expertise.

Web Application Development with Yii 2 and PHP

ISBN: 978-1-78398-188-5   Paperback: 406 pages

Fast-track your web application development using the new generation Yii PHP framework

1. Implement real-world web application features efficiently using the Yii development framework.

2. Each chapter provides micro-examples that build upon each other to create the final macro-example, a basic CRM application.

3. Filled with useful tasks to improve the maintainability of your applications.

Yii Application Development Cookbook

Second Edition

ISBN: 978-1-78216-310-7   Paperback: 408 pages

A Cookbook covering both practical Yii application development tips and the most important Yii features

1. Learn how to use Yii even more efficiently.

2. Full of practically useful solutions and concepts you can use in your application.

3. Both important Yii concept descriptions and practical recipes are inside.

Please check **www.PacktPub.com** for information on our titles

www.ingramcontent.com/pod-product-compliance
Lightning Source LLC
LaVergne TN
LVHW081330050326
832903LV00024B/1106